RICE

from perfect paella to sensational sushi

RICE

from perfect paella to sensational sushi

CHRISTINE INGRAM

HERMES
HOUSE

Publisher: Joanna Lorenz
Managing Editor: Linda Fraser
Editor: Sarah Ainley
Copy Editor: Jenni Fleetwood
Designer: Penny Dawes
Indexer: Vicki Robinson
Photography: Dave King (recipes) and David Jordan (cutouts and techniques)
Food for Photography: Jennie Shapter (recipes) and |
Sara Lewis (cutouts and techniques)
Stylist: Jo Harris
Recipes: Carla Capalbo, Kit Chan, Roz Denny, Rafi Fernandez, Silvana Franco,
Deh-Ta Hsiung, Shezad Husain, Christine Ingram, Soheila Kimberley, Masaki Ko,
Elizabeth Lambert Ortiz, Ruby Le Bois and Sallie Morris

Front cover shows Peruvian Duck with Rice. For recipe see page 203.
Previously published as *Rice & Risotto*

1 3 5 7 9 10 8 6 4 2

NOTES
Standard spoon and cup measures are level.

Large eggs are used unless otherwise stated.

CONTENTS

INTRODUCTION

The rice grain is famous for its versatility, and has been a favorite ingredient with cooks worldwide for thousands of years. Rice cultivation has certainly played a part in man's development, and this fascinating book opens with a look at its history, and at the mystical reverence with which some cultures regard rice, even today. For reference, there is a photographic directory to the world's rices, plus information on the different ways of cooking rice. Each of the world's major cuisines has its own way of dealing with rice, and the recipes here include the very best of them, to help you explore and appreciate this highly important and endlessly versatile, staple food.

Rice is a supremely important crop. It is a food that feeds half the population of the world, and is the grain that has sculpted the culture of Asia, linking Heaven and Earth, mortal to gods. In Bangladesh, Thailand and China, a common greeting, instead of "How are you?", is "Have you eaten rice today?" And at New Year, the traditional saying is "May your rice never burn." To upset a bowl of rice is a sign of bad luck, while deliberately upending a fellow diner's rice bowl is a deadly insult.

Festivals and traditions all over South-east Asia celebrate the importance of rice. In Cambodia, for instance, where people believe the rice spirit, Yiey Tep, lives on in the rice fields, farmers show their devotion by praying and making offerings of sweet rice. The Balinese have numerous rice rituals, from laying pinches of rice along the edges of fields to keep away evil spirits, to fabulous celebrations in the island's many temples.

There are two distinct attitudes to rice and two distinct types of rice eater. For many of us in the West, rice is just another grain, albeit a valued one.

We view rice as a pleasant alternative to potatoes, pasta or bread; we make pilafs and risottos; or use rice to serve with curry or as a salad.

But for the peoples of Indonesia, Thailand and other South-east Asian countries, rice is central to life itself. Many Asians eat rice three times a day and in some languages, such as Thai, the phrase for eating rice is the same as for eating food. For many Chinese or Malays, for instance, rice is the food that you eat; the rest is merely relish. On average, in the West, we each consume 4 pounds of rice a year, compared with the 330 pounds a year average annual consumption per person in Asia. In this book we suggest cooking 8 ounces of rice – a generous cupful – to serve four people, yet that would scarcely satisfy a single hungry Indonesian or Chinese adult. The world produces about 386 million tons of rice each year and over half of this amount is consumed within 30 miles of where it was grown.

Paddy fields are one of the most defining images of South-east Asia. The sight of the two-thousand-year-old

terraces of the Ifugao of Luzon in the northern Philippines is one of the wonders of the world. Rice that is growing in the field is called paddy, which comes from the word *padi*, meaning "rice growing in deep water." Rice is known as paddy until it has been threshed.

In Asia, most rice is still planted, tended and harvested by hand. By direct contrast, in the USA and Australia the process is highly mechanized and involves lasers, low-flying aircraft, combine harvesters and computers.

Yet the lack of technology in the Asian paddy fields belies the complex organization that is rice farming. Entire families are involved in the growing and harvesting of the rice they eat, and each member has a specific role to play in the process. Rice provides the family with a living, so long as the weather is predictable and the rains forthcoming, and rice cultivation shapes their way of life.

Below: Rice is farmed throughout France, including here in Provence, although the country is not a major exporter.

THE STORY OF RICE

Study the history of rice and you will discover that it is bound up with many strange and fascinating myths. Rice has fed more people than any other crop, and the story of its cultivation must rank as one of the most important developments in history. Almost every culture in the East has its own rice legend, and in many Asian countries these stories are still celebrated today.

In Bali and other parts of Indonesia, puppets act out a creation myth, which tells of how Lord Vishnu caused the Earth to give birth to rice, and the god Indra taught the people how it should be grown. From China comes the story of a devastating flood, which left all the crops destroyed. Facing certain starvation, the people of the town one day saw a dog with strange yellow seeds hanging from its tail. Rice grew when the seeds were planted in the waterlogged soil.

In the many myths from around Indonesia, Thailand and Japan, the rice spirit is always feminine. She is young and tender – a beautiful maiden, dusted with rice powder to emphasize her perfect white skin. In almost all of the many Asian cultures, the femininity of rice is reflected in the way it is grown. Men prepare the land, build the dikes and attend to irrigation, but it is the women who plant the rice, tend it in the fields, cut it and, finally, cook it.

There are numerous signs all over South-east Asia that rice is still highly revered today. A family will traditionally store its rice in a rice barn. These beautiful and elaborate buildings are where the rice spirit is said to reside until the time of the next planting, and there are often strict rules about who may enter these barns. Usually, only the women are allowed inside, and even then only once a day.

The myths of these rich cultures tell us a great deal about the history of rice, and highlight its central role in people's lives. How and when it was first grown is more difficult to discover. What is certain is that it is native to South-east Asia and has been cultivated there for perhaps 8000 years. Evidence from a cave in northern Thailand proves that rice was being cultivated from around 6000 BC.

Rice, which is a member of the grass family, grew extensively in Thailand. It is likely that early man first grew wild rice, and only later began cultivating local species. Some scholars believe that this first rice would have been dry and that wet rice was a later development. Others say that people grew whatever rice was best suited to their particular environment. Certainly rice is adaptable, and will accommodate itself to the habitat; some varieties tolerate floods and cold nights, while others survive hot temperatures and relatively little water.

Gradually, people realized the value of this sustaining crop, and rice began to travel. From north-east India and Thailand, rice spread first through South-east Asia, and then further afield.

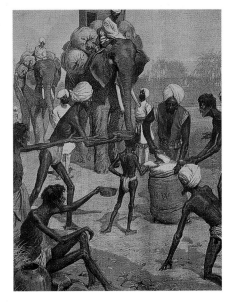

Above: Famine in the streets of Bombay in 1900. Rice is given to the starving.

Rice cultivation is believed to have begun in China in the Yangtze River delta around 4000 BC, although the rice may at first have been considered nothing more than a weed, as taro root was cultivated in parts of this region around this time. Rice isn't thought to have become an important part of the Chinese diet until around 800 BC.

By the 9th century AD, it was widely eaten in southern China, but in the north, where it could not be grown, it was food only for the wealthy. Remarkably, rice was not cultivated in Japan until the second century BC and even then, millet remained the principal cereal for most Japanese. Twelve hundred years later, in spite of famine, rice was still mainly a food for the rich and was not to be consumed in any large quantity for another 800 years.

THE REST OF THE WORLD

It is difficult to chart exactly how and when the cultivation of rice spread beyond Asia. In the Middle East and the Mediterranean, wheat was initially the main crop, while in America, maize was by far the most important cereal. Rice was not known here until the Spanish introduced it in the late 16th century.

Rice is enjoyed in many Middle Eastern countries, and basmati rice, in particular, has a special place in people's affections. Today, the Middle Eastern repertoire of rice dishes is wide-ranging,

but it clearly wasn't always so. Rice was probably introduced via northern India and Afghanistan through conquest, expansion and trading. However, even in the 13th century, rice was still regarded as a luxury item in Baghdad.

Rice came to Europe by various routes. Its popularity was determined not so much by its versatility, but by whether or not the crop could be cultivated. Unless rice could be produced locally, the cost of transporting it made the price high, and limited supply and demand. By the middle of this century, the cost of transporting foodstuffs became relatively cheap and foods such as rice, once thought of as exotic, became affordable to the majority and not just the élite.

In Spain, rice was introduced by the Moors, who ruled that country for about 300 years, from the beginning of the 8th century. It was the Moors who built the irrigation canals around Valencia and in the hills around Murcia, which are still used today for rice growing.

The Arabs introduced a dry or upland rice to Sicily, and shortly afterwards there is evidence of paddy fields in northern Italy, around Piedmont and on the Lombardy plains. Here, a wet short grain rice was cultivated, which most scholars believe was introduced not via the south of the country, but from Spain, where another short grain variety of rice had long been

Above: Rice irrigation in China, during the Yuan Dynasty, 13–14th century.

grown. Either way, from around the 14th century onwards, rulers around Pisa and Milan became aware that rice was a good alternative to wheat as a staple food. After a series of devastating famines, they began in earnest to encourage the cultivation of rice. In the 18th century, Piedmont rice was of such high quality that Thomas Jefferson, then US Minister in France, smuggled some out of Italy and sent it to friends in Charleston with instructions for its cultivation. (This was the same Thomas Jefferson who had written the Declaration of Independence and who was later to become the third president of the United States.)

In parts of Europe where cultivation was not an option, rice was often regarded with suspicion, and there appears to have been some resistance to eating it. In Britain at least, it has taken many years, notwithstanding the ubiquitous rice pudding, for rice to become truly accepted. However, rice was not totally unknown in England; in the 13th century, knights returning from the Crusades brought back rice along with other Arabian products such as sugar and lemons.

For a long time in Britain, rice was regarded in the same way as the newly arrived spices. Expensive to buy, it was used by chefs to the aristocracy to make delicate sweets and desserts,

Left: Men and women harvesting rice in China during the 13–14th century: threshing, winnowing and sorting rice.

Above: A flooded rice field in Queensland, Australia. The water will be drained from the field before the rice is harvested.

but was not considered a food for working people. Apart from rice pudding, its most famous appearance was in the savory breakfast dish, kedgeree, developed in India during 19th-century colonial rule. Based on the Indian dish *kitchiri*, kedgeree is a creamy mixture of finnan haddock, eggs and basmati rice, flavored with nutmeg and often lightly curried. It gained great popularity in Victorian England and is now an established national favorite.

Rice was introduced to the Americas by the conquering Spanish and Portuguese, and it has flourished ever since. Nowadays, rice is a hugely important crop in many Latin American countries, most notably Brazil, which grows as much rice as Japan yet still cannot meet its own needs. Brazil is second only to Europe as the world's largest importer of rice.

Some scholars believe rice came to North America with the slaves, who brought the seeds with them from West Africa. It was said that only they had the knowledge of how to grow rice. Another story talks of a ship from Madagascar that was blown off course and put into harbor in Charleston, South Carolina. As a gift of thanks, the captain presented the town with some "seeds of gold", which is a type of rice named for its color. The reality is probably a combination of these legendary stories.

The first Spanish colonists in Florida brought rice with them from the Old World, along with wheat and bread. While Florida proved a congenial environment for growing rice, it was South Carolina which became the main focus for rice cultivation. Attempts to grow upland rice in North Carolina had failed but Carolina Gold, grown in the freshwater island swamps of South Carolina, proved successful. By the late 17th century Carolina Gold was being produced in large quantities.

South Carolina's rice fields were worked entirely by slaves, and it was this situation that contributed directly to the collapse of the rice industry in the Carolinas. When the slaves were freed after the American Civil War in the 1860s, the rice fields were left empty. The war put an end to large-scale rice cultivation in the Carolinas and Georgia, but it did continue along the Mississippi River, in Louisiana, Arkansas and Texas. In the early 20th century rice cultivation spread to California, where rice is still a major crop today. The United States is now the world's second major rice exporter.

Left: The combine harvester has a central role in the modern-day rice harvest.

THE RICE FIELD

Just before harvest time, the paddy fields of Asia are a spectacular sight. On the mountain sides and in the valleys, the land is a sea of soft, luminescent shades of green, and from a distance seems to sway as if in perpetual motion. View it from the air, and you'll notice that some fields are flooded, but many are dry. These are the fields ready for harvest, where the farmer has drained the paddy while the grain continues to ripen, so that the ground is easy to walk upon. It is a mistake to think that the rice plant spends its entire life under water. Water is used to flood the fields, and the plant will remain under water for some weeks or months, but the careful farmer will always regulate this flooding.

Classification

There are numerous varieties of rice although all stem from a single species. In simple terms, each of these varieties can be classified as one of three main types of grain: indica, japonica and javonica. Indica, as the name suggests, is the rice of India. The grains are long and tend to remain separate after cooking. Japonica, which is grown in other parts of Asia, has short grains that are sticky or glutinous when cooked. The third group, javonica, is long grained but has sticky properties.

Cultivation

Rice is the only important cereal to grow in water. The water brings nutrients to the plant, insulates it against extreme heat and cold and, some believe, helps to keep down weeds, although weeding is still required.

In America the rice checks (rice fields) are flooded through a system of canals, which introduce fresh water from a nearby river to wherever it is needed. In much of South-east Asia, water for the paddy fields flows constantly, but relying on Nature for the supply can be problematic. Either there is too much or too little, or the water flows too quickly or not at all. The plant will survive wet or dry periods, and can grow in still water, but ideally the paddy should be flooded after the plant has flowered, and drained dry before harvest.

Rice today is grown throughout the world, but the principal growing regions are the southern United States, Brazil, Egypt, Spain and Italy. The biggest rice-producing area is South-east Asia, from Pakistan in the east to Japan and the Philippines in the west.

In the West, as you would expect, mechanization has taken over the jobs that in Asia are still carried out by manual labor. The rice fields of Texas and Louisiana look very different from those of Bali or Thailand. It is only in Asia where you will find the traditional images associated with rice growing: water buffalo harrowing the paddy fields, men hoeing the flooded fields before planting, and women in conical hats, planting rice seeds.

In many parts of Asia, farmers aim to achieve two crops a year, and the first job is to prepare the land. A hoe is used to break up the soil, which is then flooded prior to planting. In mountainous areas, rice is planted in the highest fields first, and the water is allowed to flow downhill to the lower terraces once the first fields are soaked. Oxen or water buffalo may be used for harrowing the flooded field, which is then planted, often by women. It can take several days to plant one paddy field, and during the growing season all members of the family are needed to help with the ongoing work of adding fertilizers and pesticides, and weeding.

Harvesting

In many Asian countries, come harvest, the women once again move back into the fields to cut the rice stalks, using a small, sharp knife. Rice is so central to people's lives here that people continue to honor the old traditions; women will conceal the cutting knife in order to protect the rice spirit from the knowledge that she must die.

Once they have been cut, the rice stalks are stacked in bundles and threshed – beaten over hard ground with flails or drawn over spikes to release the rice grains. Mechanization is creeping in, predominantly in the developed world, but you may still see hand threshing in parts of Java and Bali. Here, the grain is manually husked and winnowed to dispel the straw and chaff before being stored in the traditional family rice barn, the highly elaborate shrine to the rice spirit.

Below: Modern rice production in Spain. The milled grains are laid out to dry under the hot summer sun (bottom) before being bagged and weighed (top).

Milling

Unless it has been threshed and husked manually, paddy, once cut, is taken to the mill where the bran and husk is removed to give fully milled or "polished" white rice. Unmilled rice that has had only the husk removed is known as cargo rice. It is in this form that rice is imported into Europe from both Asia and America, so that the milling process can be completed at one of the modern mills that exist in Europe, most notably in the Netherlands.

In Europe, milling is a mechanized procedure, although the basic principle is much the same as in the small, noisy mills of Asia. The brown rice passes between rubber rollers that rub away the brown outer skin, leaving the white grain. Once fully milled this is known as "polished" rice, and while once this did imply that the grain had been treated with glycerin or talc to make the grains glossy, this operation is now fairly rare.

Marketing

Until recently, all the rice grown on a typical Asian plot would have been for the family's own consumption, and even today less than 4 per cent is traded between countries. Demand for rice is growing worldwide, however, and as agriculture and jobs diversify, a greater proportion of the rice farmer's annual crop will be sold either for the local market or for export.

Europe is the biggest importer of rice, followed by Brazil and the Middle East. Many rice-growing countries import rice to supplement their own crop, as in the case of Brazil, or so that the home-grown rice can be exported. In order to earn foreign currency, China exports the greater part of its high grade rice and imports a low grade rice for its own population. In parts of the Punjab where basmati rice is grown, almost the entire crop is exported. The price that basmati can fetch means that there is a huge incentive to sell this quality rice. Paradoxically, within the region, bread is more commonly eaten than rice.

NUTRITION

Rice is a non-allergenic food, rich in complex carbohydrates and low in salts and fats. Because brown rice retains the bran, it has twice the nutritional content of white rice and is therefore considered the healthy choice. This shouldn't deter you from eating white rice, however, as all rice is known to be good for you.

Starch/Carbohydrate Rice contains two main starches. It is these starches that determine how sticky or glutinous a rice is. Rice is an excellent carbohydrate food, supplying energy without increasing fat intake.

Protein Brown and white rice contain a small amount of easily digestible protein.

Minerals Rice contains small amounts of phosphorus, magnesium, potassium and zinc. Since these minerals are contained in the bran, they are mostly found in brown rice and, to a lesser extent, in parboiled rice, the production of which involves a process that "glues" nutrients into the grain.

Fiber The rice bran in brown rice provides some fiber. Little fiber remains in white rice after the bran has been taken out.

Vitamins Rice contains small amounts of Vitamin E, B vitamins, Thiamine, Riboflavin, Niacin, Vitamin B6 and folic acid, although since most of the vitamins are contained in the bran, brown rice is a richer source. Parboiled rice also contains a higher proportion of vitamins than white rice.

TYPES OF RICE

There are thousands of varieties of rice. In the world's major rice-growing areas, it is not unknown for each paddy field to yield its own particular strain. This does not mean, however, that people who live in these areas are faced with a bewildering choice; on the contrary, most only eat the rice that is grown locally. It is said that, with just one or two exceptions worldwide, 65 percent of rice is eaten within 550 yards of where it is grown.

There are several possible ways of classifying rice: by region; by color; by cooking properties; even by price. Visit an specialty store and you are likely to find rice grouped in one of these ways, but the most common classification, and the one most supermarkets favor, is by the length of the grain, which can be long, medium or short. As a general rule long and medium grain rices are used for savory dishes, while short grain is used for desserts, although there are exceptions: risotto is only ever made with special short grain rices, for example. In America the terms Patna, rose and pearl are used by millers to describe long, medium and short grain rice respectively.

Left: From left, white and brown long grain rices.

Below: Organic rice is grown entirely free of chemicals.

Organic Rice

This is rice that has been grown without the use of pesticides or fertilizers. It can be long, medium or short grain.

Long Grain Rices

Long grain rice is three or four times as long as it is wide. When cooked, the individual grains separate. Long grain rice can be used in a variety of recipes.

White Long Grain Rice This is the most commonly available white rice and may come from any of a number of countries. America is the most significant producer of long grain rice sold in Europe. China, India, Malaysia and Thailand, among others, produce far greater amounts of this rice than does America, but their production is principally used for the home market and is not exported.

In China long grain rice is called simply *xian* or *indica* (*oryza indica* is the generic name for all long grain rice). In the rice eating areas of China it is the cheapest and most widely available rice for everyday consumption.

The white variety of long grain rice has been fully milled, and all of the bran and outer coating has been removed. The grains are white and slightly shiny, a feature often described by the expression "polished", although strictly speaking, this would mean that glycerine or talc has been used to polish the grains, giving them a smooth and glossy appearance. This practise is relatively rare these days, although the term "polished rice" still persists in some quarters. While white rice hasn't the flavor of basmati or Jasmine rice, it is still a firm favorite and is a good choice for a large number of Western-style and Asian dishes.

Below: From left, white and brown basmati rices, admired for their fragrance and for the slender grains, which provide such a unique texture.

Brown Long Grain Rice Sometimes called whole-grain rice, this is the whole of the grain complete with bran – the rice equivalent of whole-wheat bread. In countries where rice is a staple food and thus eaten in large quantities, brown rice is generally disliked and is seldom eaten. Most brown rice is consumed in the West, where it is considered a healthier alternative to white rice, and is enjoyed for its pleasant texture and nutty flavor. Almost all brown rice is long or medium grain. Short grain rice, perhaps because it is generally used for desserts, is almost always milled first to remove the bran, although it is possible to buy brown short grain rice from health food stores.

Right: American long grain rice

Basmati Rice

This rice is grown in northern India, in the Punjab, in parts of Pakistan adjacent to West Punjab and in the foothills of the Himalayas. The particular soil and climate of this region is thought to account for basmati's unique taste and texture. The word "basmati" means "the fragrant one" in Hindi, and it is rightly considered by most rice lovers around the world to be the prince of rice. Basmati has a fine aromatic flavor. The grains are long and slender and become even longer during cooking, which partly accounts for its wonderful texture. There are various grades of basmati, but it is impossible to differentiate between them except by trying the brands to discover the variety with the best fragrance and flavor. Basmati is excellent in almost any savory rice dish and is perfect for pilafs or for serving with curries. It is also an essential ingredient in biryani.

Brown Basmati Like all types of brown rice, brown basmati comes with the bran. It has all the flavor of white basmati with the texture typical of brown rice. It would not be used in Indian dishes but is superb in any number of Western-style meals.

Above: Thai fragrant rice

Patna Rice

At one time, most of the long grain rice sold in Europe came from Patna in India, and the term was used loosely to mean any long grain rice. The custom persists in parts of America, but elsewhere Patna is used to describe a specific variety of long grain rice from the Bihar region of India.

Dehra Dun

A long grain, non-sticky Indian rice. It is not generally available outside India, except from specialist stores.

Domsiah Rice

A fine grained, Persian rice, available from Middle Eastern stores.

Jasmine Rice or Thai Fragrant Rice

This fragrant long grain rice is cultivated in Thailand and is widely used in Asian cooking. The rice has a faintly scented, almost milky aroma that is a perfect match for the exotic flavors of Oriental cuisine. Once cooked, the grains are slightly sticky. Thai fragrant rice is excellent both for savory dishes and for sweet ones. To fully appreciate its fragrance, it is best cooked by the absorption method.

American Aromatic Rice

America grows several familiar aromatic rices, including Jasmine, and has developed several of its own.

Texmati, an American version of basmati, is not sold outside the United States, although it can often be found in specialist American stores.

Medium Grain Rices

Medium grain rice is about twice as long as it is wide. After cooking, the grains are moist and tender, and tend to cling together more than long grain. Medium grain rice is sold in both brown and white varieties. In Spain, white medium grain rice is often used for making paella.

Short Grain Rices

Mention short grain or pearl rice and most people will either think of risotto or creamy, slow-cooked desserts. Both these dishes owe their success to the ability of short grain rice to absorb liquid, becoming soft and sticky in the process. Short grain rice is almost as broad as it is long and is sometimes described as round grain. The grains stick together when cooked.

Pudding or Dessert Rice

This is a catch-all name for any short grain rice. Virtually all pudding rice is white, with short, plump grains. Carolina rice was the original name for American short grain rice, taking its name from the state where it was first grown. The name is seldom used today, although you may occasionally find cookbooks calling for Carolina rice.

Italian Rice

Italy produces more rice, and in greater variety, than any other country in Europe. Most is grown in the north of the country, in the Po Valley around Piedmont. Italian rice is classified by size, ranging from the shortest grain, *ordinario*, to *semi-fino*, *fino* and *superfino*. Most of the varieties of risotto rice are either *fino* or *superfino*.

Right: Short grain pudding or dessert rice

rice grown is a medium short grain variety, which has a slightly sticky consistency when cooked. It is particularly popular for making paella. A longer grain rice is also grown and is generally added to soups.

Within Spain, rice is graded by the amount of whole grains included in the weight: *Categoria Extra* (red label) is the finest rice, with 95 per cent whole grains, *Categoria Uno* (green label) has 87 per cent whole grains, while *Categoria Dos* (yellow label) has 80 per cent whole grains. *Calasperra* is a top quality short grain rice that is quite easy to locate outside Spain, unlike most Spanish rices, which must be bought from specialty stores.

Grano Largo or Variedad Americana A long grain white rice. The brown equivalent is called *arroz integral*.

Bahia A medium grain rice used for making paella.

Bomba Another paella rice. Like an Italian risotto rice, the plump grain absorbs a lot of liquid.

Asian Rices

In Japan, two basic types of rice are eaten: glutinous rice (see separate entry) and a plump short grained rice, called *uruchimai*. They are often sold simply as Japanese rice. Although not a glutinous rice, even the ordinary rice has sticky properties – a non-sticky rice would be difficult to eat with chopsticks.

Sushi Rice In the West, a carton labeled sushi rice will almost inevitably contain a short grain rice that will need to be cooked before you can use it to make sushi. Typical examples are Japanese Rose, Kokuho Rose and Calrose. Ask for sushi rice in Japan, however, and you are likely to be offered rice that has been cooked with vinegar, sugar and salt, and is thus ready for making sushi.

Shinmai This is a highly esteemed Japanese rice that is sold in Japan in late summer. It is the first rice of the season. Because of its high moisture content, it needs less water for cooking.

Arborio This is one of the best known varieties of Italian risotto rice, and takes its name from a town in the Vercelli region of north-west Italy. Unlike the finer risotto rices such as Carnaroli, Arborio has a comparatively large plump grain with a high proportion of amylopectin. This is the starch that dissolves during cooking to give *risotti* their creamy texture. However, because of the length of the grain and because it contains less amylose (the firm inner starch) it is easy to overcook Arborio rice. Recipes often recommend turning off the heat when the risotto is almost cooked and "resting" it for a few minutes. The rice will continue to cook, due to its own heat, without becoming too soft.

Vialone Nano This is another popular risotto rice. It has a plump grain. Vialone Nano contains less amylopectin than Arborio and has a higher proportion of amylose, so retains a firm "bite" at the center of the grain when the rest of the rice has cooked to a creamy consistency. Risottos made using this rice tend to be of a rippling consistency, which is described in Italian as *all' onda*. Vialone Nano is especially popular for making Venetian- and Verona-style risottos.

Carnaroli This is considered the premium risotto rice. It was developed by a Milanese rice grower who crossed Vialone Nano with a Japanese rice. The outer part of the grain is made up of a soft starch that dissolves during cooking to leave the inner grain, which has a satisfying, firm "bite."

Spanish Rices

Rice is grown extensively in Spain, particularly in the swampy regions outside Valencia. The most common

Glutinous Rice

There are several types of glutinous rice. The name is misleading – the grains contain no gluten – but they are renowned for the way they stick together after cooking. Often known as sticky or sweet rice, glutinous rice is not usually eaten with savory dishes, but is sweetened and served, hot or cold, with fruit as a dessert.

Japanese Glutinous Rice   This short grained rice is sticky when cooked, a characteristic that makes it perfect for shaping. It has a slightly sweet taste.

Chinese Glutinous Rice   In China, glutinous rice is called *geng* rice. It is also known by the generic name for short grain rice (*oryza japonica*). There are white and black varieties, and also a pinkish red rice that grows along the Yangtze river. Glutinous rice is used for desserts and dim sum.

Above: Short grained white Chinese glutinous rice.

Thai Glutinous Rice   Also available in white and black grains, Thai glutinous rice is very popular in desserts. The cooked black rice grain is really a deep blue-purple color.

Red Rice

Red rice is not unheard of in rice growing areas, but its presence is not always welcome as it means the rice is reverting to a wild strain, and is likely to be brittle, shatter easily and prove difficult to harvest. In the Camargue region of France, however, a red rice has been developed that is the result of cross pollination between the local white rice and an indigenous wild red rice. The uncooked grain is a reddish brown, and as it cooks the color intensifies and the water turns a distinct shade of red. Like most whole-grain rice, red rice needs to be cooked for longer than white rice. It has a nutty flavor and a good firm texture. Use in place of brown rice or long grain white rice.

Above: The semi-wild hybrid, red rice.

Left: Sushi rices. Clockwise from top, a sweetened variety, Kokuho and sushi rice.

Wild or Indian Rice

This is not a true rice at all, but a grass that grows in the marshy areas around the American Great Lakes. Wild rice was once a favorite food of the Native American Indians, and today much of America's wild rice is harvested by Native Americans, who have treaty agreements to harvest it.

Wild rice needs to be soaked for several hours before cooking, and must be cooked for about 40 minutes until the inner grain breaks through the husk. Wild rice has acquired a fashionable status throughout the West, but its greatest popularity is still in the United States. It is used at Thanksgiving for stuffing the turkey, a symbol of the fact that wild rice was an important staple food for the early settlers when the wheat and barley they had brought with them failed to thrive in the New World.

Below: Canadian wild rice

Giant Canadian Wild Rice

Canadian wild rice is similar to the variety from the United States, but the grains are longer and the Canadian rice is considered to have a superior flavor. The rice is grown on lakes in the north and on the west coast of Canada, where it is harvested by local Indians, who traditionally beat the overhanging grass stems with canoe paddles. The grain that falls into their canoes is theirs to keep, while the remainder, which settles in the shallow water, is for next year's harvest. Like all wild rice, this giant version should be soaked in water for several hours and rinsed, before being cooked for at least 40 minutes, until the tough outer husk has burst open.

Wild Rice and Basmati

This is simply a mixture of two popular and well flavored grains. Because wild rice normally takes much longer to cook than plain basmati, the makers of this product balance the equation by using a parboiled basmati, which has a longer cooking time, matching it with a strain of wild rice that requires less cooking than usual. Check the packaging for exact cooking times.

Parboiled or Easy-cook Rice

In spite of its name, parboiled or converted rice (sometimes labeled "easy-cook") is not a quick cooking rice; indeed, it takes almost half as long again to cook as most long grain rices. Parboiling is an ancient technique that was developed in India. The whole grain rice is soaked in water and then steamed, which has the effect of locking in the nutrients that are in the bran layer. For white rice, the bran is then removed.

In parts of India and the Middle East, parboiled rice is very popular. In the West it is mainly – and mistakenly – perceived to be an easy-to-cook rice, although a better description might be "difficult to ruin" as it can stand quite a bit of abuse during cooking.

The parboiled rice grains are more yellow than those of normal rice, although this coloration disappears during cooking; when fully cooked, parboiled white rice is a brilliant white. Parboiled rice does take longer to cook than normal rice, but the advantage, for those who enjoy this rice, is that the rice grains stay noticeably separate and slightly chewy. Some people, however, dislike the over-assertive texture and complain that the flavor is bland.

If you're not sure, try both types and compare the results. There are parboiled versions of white and brown basmati and white and brown long grain rice.

Right: Nowadays, there is a wide choice of convenience rices on the market. Some are ready-mixed with flavorings or vegetables for an instant side dish.

Below: Wild and basmati rices

Quick-cook Rices

Boil-in-the-bag Rice This is a called a convenience rice, although it takes just as long to cook as regular rice; the main convenience is that the pan doesn't have to be washed afterwards. Most boil-in-the-bag rices are prepared with parboiled (easy-cook) rice.

Instant and Quick White Rice

Not to be confused with parboiled, instant rice is just that – rice that has been fully cooked in advance and only needs to be rehydrated and heated in order to be ready to serve. Quick white rice has been partially cooked in advance. There are a number of different brands available, each with different rehydrating and reheating instructions, so it is important to check carefully before cooking.

Frozen Rice Also a pre-cooked rice, this needs only to be thawed and reheated, which can often be done in the microwave; check the instructions.

Canned Rice This type of rice really couldn't be simpler to use; just open the can, tip into a bowl and reheat in the microwave or in a conventional oven. For single people with little time for cooking, canned rice may be a handy standby, but it is a hugely expensive way to eat rice, and the flavor is severely diminished.

RICE PRODUCTS

Flaked Rice

Flaked rice is commonly used in Chinese, Thai and Vietnamese cooking for stuffings and desserts. The parboiled rice is flattened with heavy rollers, so the rice cooks quickly and evenly. In the West, flaked rice is used by the food trade for breakfast cereals and snacks but it is seldom used in recipes. Flaked rice is available from Asian stores.

Ground Rice

More granular than rice flour, this is used for milk desserts, and was once particularly popular in England. Ground rice is also widely used for biscuits and baking and is a good substitute for wheat flour, especially for people who cannot tolerate gluten.

Rice Flour

Finer than ground rice, this is also used in both oriental and Western cooking for cakes, biscuits and desserts.

Glutinous Rice Flour

This is made from glutinous rice and is normally labeled rice powder or sweet rice flour. It is used for desserts.

Shiratamo-Ko

A Japanese version of glutinous rice flour.

White Rice Vinegar

Made from glutinous rice, Japanese rice wine vinegar has a subtle flavor, and is excellent not only in Asian cooking but for any dressing where you need a mild unassuming flavor. Chinese rice wine vinegar is not as delicate but it makes a good alternative to wine vinegar.

Black Rice Vinegar

Though dark in color, black rice vinegar has a surprisingly mild taste. It can be used for Asian soups and for dipping sauces.

Red Rice Vinegar

Much spicier than other rice vinegars, Chinese red rice vinegar is used mainly in hot dipping sauces to be served with seafood.

Shaoxing

This Chinese rice wine, which is made from glutinous rice, yeast and water, has a rich, mellow flavor. It is popular throughout China for cooking and drinking, and is available in Asian stores and some wine stores. Although both are rice wines, do not confuse Shaoxing with sake, which has a completely different taste. Other Chinese renditions include Chia Fai, Hsiang Hseuh and Yen Hung.

From left: Flaked rice and ground rice. Both cook quickly and evenly, which makes them good for desserts and baking.

Left: Glutinous rice flours. The top product is made from cooked glutinous rice, while the bottom product is made from uncooked rice. The difference between the two will affect recipe cooking times and flavors.

Above: From left, Japanese seasoned rice vinegar, Chinese red rice vinegar and Japanese sweetened vinegar. The mild Japanese vinegars are used for a variety of cooking purposes; the spicy Chinese vinegar is generally only used for sharper-flavored dishes and dipping sauces.

Sake

This Japanese rice wine is quite sweet with a mild flavor that belies its potency. Sake is served in small cups – about the size of egg cups – and can be chilled but is more often served warm. Nowadays, sake is often drunk with a meal, which is a radical shift in emphasis; traditionally, sake was the central attraction, and the small portions of food that accompanied it were there to enhance the flavor of this celebrated drink.

Mirin

A sweet cooking sake with a light delicate flavor, mirin is normally stirred into Japanese dishes during the final stages of cooking. It adds a mild sweetness to sauces or dips. Combined with soy sauce, it is the basis of teriyaki sauce, which is popular for basting grilled foods. Mirin is available from any Japanese food store and from many of the larger supermarkets.

Rice-stick Noodles

These flat noodles vary in thickness; each is roughly the same length as a chopstick. To cook rice sticks, soak them in warm water or stock for 20 minutes to soften before draining.

The noodles are used to thicken soups and casseroles, and for stir-fries.

Rice-flour Noodles

These hair-like noodles are very popular in Thai, Vietnamese and Indonesian cooking. Don't confuse them with bean thread noodles (which look similar) as these are made from ground mung beans. Soak rice-flour noodles in warm water for 5–10 minutes to soften, then use according to the recipe.

Japanese Harusame Noodles

Similar to rice-flour noodles, these are also made from ground rice and are sold in fragile-looking loops. Prepare the noodles in the same way as rice-flour noodles.

Below: Round and triangular rice papers. Clockwise from top, Thai, Chinese and Vietnamese varieties.

Above: Chinese and Thai rice sticks and rice-flour noodles.

Rice Paper

Sometimes called rice wrappers, these wafer-thin papers are made from rice flour, salt and water. They are sold dried in Asian stores and supermarkets, and can be round or triangular in shape. Before use, dip the rice papers into hot water for a few seconds to soften them. They are used in Vietnamese cooking to make spring-rolls, and are popular in some Chinese dishes. Don't confuse them with spring roll wrappers, which are made from wheat flour and water, nor with the edible rice paper used for lining cookie sheets.

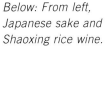

Below: From left, Japanese sake and Shaoxing rice wine.

COOKING PERFECT RICE

BOILED RICE

Choosing the Rice

Which rice you choose will depend largely on the meal you intend to cook. Basmati, with its wonderful fragrance and flavor, is for many the only rice to serve with an Indian meal. For a Chinese, Thai or Indonesian meal, Jasmine rice, with its pleasant aroma and slightly sticky texture (important if you intend to use chopsticks) is excellent, while the versatile American long grain rice is great for stir-fries, pilafs, jambalayas and gumbos.

There are a few instances where only a specific type of rice will do – risottos, for example, can only be made successfully with risotto rice – but in general, providing you know a little about the qualities of the rice, there are no hard and fast rules. Although tradition demands rice desserts be made with a short grain rice, there's no reason why you shouldn't use long grain. Jasmine rice and basmati make delicious desserts too.

Quantities

There are no absolute rules. In the West, 2⅓ cups of uncooked rice is the quantity recommended for eight people as a side dish, but would barely be enough for two Javanese workmen. The following quantities of uncooked rice apply to basmati rice, Thai fragrant rice and both brown and white long grain rices.
• For side dishes allow 2–3 ounces rice per person or 8–12 ounces rice to serve four.
• For pilafs allow 2 ounces rice per person or 8 ounces to serve four,
• For salads allow 1–1½ ounces per person or 4–6 ounces to serve four.
• For short grain rice desserts allow ½–¾ ounce per person or 2–3 ounces to serve four.
The weight of rice doubles in weight after cooking, although this depends on the type of rice, the amount of liquid and the cooking time. As a basic rule, when a recipe calls for cooked rice, use just under half the weight in uncooked rice.

Preparing Rice

Some types of rice benefit from being rinsed in cold water, while others should be left to soak before use. Precisely which procedure to follow will be outlined in individual recipes.

Rinsing

• Suitable for: basmati, brown basmati, Jasmine rice, brown and white long grain, sushi, glutinous and short grain rice.

Rinsing rice before it is cooked is not essential but it does help to remove excess starch and any dust that may have accumulated in storage. Most types of rice benefit from being rinsed. Do not rinse if using rice in a risotto. If you rinse rice which is to be used in a paella or any other dish where it is fried at the beginning of the recipe, be sure to drain it thoroughly first.

1 Cover the rice with cold water and swirl the grains between your fingers. The water will become slightly cloudy.

2 Allow the rice to settle, then tip the bowl so that the water drains away. Cover the rice once more with cold water, then rinse. Repeat several times until the water runs clear.

COOK'S TIP

In Japan, it is common practise for rice to be rinsed and then left to drain for 30 minutes or longer.

Soaking

• Suitable for: basmati, brown basmati, glutinous rice and sometimes American long grain, brown long grain rice, short grain rice and Jasmine rice.

Soaking is seldom essential but it does increase the moisture content of the grains, which means the rice will cook more quickly and will be less sticky. Soaking is particularly beneficial for basmati rice; less so for Jasmine rice, where a slight stickiness is an advantage. Risotto rice must not be soaked. Occasionally, rice that has been soaked will be fried; if this is the case, drain it very thoroughly first.

1 To soak rice, simply place it in a large bowl and cover with double the volume of cold water.

2 Leave the rice in the bowl for about 30 minutes or for the time suggested in the recipe, then drain it thoroughly in a strainer or colander.

Making Perfect Boiled Rice

Pan-of-water method

• Suitable for: most types of rice, but particularly for basmati, brown basmati, American long grain, red Carmague and brown rice. Not recommended for Jasmine rice.

In Asia, cooks often add a few drops of vegetable oil as well as salt when cooking rice by this method.

1 Put the rice in a large pan. Pour in a large amount of boiling water or stock (about 5 cups for every 1 cup rice) and add a pinch of salt. Bring the water back to a boil, then lower heat and simmer, uncovered, for the time indicated on the packet, until the rice is just tender.

2 Strain the cooked rice through a strainer or colander and rinse thoroughly with plenty of hot water.

3 Either return the rice to the pan or set the strainer over the pan. Cover with the pan lid or a dish towel and let the rice stand for 5 minutes. Fork through the rice before serving, adding butter or oil if desired.

Adding flavorings Stock can be used instead of water, and flavorings such as bay leaves, curry leaves or whole spices can be added if you like, especially if the rice is to be used for a salad, a fried rice dish or a stuffing.

Absorption method

• Suitable for: basmati, Thai, fragrant rice, short grain and glutinous rice. Sometimes used for brown basmati and American long grain rice.

This is also known as the covered pan method. The rice is cooked in a measured amount of water in a pan with a tightly fitting lid until the water has been absorbed. The proportion of rice to water, and the cooking time, will depend on the type of rice used. Use this method if you need cooked rice for stir-frying, or for a rice salad. It is also used when making some rice desserts.

1 Put the rice into a pan and pour in the measured liquid. Bring back to a boil, then reduce the heat to the lowest possible setting.

2 Cover and cook until the liquid has been absorbed. This can take up to 25 minutes, depending on the type of rice.

3 Remove the pan from the heat and let stand, covered with the lid or with foil or a dish towel, for 5 minutes. Steam holes will have appeared on the surface of the rice. If the grains are not completely tender, replace the cover tightly and let the rice stand for about 5 minutes more.

Adding flavorings If you want to flavor the rice, the absorption method provides the perfect opportunity. Lemongrass, curry leaves and whole spices can be added with the liquid, which can be water, stock, coconut milk or a mixture. This method of cooking rice is the basis of several pilaf-style dishes, where onions, garlic and other ingredients, such as spices, are fried before the rice and liquid are added.

COOK'S TIP

It is vital that the pan is covered tightly and that the rice is cooked at as low a heat as possible. If the lid of the pan is loose, cover the pan with foil or a dish towel before fitting the lid, making sure that any excess fabric is kept well away from the heat source. White rice will cook however low the heat. If, after bringing the liquid back to a boil, the pan is removed entirely from the heat, the rice would continue to cook but would take longer.

The absorption method is the best way to cook Jasmine rice, and basmati rice will retain its excellent flavor when cooked by this method.

Microwave method

• Suitable for: basmati, brown basmati, Jasmine and white and brown long grain rice.

Although no faster than conventional cooking, using the microwave is very convenient. It frees a burner on the stovetop, and the rice can be served in the dish in which it is cooked.

1 Using the same quantities of rice and liquid as for the absorption method, put the rice in a deep glass bowl or microwave container and stir in the boiling water or stock.

2 Cover with a lid or with microwave-proof plastic wrap and cook on 100% Full Power. Check your microwave instruction book for timings. Let the rice stand for 10 minutes before use.

Adding flavorings Cooking in the microwave is essentially the same as when following the absorption method and simple flavorings can be added. If using a large number of additional ingredients, consult your microwave instruction book as the cooking times may differ.

Oven method

• Suitable for: basmati, brown basmati, American long grain, brown long grain, and red Camargue rice.

This is a combination of two methods: the rice is partially cooked first in a pan on the stovetop, before being finished in the oven. It produces a slightly dry rice, with separate grains.

1 Cook the rice by the pan-of-water method or the absorption method for three-quarters of the normal cooking time. Drain, if necessary, then spoon the rice into a baking dish.

2 Dot with butter or ghee, then cover tightly and cook in a moderate oven for 10–20 minutes. The oven temperature can be between 325ºF and 375ºF but the cooking time will need to be adjusted accordingly.

Adding flavorings Flavorings can be added to the rice during the first stage of cooking, or part of the cooked rice can be colored and flavored with saffron or a spice, if you like. Fried onions, garlic or cardamoms can be dotted over the partly cooked rice before it is placed in the oven.

Steaming

• Suitable for: white basmati, American long grain and Jasmine rice.

This method is also combined. The rice is partially cooked first in a pan of simmering liquid, before being steamed. This method of cooking is used for plain boiled rice and some glutinous rice dishes.

1 Cook the rice by the pan-of-water method or the absorption method for about three-quarters of the normal cooking time. Tip the partly cooked rice into a strainer or colander.

2 Transfer the cooked rice to a cheesecloth bag set inside a pan of simmering water. Cover and steam for 5–10 minutes for white rice; 15 minutes for brown rice. If the grains of rice still feel hard, steam for a little longer.

Adding flavorings The rice can be flavored during the first stage of cooking, in the same way as for the pan-of-water or absorption methods. Replace the cooking water with stock, coconut milk or a mixture, if you like, and add bay leaves, curry leaves, lemongrass or whole spices with the liquid.

Electric rice cooker

• Suitable for: all types of rice.

1 Put the rice into the cooker and add the required amount of water as indicated in your instruction booklet. Do not add salt. Cover the cooker with the lid and switch it on. The cooker will switch itself off automatically when the rice is ready, and will keep the rice hot until you are ready to serve.

Quick-cook method

Rice can be soaked in boiling water and then quickly cooked at the last minute. This works particularly well with basmati rice that is to be cooked by the pan-of-water method. It is a useful cooking method if you are entertaining and want the rice to cook quickly, and with as little fuss as possible.

1 Put the measured rice into a large bowl and pour over boiling water to cover. Let stand, uncovered, for at least 30 minutes or up to 1 hour.

2 Bring a pan of lightly salted stock or water to a boil. Drain the rice, add it to the pan and cook for 3–4 minutes until the rice is tender.

Adding flavorings Flavorings can be added in the same way as for boiled rice.

Cooking Brown Rice

Brown rice takes longer to cook than white rice, but how much longer will depend on the type of rice; always check the packaging instructions. Soaking brown rice in a bowl of water first will soften the grains but it will not shorten the cooking time.

Cooking Glutinous Rice

Glutinous rice should be soaked before cooking, for at least 1 hour and up to 4 hours. After being drained, the rice can then be simmered with coconut milk and sugar if it is to be served as a dessert. For a savory side dish, steam the drained rice for about 10–15 minutes, until it is tender.

Cooking Wild Rice

Although this is not strictly a rice, wild rice can be treated in the same way. It takes a lot of cooking, and for best results, should be soaked in water for 1 hour before being boiled in lightly salted water for 45–60 minutes. Check the instructions on the packaging as cooking times differ according to the size of the grains. Wild rice is cooked when the inner white grain bursts out of the black husk.

Cooking Parboiled (Easy-cook) Rice

This takes longer to cook than regular rice. Check the packaging for instructions. Parboiled rice can be cooked by the pan-of-water or the absorption method. It can also be cooked in the microwave or in a rice cooker. This type of rice is fine as a side dish, but is not as good for fried rice dishes.

Cooking/Heating Frozen or Canned Rice

Follow the instructions on the packaging. Most can be reheated or cooked on the stovetop or in the microwave.

Storing Rice

Raw (uncooked) rice can be kept in a cool, dark place for up to three years in the unopened packaging or in an airtight container. It should be kept perfectly dry; if the moisture content creeps up, the rice will turn moldy. If the rice is very old, it may need more water or longer cooking. Check the packaging for "best before" dates.

Cooked rice can be stored for up to 24 hours if cooled, covered and kept in the fridge. You can also freeze the cooled rice; reheat it in a covered casserole in the oven or thaw it and use for fried rice or in a salad. Reheated rice should be piping hot all the way through.

RICE COOKING TIPS

• Always let cooked rice stand for 5 minutes after draining and before serving to "rest" it and complete the cooking process.

• Remember that rice absorbs water as it cooks. If you use too much water with the absorption method, or cook the rice for too long, it will become soggy.

• If rice is still a little undercooked after cooking (by whatever method), cover it tightly and set aside for 5–10 minutes. It will continue to cook in the residual heat.

• If cooking rice for a rice salad, use the pan-of-water method and rinse the drained, cooked rice under cold water. Drain it thoroughly before mixing with the other ingredients.

• If cooked rice is required for a fried rice dish, cook it either by the absorption method (Jasmine rice) or the pan-of-water method (basmati rice). Avoid overcooking. The rice should be dry and fluffy.

• Be sure to use a pan with a tight fitting lid if you are cooking rice by the absorption method.

Above: Cooked, cooled rice freezes well.

RISOTTO

This simple Italian dish is very much a peasant food and it says a great deal about the changing attitudes towards food and healthy eating that in the last decade or so, this dish, like much *cucina povera*, has come to be so widely appreciated. Nowadays you will see risotto on the menu at some of the classiest restaurants in town, enjoyed for the same reasons it has always been valued, because it is healthy, satisfying and extremely good to eat. Yet what could be simpler than a risotto? Although there are complicated and elaborate versions, some of the best risottos are made using little more than rice, a good stock and a few fresh herbs or cheeses. These simple risottos, like *Risi e Bisi* (Rice and Peas) or *Risotto alla Parmigiana* (Rice with Cheese) are probably the most traditional of all, and are no less tasty for their plain ingredients.

Since the first risottos were the food of poorer people, there is no long line of recipes that chart the popularity of this dish. Recipe books written in Italy during risotto's infancy tended to concern themselves with costly meats or spices and were written for the wealthy who could afford these expensive ingredients. Peasants and poor farmers had neither the time, the ability nor the inclination to read what they knew already: that rice was a cheap and sustaining food that was also delicious when cooked with care.

Short grain rice, which is the central ingredient in risotto, has been grown in Italy for several hundred years. The Arabs introduced rice into Italy during the Middle Ages, but this early rice was a longer grained variety and was grown in Sicily and the south of the country.

At some point though, rice was introduced to Lombardy in northern Italy, and by the 15th century, rice cultivation had become an established part of the Italian way of life. It was around this time that the custom of cultivating rice in fields flooded with water was adopted in Italy; this method of growing rice followed the process used in Asia, as opposed to the method of dry cultivation favored by the Arabs.

Today, Italy shares with Spain the honor of being Europe's leading rice producer. Risotto rices are still grown in the north of the country, where the rice fields are irrigated with water running down from the Alps. The varieties of rice grown today have been improved and refined since earlier times, yet the characteristic starchy short grain has remained the same.

The method of cooking rice in stock may have been influenced by cooking styles in France and Spain but, whether by accident or design, it is difficult to imagine a better way of doing justice to fine rice than to serve it as a risotto.

Risotto is traditionally eaten as a separate course before the meat and vegetables. Only rice and stock are the essential ingredients, but you should choose these carefully. The stock must be home-made (or the very best you can afford) and the rice must be one of those recommended for the purpose. Have the stock simmering in a pan adjacent to the risotto pan, and add it slowly and lovingly. Observe the standing time at the end, as this allows the rice to rest and reach perfection. Do all this – and it is not difficult – and you'll find risotto one of the most simple and rewarding rice dishes you can make.

Types of Risotto Rice

It is essential to use a risotto rice, but precisely which one is up to you. Named risotto rices are becoming more widely available, but you will often find packages labeled simply Italian risotto rice. Of the named varieties, Arborio is the most widely available, with Carnaroli and Vialone Nano becoming increasingly easy to find in Italian specialty stores and good supermarkets. Other specific types of risotto rice include Baldo, Vialone Nano Gigante and Roma. Each has its own particular qualities, which will be familiar to those who specialize in cooking *risotti*. Some recipes call for a named risotto rice, but most are non-specific and any risotto rice will give a good result.

INSTANT RISOTTOS

There are several instant risottos on the market, available from supermarkets and specialty stores. They are easy to make, all you need to do is add water, heat and stir. They are supplied with simple instructions and recommend simmering for about 10 minutes – roughly half the time required for making a classic risotto. Instant risottos come in several flavors, including four cheeses, spinach, saffron, tomato and black cuttlefish. They are handy for a quick meal, and the colors supplied by the flavorings make them pretty to serve. More importantly, these risottos taste surprisingly good.

Left: Clockwise from top, instant risottos flavored with cuttlefish, tomatoes, saffron and spinach.

Making Perfect Risotto

1 In a large, deep pan, cook the onion, garlic and any other vegetable(s) in extra virgin olive oil over medium heat for a few minutes, stirring constantly. Unless the recipe specifies otherwise, the onion and other vegetables should be softened but not browned.

2 If using any uncooked meat or poultry, add these ingredients to the onions in the pan, unless the recipe specifies otherwise. Turn up the heat to high and cook, stirring frequently, until browned on all sides.

3 Tip the risotto rice into the pan, and stir, so that every grain is coated in the oil. Cook the rice over high heat for 3–4 minutes, stirring constantly. You will notice that the grains of rice become transparent as they are stirred into the hot oil, except for the very center of the grain, which remains opaque.

4 Add a little wine, if this is what is called for in the recipe, or a ladleful of hot stock. Stir the rice until all the liquid has been absorbed.

5 Lower the heat to moderate, then add another ladleful of hot stock and stir it into the rice. Keep the pan over moderate heat so that the liquid bubbles but the rice is in no danger of burning. Stir the rice frequently.

6 Add the remaining stock a ladleful at a time, making sure that each ladleful is used up before adding the next. This process will take about 20 minutes. As the risotto cooks, the grains of rice will begin to soften and merge together.

7 When the risotto begins to look creamy, shred in the cheese or add any extra butter. The rice should be virtually tender, but still a little hard in the center. At this point remove the pan from the heat, cover with a dish towel and let rest for about 5 minutes. The risotto will cook to perfection in the residual heat.

RISOTTO TIPS
- To begin, cook the rice in hot oil, stirring all the time, until the grains are coated and begin to turn translucent.
- Add any wine or sherry to the risotto before adding the stock. The alcohol will evaporate, but the flavor will remain.
- Use a good quality, home-made stock for your risotto. Alternatively, buy cartons of fresh stock, which are available from supermarkets.
- The stock added to a risotto must always be hot. Have it simmering in a separate pan adjacent to the pan in which you are cooking the risotto.
- Add the hot stock slowly, ladleful by ladleful. Make sure all the liquid has been absorbed before adding the next ladleful.
- Avoid overcooking the risotto. Remove the pan from the heat while the rice is still slightly undercooked.
- For best results, season the risotto after cooking but before letting it rest. Stock, salted butter and Parmesan cheese will all contribute some saltiness, as may other ingredients, so always taste the risotto before adding any extra salt.
- Don't use ready-grated Parmesan. For the best flavor, buy good quality Parmesan in one piece and shred it yourself.

Equipment

There are only three essential pieces of equipment needed for cooking a risotto, and with luck you'll have them already.
- A heavy pan. Ideally, this should be a wide, straight-sided pot, deep enough to contain the cooked risotto. A deep skillet can be used for smaller risotto quantities.
- A wooden spoon.
- A pan for the simmering stock.

Adding Risotto Ingredients

Recipes will tell you when to stir in any additional ingredients needed for the risotto, but this guide may be helpful when devising your own risotto recipes.

Vegetables   Onions and garlic are cooked until soft at the beginning, before the rice is added. Most other vegetables, such as eggplant, carrots, zucchini and pepper, are sauteed with the onions. Vegetables that require little cooking, such as spinach and asparagus, should be stirred in towards the end of cooking. Mushrooms are usually cooked at the same time or just after the onions, before adding the rice.

Above: Onions and garlic are essential ingredients in a good risotto. Use red onions or shallots for variations in flavor.

Above: Fresh green vegetables, such as zucchini, spinach and asparagus, add texture to the risotto. They retain their shape and color during cooking, and always look impressive.

Fish and shellfish   These are generally cooked before being added to the risotto. It is usual for fillets of fish, such as salmon, flounder or sea bass to be poached, then flaked. Scallops should be lightly cooked, then sliced. Stir fish or shellfish into the risotto about three-quarters of the way through cooking.

Above: Almost any fresh fish and seafood can be used in a risotto, including salmon fillets, haddock, flounder and shrimp.

Meat and poultry   These are usually added at an early stage, at the same time as the onions; the rice is added later, so that both ingredients cook together. The exception is cooked meats, such as sausage or ham, which tend to be stirred into the risotto towards the end of cooking.

Above: Chicken fillets and gammon are both very successful ingredients for risottos, but the choice really is endless. Cut the meat into small pieces and brown with the onions before stirring in the rice.

Herbs   Robust herbs are sometimes cooked with the onions, but more delicate herbs, such as parsley or cilantro, are usually added at the end of cooking, at the same time as the Parmesan cheese or butter.

Above: Delicate-flavored herbs, such as thyme, sage, cilantro and tarragon, can all be stirred into the cooked rice for a simple risotto.

Cheese   Where cheese is the dominant flavoring, as in a four-cheese risotto, it can be added halfway through cooking, but it is more usual for shredded Parmesan to be added just before the risotto is left to rest.

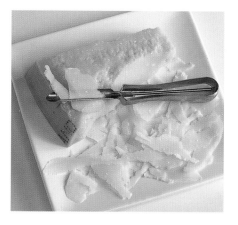

Above: Most cheeses can be used in risottos but the one essential cheese is Parmesan. Use it either on its own as a simple flavoring or to complement other ingredients in the recipe. Fresh shavings of Parmesan can be used to garnish the risotto, or supply a bowl of Parmesan, shredded fresh from the block, to be passed separately when serving.

MAKING STOCKS

Chicken Stock

MAKES ABOUT 6¼ CUPS

INGREDIENTS
    1 onion, quartered
    2 celery stalks, chopped
    1 carrot, coarsely chopped
    about 1½ pounds fresh chicken,
      either ½ whole chicken or
      2–3 chicken quarters
    1 fresh thyme or marjoram sprig
    2 fresh parsley sprigs
    8 whole peppercorns
    salt

1 Put all the prepared vegetables in a large, heavy pan and lay the chicken on top. Pour enough over cold water to cover the chicken (this will be about 6¼ cups).

2 Bring to a boil slowly. Do not cover the pan. When bubbling, skim off any fat that has risen to the surface.

3 Add the herbs, peppercorns and a pinch of salt. Lower heat, cover the pan and simmer the stock gently for 2–2½ hours, until the chicken is tender.

4 Using a slotted spoon, transfer the chicken or chicken pieces to a plate. Remove any skin or bones; the chicken can be used in another recipe. Strain the stock into a clean bowl, let cool, then chill in the fridge.

5 A layer of fat will form on the surface of the chilled stock. Remove this just before use. The stock can be kept in the fridge for up to 3 days or frozen for up to 6 months.

Fish Stock

MAKES ABOUT 10 CUPS

INGREDIENTS
    2 pounds white fish bones and
      trimmings, but not gills
    10 cups water
    1 onion, roughly chopped
    1 celery stick, chopped
    1 carrot, chopped
    1 bay leaf
    3 fresh parsley sprigs
    6 peppercorns
    2-inch piece of pared lemon rind
    ⅓ cup dry white wine

1 Put the fish bones and fish heads in a large, heavy pan. Pour in the measured water.

2 Bring the liquid to a boil, using a spoon to skim off any scum that rises to the surface. Add the onion, celery, carrot, bay leaf, parsley, peppercorns, lemon rind and white wine.

3 Lower heat, and cover the pan with the lid. Simmer the stock gently for 20–30 minutes, then cool.

4 Strain the cooled stock through a cheesecloth bag into a clean bowl. Keep the stock in the fridge for up to 2 days or freeze it for up to 3 months.

COOK'S TIP
Do not allow the fish stock to boil for a prolonged period or the bones will begin to disintegrate and the stock will acquire an unpleasant, bitter flavor.

Vegetable Stock

MAKES ABOUT 5 CUPS

INGREDIENTS
    3–4 shallots, halved
    2 celery stalks or 3 ounces celery
      root, chopped
    2 carrots, coarsely chopped
    3 tomatoes, halved
    3 fresh parsley stalks
    1 fresh tarragon sprig
    1 fresh marjoram or thyme sprig
    1-inch piece of pared orange rind
    6 peppercorns
    2 allspice berries
    6¼ cups water

1 Put all the vegetables into a heavy pan. Add the fresh herbs, orange rind and spices. Pour in the water.

2 Bring the liquid to a boil, then lower heat and simmer the stock gently for 30 minutes. Let cool completely.

3 Strain the stock through a strainer into a large bowl, pressing out all the liquid from the vegetables using the back of a spoon. Store the cold stock in the fridge for up to 3 days or in the freezer for up to 6 months.

PAELLA

In Spain, paella is not just a meal, it is an occasion. Come fiestas and holidays (and there are many of these in Spain), it is not unknown for someone to say, "How about a paella," and, the weather being good, and the company convivial, ingredients, utensils and plenty of red wine will then be gathered up and the party will head outdoors, to the beach or into the mountains. The ingredients can be many and various. Rice – the short grain variety – is an obvious essential, but saffron, garlic and olive oil will inevitably be included, too. Everyone will help to gather wood and light a fire, after which one of the men will prepare and cook the paella. Other men will doubtless make their contribution. There will be advice for the chef on when to add the rice, how much stock to use and whether to add herbs early or late, but the principle is that men do the cooking.

Traditionally, a paella should always be cooked out of doors, over a wood fire by a man. The indoor version, cooked more conventionally over a stove, and by a woman, is strictly speaking not a paella at all but an *arroz* – a rice.

There are other conventions concerning paella, some more imperative than others. Short grain rice and saffron are essential ingredients. Purists believe that an authentic paella should contain only eels, snails and beans, the ingredients used in the original Valencian paella, but most Spanish people today are fairly relaxed about using other ingredients. Fish, shellfish, meat and poultry are routinely used, sometimes together.

More important in Spain is the manner in which the paella is eaten. For the Spanish, paella is the epitome of convivial eating: it is always served with generous amounts of wine and is inevitably made for a large party of people. The paella dish – the *paellera* – is placed on the table as a spectacular centerpiece, and everyone helps themselves to the food, while the conversation, lubricated by the wine, is, in true Spanish fashion, animated and lively.

For all these reasons, paella has become one of the world's best loved rice dishes. There are hundreds of variations, with restaurants up and down the country producing their own speciality. Although tradition dictates that paella should be cooked out of doors, superb paellas can be made in conventional kitchens, albeit on a more modest scale. A paella can be simple or elaborate and you can vary the combination of meat, poultry, fish and shellfish to suit your taste, your pocket and the occasion.

Making Perfect Paella

1 Cut the meat or joint the poultry into large pieces; season if the recipe requires. Cook the meat or poultry in olive oil in the paella pan or in a large skillet until it turns an even deep golden brown. Transfer the cooked meat or poultry to a plate. Slice the sausage.

2 Prepare any fish and shellfish that is to be included according to type: steam mussels (discarding any that fail to open), prepare squid and peel shrimp. Cook the fish and shellfish briefly, if required by the recipe, and transfer to a plate.

3 In a paella pan, cook the onions in olive oil until golden. Add the garlic, tomatoes and any firm vegetables. Stir in cooked dried beans, if using. Stir briefly, then add water or stock and any seasonings. Bring to a boil.

4 Add the rice, stirring so that it is evenly distributed, then add the meat or poultry, and any sausage. Cook, uncovered, over medium heat (so that the liquid simmers nicely) for 15 minutes.

5 Lower the heat, and add any softer vegetables, fish or shellfish. Add saffron to give the paella its distinctive color. Cook over low heat for 10 minutes until the liquid has been absorbed, then cover and rest for 5–10 minutes.

To Stir or Not to Stir

Read any guide to making paella, and you'll be told that the paella mustn't be stirred or disturbed in any way. This is fine advice for a true paella – cooked over an open fire so that the heat is distributed evenly over the base of the pan. But if you're using a gas or electric flame, the uneven heat distribution will mean that the center will cook more quickly than the outside. To get around this problem, you can either break the rules and stir occasionally, or cook the paella in the oven. That way it will cook evenly, although technically, in Spain, it would be a "rice" (*arroz*) and not a paella.

A GUIDE TO PAELLA QUANTITIES

Individual paella recipes will usually specify quantities of rice, liquid and other ingredients, although the following can be used as a rough guide.

Amount of rice	Amount of liquid	Servings
1 cup	2¼ cups	2–3
1¾ cups	3¾ cups	4–6
2⅓ cups	5 cups	6
3 cups	5½ cups	8

Allow between ⅓–½ cup rice per person

PAELLA TIPS

• Use the right type of rice. The Spanish will occasionally use a medium grain rice, although the traditional choice is a short grain rice that absorbs liquid well. The round grained and stubby Spanish rice Calasperra would be ideal, or use Italian Arborio risotto rice.

• It is important to use a large pan. The rice needs to be cooked in a shallow layer so there should be plenty of room to spread it out. If at all possible use a paella pan (called a *paellera*), which is a wide flat metal pan. If you don't have a paella pan, you can use a skillet – the largest you have – but this will probably only be large enough for a paella for three or four people.

• Always use fresh ingredients, especially the fish and seafood. Paella is not a dish for leftovers.

• Cook other ingredients carefully before you start to cook the paella. Meats should be cooked until golden brown, as should onions, as this will add flavor to the dish. Fish should be seared lightly, and added to the rice towards the end of cooking, to avoid overcooking it.

Below: The width and shallow depth of the paella pan allow an even distribution of heat when the rice is cooking.

• Less tender cuts of meat or larger pieces of poultry may require longer cooking. Always check instructions in the recipe for timings.

• Use a well-flavored stock – preferably home-made chicken, meat, fish or vegetable.

• Bring the stock or other liquid in the pan to a fierce boil before adding the rice. (This is the opposite of the technique used when making a risotto, where the stock is added slowly to the rice.)

• Use saffron strands rather than turmeric or any other coloring.

• Once the liquid has been absorbed by the rice, cover the paella with a dampened dish towel and allow it to rest for a few minutes before serving, to complete the cooking.

SUSHI

Sushi is wonderful food. Sushi bars, or *sushiya*, are to be found everywhere in Tokyo and are now a familiar sight in London, New York, Sydney and other large cities. The little snacks are a superb treat – clean-tasting yet surprisingly filling. They are not difficult to prepare at home and make an attractive and impressive snack or starter.

A Japanese short grain rice should be used for sushi. Some supermarkets sell a rice labeled sushi rice, which takes the guesswork out of the process. Japanese short grain rice is slightly sticky, which makes it easy to pick up with chopsticks and ideal for sushi, as the grains of rice cling together. Glutinous rice is not suitable for making sushi, as it is too sticky.

The rice should be rinsed and left to drain for 30 minutes before being cooked by the absorption method. You can use an electric rice cooker but don't be tempted to use the pan-of-water method as the results will be disastrous.

Nori This dried seaweed is sold in paper-thin sheets. It is dark green to black in color and almost transparent in places. Some nori comes ready-toasted (yakinori), often seasoned with soy sauce and sesame oil (ajijsuke-nori). Alternatively, toast the nori under a hot broiler before use.

Shoga Pale pink (amazu shoga) or bright red (beri shoga) ginger pickles, which are excellent for serving with sushi.

Shoyu This Japanese soy sauce is milder than Chinese soy sauce. Serve with sushi.

Wasabi A hot green horseradish to serve with fish. It is sold as a paste or as a powder, to which water is added.

Above: Clockwise from top, bamboo sushi mat, amazu shoga, wasabi paste, shoyu and nori sheet.

Making Perfect Sushi

1 Rinse the rice and drain for 30–60 minutes, then put in a heavy pan and add a piece of dried kelp (kombu). Add water (see Quantities below), and bring to a boil. Remove the kelp, cover the pan and cook gently over low heat for about 15 minutes. Increase to high for 10 seconds, then remove from heat and let stand for 10 minutes. Lift the lid. Steam holes will have appeared in the rice and it will be tender.

2 Prepare the sushi vinegar. For every 2⅓ cups rice, mix together 4 tablespoons rice vinegar, 1 tablespoon granulated sugar and ½ teaspoon salt.

3 Stir the sushi vinegar into the rice, cover with a damp cloth and leave to cool. Do not put the rice in the fridge as this will make it go hard.

Quantities

Use between 2½ cups and 3 cups water for every 2⅓ cups sushi rice, depending on the type of rice; always check the instructions on the packaging. If you prefer, you could use sake instead of 2 tablespoons of the water.

Rolled Sushi with Smoked Salmon

MAKES 24 SLICES

1 Line a bamboo sushi mat with plastic wrap. Arrange the smoked salmon across the mat, overlapping if necessary, so that there are no gaps or holes. Spread a generous layer of the dressed rice over the salmon.

2 Roll the mat away from you so that the salmon rolls up around the rice. Do not roll up the plastic wrap with the fish. Make more rolls in the same way.

3 Chill the rolls in the fridge for about 10 minutes, then unwrap and cut each roll into six slices, using a wet knife. Cover with a damp cloth and keep cool.

Rolled Sushi with Nori and Filling

MAKES 24 SLICES

To make this sushi you will need
sheets of yakinori (toasted seaweed).
Two sheets will make four rolls.

1 Cut the yakinori in half lengthwise
and place a half-sheet, shiny side
down, on the bamboo sushi mat.

2 Spread a layer of the dressed rice
over the yakinori, leaving a ½-inch clear
edge at the top and bottom.

3 Arrange a line of filling horizontally
across the middle of the rice. The
filling could be raw salmon or raw tuna,
cut into ½-inch square long sticks,
sliced raw scallops, Japanese omelet,
roasted bell pepper, scallions,
cucumber or a selection of two or
three of these.

4 Using the sushi mat as a guide, and
working from the nearest edge of yakinori,
roll up the yakinori and rice into a cigar
(do not to include the mat in the roll).
Roll the mat in the palms of your hands
so that the edges stick together.

5 Wrap the rolls in plastic wrap and
chill in the fridge for 10 minutes, then
unwrap the rolls. Use a wet knife to
cut each roll into six slices, rinsing the
knife occasionally.

Shaped Sushi

1 Wet your hands. Take about
2–3 tablespoons dressed sushi rice at
a time and shape it into a rectangle,
measuring about ¾ x 2 inches and
½ inch high.

2 Repeat this process until all the rice
is used up. Gently spread a little wasabi
paste in the middle of each of the
rectangles of rice, then add your
chosen topping.

Sushi Toppings

Make plain rolled sushi and top them
with any one of these suggestions.
Raw sushi-grade salmon, raw sushi-grade tuna, salmon roe or other fish roe
Cut the salmon and tuna into pieces
that are roughly the same size as the
rice portions.
Peeled raw shrimp tails Cook the
shrimp for about 1 minute in a pan
of simmering water, then drain. Slit
each shrimp along the belly and
remove the dark vein, then carefully
open out each shrimp like a book.
Mix together 1 tablespoon rice vinegar
and 1 teaspoon sugar in a small bowl.
Add the shrimp, turn to coat, and
let marinate in a cool place for about
10 minutes.
Blanched squid and boiled octapus
Slice the squid and octopus into strips
that are roughly the same size as the
rice portions.
Rolled omelet slices Beat together
1 egg, 1 tablespoon sake, 1 tablespoon
sugar, 1 tablespoon water and a pinch
of salt. Heat a little groundnut oil in
a small skillet, then pour in the
egg mixture. Cook over medium to
high heat until the egg is just set
but not browned. Roll up the omelet
and slice.

Garnishes

Fish sushi can be garnished with
fresh chives, cilantro or toasted sesame
seeds. Omelet sushi can be garnished
by wrapping strips of yakinori around
the molded rice.

COOK'S TIP

Sushi rice should be cooked either by
the absorption method or in an electric
rice cooker. The pan-of-water method
should not be used.

Sushi rice is very sticky when cooked.
If you find it becomes unmanageable,
rinse your hands in a bowl of water to
which 1 teaspoon of oil has been added.
Pat your hands dry; they will be slightly
oily, and the rice will no longer stick
to them.

BIRYANI

This is one of India's most famous rice dishes. Perfect for parties and other festivities, biryani is served with other vegetables and meats, but essentially takes center stage itself. It is basically an all-in-one dish. The rice is piled on top of a meat or vegetable curry, with saffron milk dribbled over the top to give the rice a splash of golden color.

Although biryani takes a little time to prepare, it is straightforward and simple. The only rule is to use basmati rice, which should be soaked for 4 hours, preferably in lightly salted water, a technique which the Persians, who are credited with inventing this dish, believed made the rice a brilliant white.

Lamb, chicken and beef are commonly used in biryanis, but duck and game work well, and vegetarian biryanis are popular, too. Biryanis should never be very hot, but are traditionally flavored with fragrant spices. They can be made using coconut milk, but plain yogurt is more common. The sauce should be sweet and fragrant, with a creamy consistency.

Making Perfect Chicken Biryani

1 First make the saffron milk. Crumble a generous pinch (about 1 teaspoon) of saffron strands into 2 tablespoons of warm milk in a small bowl. Stir, then let soak for about 3 hours.

2 Meanwhile, wash 1½ cups basmati rice in cold water. Drain the rice thoroughly, then put it into a large bowl and cover with more cold water. Stir in 2 teaspoons salt and let soak for about 3 hours.

3 Prepare a chicken curry. Heat 3 tablespoons oil in a skillet and add 3 sliced onions. Cook until soft. Add 6 ounces cubed chicken breasts, along with any spices you are using. Stir to coat the chicken in the spices, then add ½ **teaspoon salt**, 2–3 chopped garlic cloves and lemon juice to taste. Stir-fry for 5 minutes more, until the chicken is browned. Drain the rice and cook it in boiling salted water for 4–5 minutes until three-quarters cooked.

4 Spoon a little drained rice into a flameproof dish, just enough to cover the bottom, then add the chicken curry. Spoon ⅔ cup plain yogurt over the curry and spread it evenly. Preheat the oven to 300°F.

5 Pile the remaining rice in a hillock on top of the curry, then, using the handle of a wooden spoon, make a 1-inch hole down from the peak to the bottom.

6 Dribble the saffron milk and ⅔ cup hot chicken stock over the rice, and dot with butter or ghee. Scatter over fried onions, golden raisins and toasted almonds. Cover the dish tightly with a double piece of foil held in place by the lid. Cook in the oven for 40 minutes.

Spices for Chicken Biryani

For 6 ounces chicken use 10 whole green cardamom pods; ¼ teaspoon ground cloves; 2–3 whole cloves; 2-inch cinnamon stick; 1 teaspoon ground cumin; ½ teaspoon ground black pepper; 1 teaspoon ground coriander; 1 teaspoon finely chopped fresh ginger root; ¼ teaspoon chili powder.

LONTONG (COMPRESSED RICE)

This is a speciality of Indonesia and Malaysia. The rice is cooked in a confined space for longer than normal to form a compact solid mass, which when cooled, can be cut into squares. Lontong is eaten cold, usually with salads and satay, when it absorbs the spicy dressings and sauces.

Lontong is traditionally cooked in a banana leaf, although a cheesecloth bag is generally easier to use.

Jasmine rice, basmati or any other long grain rice can be used for lontong. Do not be tempted to use parboiled (easy-cook) rice, as it will not form a solid mass.

Making Perfect Lontong

1 You will need several cheesecloth bags, each about 6 inches square. Leave the top of each bag open. Spoon in enough long grain rice to fill each bag one-third full (about a generous ½ cup), then sew the opening closed.

2 Bring a pan of salted water to a boil, lower in the bags of rice and allow to simmer gently, uncovered, for about 75 minutes, making sure the pan doesn't boil dry and adding more water if necessary.

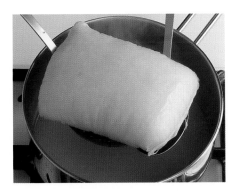

3 Remove the bags from the water and drain them thoroughly. Each bag should feel like a rather hard and solid lump.

4 When the lontong is completely cold, open the cheesecloth bags, remove the blocks of compressed rice and cut each block into squares or oblongs, using a wet, sharp knife.

FRIED RICE TIPS

• Rice must be cooked and completely cold before frying. Warm rice will become soggy and oily if fried. If you are cooking rice especially for frying, spread it out on a cookie sheet as soon as it has been cooked so that it cools rapidly. Let stand for at least 2–3 hours.

• Use long grain white or brown rice for frying.

• Other ingredients should be cooked before the rice is added.

• Always cook the rice over low heat. It is important to heat the rice through completely, but take care not to overcook it.

FRIED RICE

Wherever rice is a staple food, every region, even every family, has its own fried rice recipe. When rice is served at almost every meal, there are inevitably leftovers, and it's a simple matter to fry these with other ingredients for breakfast, for a lunchtime snack or for a more elaborate evening meal.

There are several classic fried rice dishes – Nasi Goreng, one of the most famous, comes from Indonesia, but is more commonly associated with the Dutch *Rijstafel* (rice table). There are also several well known Chinese fried rices: Egg Fried Rice and Special Fried Rice are two of the most popular. Recipes for any of these dishes are extremely flexible. Provided you follow a few simple rules, the best way with any fried rice dish is to make up your own favorite mixture.

The choice of ingredients is up to the individual cook, but here are some suggestions.

Aromatics Sliced scallions or shallots; red or yellow onions, sliced or cut into wedges; sliced or crushed garlic. Stir-fry in oil for 3–4 minutes, then add the meat, fish, vegetables and/or eggs. If choosing two or more different ingredients, stir-fry them individually before stirring together.

Meat Any tender cut of poultry or meat, such as chicken, duck, beef, lamb or pork tenderloin can be used. Slice meat thinly so that it cooks quickly. Meats can be marinated for 30 minutes before cooking (see individual recipes for marinade ingredients). Stir-fry with onions until cooked. Cooked meats only require heating through.

Fish Raw fish and shellfish work well and should be stir-fried after any meat. Cooked fish or shrimp can be stirred in at the end.

Vegetables Choose colorful vegetables such as carrots, bell peppers, zucchini and mushrooms. Cut them into thin strips so that they cook quickly and evenly. Stir-fry until just tender.

Eggs Beat together and scramble with the onions. Or use the eggs to make an omelet; roll it up, cut into slices and use to garnish the rice.

Making Perfect Fried Rice

1 Stir-fry any uncooked meat in oil in a wok or large, deep skillet, then add onions. Transfer the meat to a plate.

2 Add beaten egg to the skillet and scramble with sliced scallions.

3 Add spices and flavorings such as soy sauce, rice wine, fresh chilies, tomato paste or spices.

4 Add the cold rice to the skillet and mix with the scrambled egg. Return any cooked meats, cooked fish or cooked vegetables to the pan at this stage, or add chopped herbs. Cook over low heat, stirring occasionally, to warm the rice through completely.

RICE DESSERTS

In one form or another, rice pudding is enjoyed all over the world. It is England's best known rice dish. Most other European countries have at least one favorite rice pudding or dessert to call their own.

Perhaps the popularity of the traditional rice pudding arose from the fact that it is difficult to overcook it. In the 18th century, food was often badly cooked, and overcooked, stodgy savory rice dishes were probably despised then as they are now. Rice pudding was one of the few foods that could stand up to such abuse. With its meltingly tender grains slowly cooked in creamy milk, flavored with vanilla or nutmeg and sweetened with sugar, rice pudding quickly became a firm favorite in Britain and beyond.

English rice pudding is made with short grain rice but this is not essential. Jasmine rice and basmati rice can be used equally successfully. In Asia, glutinous rice, which is stickier than short grain, is the favored rice for making desserts.

Making Perfect English Rice Pudding

Oven method

1 Preheat the oven to 300°F. Following your chosen rice pudding recipe, put the rice and sugar in a shallow baking dish and pour in cold milk. Stir well to mix and then dot the surface with a little butter.

2 Bake in the preheated oven for about 45 minutes, by which time a thick skin will have formed on top of the pudding.

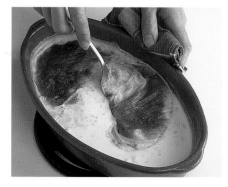

3 Stir the skin into the pudding and bake the pudding for about 1¼ hours more, stirring once or twice.

Pan method

1 Place the rice in a large pan. Add the quantity of milk and sugar as specified in the recipe and stir well to mix.

2 Bring to a boil, then lower heat, cover the pan and simmer very gently for 1¼ hours, stirring frequently.

3 Remove the lid and simmer for about 15–20 minutes more until the rice mixture is thick and creamy.

Combination method

1 Partially cook the rice using the absorption method. Put the rice in a pan and add a third of the measured liquid. Simmer gently over low heat.

2 When the liquid has been absorbed, stir in half the remaining liquid and simmer for about 6 minutes more.

3 Stir in the sugar, any flavorings and the remaining milk, then pour the mixture into a buttered baking dish.

4 Dot with butter and bake for 1–1½ hours at a temperature between 300°F and 350°F. The lower temperature cooks slower but will give the pudding a creamier taste.

Making Perfect Glutinous Rice Dessert

1 Place the rice in a large bowl, add cold water to cover and leave to soak for 3–4 hours.

2 Drain the rice, put it in a large pan and pour in coconut milk or cow's milk. Bring to a boil, then lower heat, cover the pan and simmer gently for 25–30 minutes, stirring frequently.

3 Add sugar, creamed coconut and any flavorings, and cook for 5–10 minutes more, uncovered, until the rice reaches the consistency you like. Serve with slices of exotic fruits such as mango, papaya and pineapple, if you like.

Making Perfect Thai Rice Dessert

This is quick, easy and quite delicious. Cook Jasmine rice in boiling water using the absorption method. Let stand for a few minutes, then stir in milk and sugar to taste, and creamed coconut, if desired. Serve the dessert hot, with fresh fruit.

Quantities

• For short grain rice dessert, use 2½ cups milk for every generous ¼ cup rice. Stir in 3 tablespoons sugar. This should be sufficient to serve four.
• For glutinous rice dessert, use 1¼ cups liquid for every scant ½ cup rice to serve four.
• For Thai rice dessert, use 2 cups water, ½ cup milk and 4 tablespoons creamed coconut for every generous ¼ cup rice to serve four.

COOK'S TIPS

To give an English rice pudding a richer flavor, try any one of the following suggestions.
• Replace half the liquid with evaporated milk and add light brown sugar.
• If using the pan method, stir in a little cream just before serving.
• Beaten eggs can be stirred into the hot, cooked rice, or added to the part-cooked rice (see combination method).

Flavorings

Vanilla Give the milk a delicate vanilla flavor by heating it with a vanilla pod until the milk is hot but not boiling. Remove from the heat and let infuse for 1–2 hours. Strain the flavored milk over the rice.
Nutmeg This is another very popular addition. Either shred it over the surface of a rice dessert that is to be baked, or stir shredded nutmeg into the mixture in the pan. Ground cinnamon could be used instead.

Above: Aromatic nutmeg will add sweetness and warmth to the dessert.

Raisins Stir into the rice or scatter at the bottom of the dish.
Spices Add lemongrass, cardamom pods, or pared orange, lemon or lime rind to the rice as it is cooking.
Nuts Chopped pistachios or almonds can be added during cooking to a rice pudding which is being cooked by the combination or pan method.

Above: Pistachios stirred into the dessert with shreds of fresh mint will provide texture and a slightly sweet flavor.

EQUIPMENT

Electric Rice Cooker

In Japan and other more affluent rice-eating countries, electric rice cookers have now replaced more conventional means of cooking rice. In the West they are also becoming increasingly popular, and cooks who use them often swear by them. The cookers cook rice perfectly and have the added advantage of keeping it warm throughout the meal, without it drying or becoming soggy. Another bonus of the rice cooker is that it frees stovetop space.

Pans

Even if you have invested in a rice cooker, you will always need a selection of pans. For plain boiled rice and for risottos, a heavy pan is the best choice – the actual size will depend on the quantities you are likely to be making but in general, bigger is better; small amounts of rice can be cooked in a large pan but you'll run into difficulties if you try cooking lots of rice in a pan that is too small. For risottos, some

Below: Pans

Left: Electric rice cooker

Right: Colander and strainer

cooks prefer to use a deep skillet. A small skillet or crêpe pan will be useful for frying the omelets often used to garnish Asian rice dishes.

Colanders and Strainers

A colander or strainers is essential for draining boiled rice. Buy a good quality colander with a long handle, so that you can stand well back to pour the steaming rice out of the pan.

Measuring Cups and Scales

It is important to measure rice accurately, and to add the correct quantity of water or other liquid, as specified in the recipe or on the packaging, especially when cooking by the absorption method. In most recipes the rice is measured by weight, although it can also be measured by volume. Use a measuring cup when adding stocks and other liquids.

Flameproof Casserole

Several rice dishes are started on the stovetop, then finished in the oven. A flameproof casserole is perfect for this, and will also prove useful for dishes that are entirely oven-baked. Casseroles should have well-fitting lids; if lids are at all loose, cover the casserole with foil before fitting the lid in place.

Earthenware Casserole

These cannot be used on the stovetop, but are very useful for oven-cooked pilafs. It is essential for the casserole to have a well-fitting lid.

Parmesan Shredder

Freshly shredded Parmesan cheese is an essential ingredient in risottos. Although many supermarkets now stock freshly shredded Parmesan, it is fairly expensive, and buying Parmesan as one whole piece and shredding it yourself is a much better option. Small metal Parmesan shredders are available, but the mouli shredder, where you pop the cheese in the top and turn the handle, allows you to shred only the amount you need.

Left: Earthenware and flameproof casseroles

Left: Bamboo steamer

Above: Chopsticks and chopstick stands

Left: Japanese bamboo sushi mat

Mortar and Pestle

Spices are not necessary for cooking rice, but if for interesting meals, particularly those with an Asian flavor, they are essential. The advantage of grinding your own spices is that you can be sure they are absolutely fresh; you'll notice the difference at once compared with ready ground spices. A mortar and pestle is the traditional piece of equipment for grinding spices, and has the advantage that you can grind very small quantities. The mortar is the container, while the pestle is used to pulverize spices, seeds, garlic or herbs. Mortar and pestle sets can be made of stone, wood or marble.

Spice Grinder

A spice grinder can be used instead of a mortar and pestle. It will grind spices very finely with very little effort.

Cooking Knives

Not specifically required for cooking rice, but good quality kitchen knives in a range of sizes and weights are essential for preparing other ingredients.

Paella Pan

If you are likely to make paella on a regular basis – or fancy bringing back a useful souvenir of your Spanish holiday – do invest in a paella pan. Bigger pans obviously make bigger paellas, but very large pans will probably turn out to be bigger than the ring on your stovetop, which will mean the food will cook unevenly.

Wok

You will need a wok for any stir-fried rice dish and will also find one useful for making a wide variety of sauces and stir-fries to accompany rice dishes. Buy the appropriate wok for your stove. Round-bottomed woks can only be used on gas stovetops; a flat-bottomed wok should be used on an electric stovetop.

Steamers

You can use a rice steamer to cook rice and for "finishing" rice if you do not have an electric rice cooker.

Japanese Bamboo Sushi Mat

Essential for rolling rice when making sushi, this simple but very useful piece of equipment is flexible in one direction but rigid in the other.

Cheesecloth Bag

This is not essential, but is useful for making your own lontong (compressed rice). If you don't have a bamboo steamer, the bag containing the rice can be set inside a pan of boiling water. You can make your own cheesecloth bag by cutting two 10-inch squares of cheesecloth and sewing them together around three sides, leaving one edge open.

Chopsticks and Chopstick Stands

Asian cooks use long chopsticks for manipulating foods when stir-frying. You may like to have good quality chopsticks to use when serving a Chinese or Thai meal, as they add authenticity. Chopstick stands are used for chopsticks at the table; less elaborate ones can be used when cooking.

Rice Bowls

Not essential pieces of equipment, but very attractive accessories: Chinese or Japanese rice bowls will make a huge difference to the look of an Oriental meal. Buy genuine sets from Oriental markets, or when traveling, for use on special occasions.

Right: Rice bowls

RICE
AND
RISOTTO
RECIPES

INDIA

We have India to thank for a large number of our favorite rice dishes. Whether side dishes or main meals, there are countless rice recipes from India. Some, like Chicken Biryani, are known and loved across the world. Others, like Saffron Rice with Cardamoms, made with fragrant basmati rice, are an essential side dish to curries.

CHICKEN BIRYANI

EASY TO MAKE AND VERY TASTY, THIS IS THE IDEAL DISH FOR A FAMILY SUPPER.

<u>SERVES FOUR</u>

INGREDIENTS

10 whole green cardamom pods
1½ cups basmati rice, soaked
  and drained
½ teaspoon salt
2–3 whole cloves
2-inch cinnamon stick
3 tablespoons vegetable oil
3 onions, sliced
4 chicken breasts, each about
  6 ounces, cubed
¼ teaspoon ground cloves
¼ teaspoon hot chili powder
1 teaspoon ground cumin
1 teaspoon ground coriander
½ teaspoon ground black pepper
3 garlic cloves, chopped
1 teaspoon finely chopped fresh
  ginger root
juice of 1 lemon
4 tomatoes, sliced
2 tablespoons chopped fresh cilantro
⅔ cup plain yogurt
4–5 saffron strands, soaked in
  2 teaspoons hot milk
⅔ cup water
toasted slivered almonds and
  cilantro sprigs, to garnish
plain yogurt, to serve

1 Preheat the oven to 375°F. Remove the seeds from half the cardamom pods and grind them finely, using a pestle and mortar. Set them aside. Bring a pan of water to a boil and add the rice, salt, whole cardamom pods, cloves and cinnamon stick. Boil for 2 minutes, then drain, leaving the whole spices in the rice.

2 Heat the oil in a skillet and cook the onions for 8 minutes, until softened and browned. Add the chicken and the ground spices, including the ground cardamom seeds. Mix well, then add the garlic, ginger and lemon juice. Stir-fry for 5 minutes.

3 Transfer the chicken mixture to a casserole and arrange the tomatoes on top. Sprinkle on the fresh cilantro, spoon the yogurt evenly on top and cover with the drained rice.

4 Drizzle the saffron milk over the rice and pour over the water. Cover tightly and bake for 1 hour. Transfer to a warmed serving platter and remove the whole spices from the rice. Garnish with toasted almonds and cilantro sprigs and serve with the plain yogurt.

BASMATI AND NUT PILAF

VEGETARIANS WILL LOVE THIS SIMPLE PILAF. ADD WILD OR CULTIVATED MUSHROOMS, IF YOU LIKE.

SERVES FOUR

INGREDIENTS
  1–2 tablespoons sunflower oil
  1 onion, chopped
  1 garlic clove, crushed
  1 large carrot, coarsely shredded
  generous 1 cup basmati
    rice, soaked
  1 teaspoon cumin seeds
  2 teaspoons ground coriander
  2 teaspoons black mustard seeds
    (optional)
  4 green cardamom pods
  scant 2 cups vegetable stock
    or water
  1 bay leaf
  ¾ cup unsalted walnuts
    and cashews
  salt and freshly ground black pepper
  fresh parsley or cilantro sprigs,
    to garnish

1 Heat the oil in a large, shallow skillet and gently cook the onion, garlic and carrot for 3–4 minutes. Drain the rice and then add to the pan with the spices. Cook for 1–2 minutes more, stirring to coat the grains in oil.

2 Pour in the stock or water, add the bay leaf and season well. Bring to a boil, lower heat, cover and simmer very gently for 10–12 minutes.

3 Remove the pan from the heat without lifting the lid. Let stand for about 5 minutes, then check the rice. If it is cooked, there will be small steam holes on the surface of the rice. Remove and discard the bay leaf and the cardamom pods.

4 Stir in the nuts and check the seasoning. Spoon onto a platter, garnish with the parsley or cilantro and serve.

COOK'S TIP
Use whichever nuts you prefer in this dish – even unsalted peanuts taste good, although almonds, cashews or pistachios are more exotic.

SAVORY RICE WITH MADRAS CURRY

BITE-SIZE CUBES OF BEEF SIMMER GENTLY WITH SPICES UNTIL THEY ARE TENDER ENOUGH TO MELT IN THE MOUTH. THEY ARE SERVED WITH BASMATI RICE, COOKED UNTIL LIGHT AND FLUFFY.

SERVES FOUR

INGREDIENTS
generous 1 cup basmati rice
1 tablespoon sunflower oil
2 tablespoons ghee or butter
1 onion, finely chopped
1 garlic clove, crushed
1 teaspoon ground cumin
½ teaspoon ground coriander
4 green cardamom pods
1 cinnamon stick
1 small red bell pepper, seeded
  and diced
1 small green bell pepper, seeded and
  diced
1¼ cups chicken stock
salt and freshly ground black pepper
For the curry
2 tablespoons vegetable oil
2 tablespoons ghee or butter
1½ pounds chuck beef steak, cut into
  bite-size cubes
1 onion, chopped
3 green cardamom pods
2 fresh green chilies, seeded and
  finely chopped
1-inch piece of fresh ginger root, shredded
2 garlic cloves, crushed
1 tablespoon Madras curry paste
1 teaspoon ground cumin
1 teaspoon ground coriander
⅔ cup beef stock

1 Start by making the curry. Heat half the oil and ghee or butter in a skillet and fry the meat, in batches if necessary, until browned on all sides. Transfer to a plate and set aside.

2 Heat the remaining oil and ghee or butter and cook the onion for about 3–4 minutes until softened. Add the cardamom pods and fry for 1 minute, then add the chilies, ginger and garlic and cook for 2 minutes more.

3 Stir in the curry paste, ground cumin and coriander, then add the meat and stock. Season with salt, bring to a boil, then lower the heat and simmer very gently for 1–1½ hours, until the meat is tender.

4 When the curry is almost ready, prepare the rice. Put it in a bowl and pour over boiling water to cover. Set aside for 10 minutes, then drain, rinse under cold water and drain again. The rice will still be uncooked but should have lost its brittleness.

5 Heat the oil and ghee or butter in a flameproof casserole and cook the onion and garlic gently for 3–4 minutes until softened and lightly browned.

6 Stir in the cumin and ground coriander, cardamom pods and cinnamon stick. Cook for 1 minute, then add the diced bell peppers.

7 Add the rice, stirring to coat the grains in the spice mixture, and pour in the stock. Bring to a boil, then lower the heat, cover the pan tightly and simmer for about 8–10 minutes, or until the rice is tender and the stock has been absorbed. Spoon into a bowl and serve with the curry. Offer a little mango chutney, if you like.

COOK'S TIP
The curry should be fairly dry, but take care that it does not catch on the bottom of the pan. If you want to leave it unattended, cook it in a heavy-based pan or flameproof casserole, on the stovetop or in an oven preheated to 350°F.

LAMB PARSI

THIS IS SIMILAR TO BIRYANI, BUT HERE THE LAMB IS MARINATED WITH THE YOGURT, A TECHNIQUE WHICH IS A PARSI SPECIALITY. SERVE WITH A DHAL OR WITH SPICED MUSHROOMS.

SERVES SIX

INGREDIENTS
   2 pound boneless leg of lamb, cut
      into 1-inch cubes
   4 tablespoons ghee or butter
   2 onions, sliced
   1 pound potatoes, cut into large
      chunks
   chicken stock or water
      (see method)
   3½ cups basmati rice, soaked
   generous pinch of saffron strands,
      dissolved in 2 tablespoons milk
   cilantro sprigs, to garnish
For the marinade
   2 cups plain yogurt
   3–4 garlic cloves, crushed
   2 teaspoons cayenne pepper
   4 teaspoons garam masala
   2 teaspoons ground cumin
   1 teaspoon ground coriander

1 Make the marinade by mixing all the ingredients in a large bowl. Add the meat, stir to coat, then cover and let marinate for 3–4 hours in a cool place or overnight in the fridge.

2 Melt 2 tablespoons of the ghee or butter in a large pan and cook the onions for 6–8 minutes until lightly golden. Transfer to a plate.

3 Melt a further 1½ tablespoons ghee or butter in the pan. Fry the marinated lamb cubes in batches until evenly brown, transferring each batch in turn to a plate. When all the lamb has been browned, return it to the pan and scrape in all the remaining marinade.

4 Stir in the potatoes and add about three-quarters of the fried onions. Pour in just enough chicken stock or water to cover the mixture. Bring to a boil, then cover and simmer over very low heat for 40–50 minutes until the lamb is tender and the potatoes are cooked. Preheat the oven to 325°F.

5 Drain the rice. Cook it in a pan of boiling stock or water for 5 minutes. Meanwhile, spoon the lamb mixture into a casserole. Drain the rice and mound it on top of the lamb, then, using the handle of a wooden spoon, make a hole down the center. Top with the remaining fried onions, pour the saffron milk over the top and dot with the remaining ghee or butter.

6 Cover the pan with a double layer of foil and a lid. Cook in the oven for 30–35 minutes or until the rice is completely tender. Garnish with cilantro sprigs and serve.

COOK'S TIP
Take care not to overcook the rice when parboiling it. The grains should still be quite hard, but should have a slightly powdery consistency.

GOAN SHRIMP CURRY WITH SOUTHERN-STYLE RICE

MAKE THIS CURRY AS MILD OR AS FIERY AS YOU WISH. GOANS TRADITIONALLY LIKE THEIR SEAFOOD DISHES FAIRLY HOT, BUT A MILDER CURRY IS JUST AS DELICIOUS, FLAVORED WITH HERBS AND SPICES.

SERVES FOUR

INGREDIENTS
 1 tablespoon ghee or butter
 2 garlic cloves, crushed
 1 pound small shrimp, shelled and
   deveined
 4 cardamom pods
 4 cloves
 1 cinnamon stick
 1 tablespoon mustard seeds
 about 1 tablespoon groundnut oil
 1 large onion, chopped
 ½–1 fresh red chili, seeded and
   finely sliced
 4 tomatoes, peeled, seeded and
   chopped
 ¾ cup fish stock or water
 1½ cups coconut milk
 3 tablespoons fragrant spice mix
   (see Cook's Tip)
 2–4 teaspoons cayenne pepper
 salt
For the rice
 1¾ cups basmati rice, soaked
   and drained
 1 teaspoon coriander seeds
 1 teaspoon cumin seeds
 2 tablespoons urad dhal, rinsed
   (optional)
 ½ teaspoon ground turmeric
 1 teaspoon brown mustard seeds
 1 cup unroasted cashews
 1 tablespoon groundnut oil
 1 tablespoon ghee or butter

COOK'S TIP
To make a fragrant spice mix, dry fry
1½ tablespoons coriander seeds,
1 tablespoon mixed peppercorns,
1 teaspoon cumin seeds, ¼ teaspoon
fenugreek seeds and ¼ teaspoon fennel
seeds until aromatic, then grind finely
in a spice mill. Alternatively, use ready-
ground spices, in which case 1 tablespoon
ground coriander will be required.

1 Melt the ghee or butter in a flameproof casserole, add the garlic and stir over low heat for a few seconds. Add the shrimp and stir-fry briefly to coat. Transfer to a plate.

2 Dry fry the cardamom pods, cloves and cinnamon stick for 2 minutes. Add the mustard seeds and fry for 1 minute. Heat the oil and cook the onion and chili for 3–4 minutes. Add the remaining curry ingredients. Set aside.

3 Preheat the oven to 350°F. Cook the rice for 5 minutes. Drain well. Meanwhile, dry fry the coriander and cumin seeds with the urad dhal, if using, for a few minutes. Add the turmeric and grind the mixture finely in a spice grinder.

4 Cook the mustard seeds and cashews in oil for a few minutes and stir into the rice with the ground spice mix.

5 Spoon the rice mixture into a large casserole and dot with ghee or butter. Cover tightly with foil or cheesecloth before fitting the lid securely. Cook in the oven for 20 minutes.

6 About 10 minutes before the rice is ready, reheat the curry sauce and add the shrimp. Simmer gently for 5–8 minutes until the shrimp are cooked through. Spoon into a dish and serve with the rice.

CHICKEN KORMA WITH SAFFRON RICE

MILD AND FRAGRANT, THIS DISH IS — QUITE UNDERSTANDABLY — AN OLD FAVORITE.

SERVES FOUR

INGREDIENTS
    ¾ cup slivered almonds
    1 tablespoon ghee or butter
    about 1 tablespoon sunflower oil
    1½ pounds skinless, boneless
        chicken breasts, cut into bite-size
        pieces
    1 onion, chopped
    4 green cardamom pods
    2 garlic cloves, crushed
    2 teaspoons ground cumin
    1 teaspoon ground coriander
    1 cinnamon stick
    good pinch of chili powder
    1¼ cups canned coconut milk
    ¾ cup chicken stock
    1 teaspoon tomato paste
        (optional)
    5 tablespoons light cream
    1–2 tablespoons fresh lime or
        lemon juice
    2 teaspoons shredded lime or
        lemon rind
    1 teaspoon garam masala
    salt and freshly ground black pepper
    cilantro sprigs, to garnish
For the saffron rice
    1½ cups basmati rice, soaked
    3 cups chicken stock
    generous pinch of saffron strands,
        crushed, then soaked in hot water
        (see Cook's Tip)

1 Dry fry the slivered almonds in a small skillet until pale golden. Transfer about two-thirds of the almonds to a plate and continue to dry fry the remainder until they are slightly deeper in color. Transfer the darker almonds to a separate plate and set them aside for the garnish. Let the paler almonds cool, then grind them in a spice grinder or coffee grinder.

2 Heat the ghee or butter and oil in a wok or flameproof casserole and cook the chicken pieces, in batches if necessary, until evenly brown. Transfer to a plate.

3 Add a little more oil if necessary and cook the onion for 2 minutes, then stir in the cardamom pods and garlic and cook for 3–4 minutes more, until the onion is lightly flecked with brown.

4 Stir in the ground slivered almonds, cumin, coriander, cinnamon stick and chili powder and cook for 1 minute. Stir in the coconut milk, chicken stock and tomato paste, if using.

5 Bring to simmering point, then add the chicken and season. Cover and cook over a gentle heat for 10 minutes until the chicken is tender. Set aside, covered, while cooking the rice.

6 Drain the rice and put it in a pan. Add the seasoned stock and the saffron. Bring to a boil over medium heat, then cover the pan tightly with a lid and cook over low heat for about 10 minutes or according to the instructions on the packet.

7 Just before the rice is ready, reheat the korma until it is simmering gently. Stir in the cream, the citrus juice and rind and the garam masala. Taste and season as necessary. Pile the rice into a warmed serving dish and spoon the korma into a separate dish. Garnish with the cilantro sprigs and reserved browned almonds.

COOK'S TIP
Saffron should always be soaked before use. Soak the strands for about an hour in either warm water or milk, according to the recipe.

BEEF BIRYANI

THE MOGULS INTRODUCED THIS DRY, SPICY RICE DISH TO CENTRAL INDIA. IT IS A MEAL IN ITSELF.

SERVES FOUR

INGREDIENTS

2 large onions
2 garlic cloves, chopped
1-inch piece of fresh ginger root,
    peeled and coarsely chopped
½–1 fresh green chili, seeded and
    coarsely chopped
small bunch of cilantro
4 tablespoons slivered almonds
2–3 tablespoons water
1 tablespoon ghee or butter,
    plus 2 tablespoons butter,
    for the rice
3 tablespoons sunflower oil
2 tablespoons golden raisins
1¼ pounds chuck steak, cubed
1 teaspoon ground coriander
1 tablespoon ground cumin
½ teaspoon ground turmeric
½ teaspoon ground fenugreek
good pinch of ground cinnamon
¾ cup plain yogurt
1½ cups basmati rice
about 5 cups hot chicken stock
    or water
salt and freshly ground black
    pepper
2 hard-cooked eggs, quartered,
    to garnish

1 Roughly chop 1 onion and place it in a food processor or blender. Add the garlic, ginger, chili, cilantro and half the slivered almonds. Pour in the water and process to a smooth paste.

2 Finely slice the remaining onion into rings or half rings. Heat half the ghee or butter with half the oil in a heavy-based, flameproof casserole and cook the onion rings over medium heat for 10–15 minutes until they are a deep golden brown. Transfer to a plate with a slotted spoon. Cook the remaining slivered almonds briefly until golden and set aside with the onion rings, then quickly cook the golden raisins until they swell. Transfer to the plate.

3 Heat the remaining ghee or butter in the casserole with a further 1 tablespoon of the oil. Cook the meat, in batches, until evenly brown. Transfer to a plate and set aside.

4 Wipe the casserole clean with paper towels, heat the remaining oil and pour in the onion and ginger paste. Cook over medium heat for 2–3 minutes, stirring constantly, until the mixture begins to brown lightly. Stir in all the spices, season with salt and pepper and cook for 1 minute more.

5 Lower heat, then stir in the yogurt, a little at a time. When all of it has been incorporated into the spice mixture, return the meat to the casserole. Stir to coat, cover tightly and simmer over gentle heat for 40–45 minutes until the meat is tender. Soak the rice in a bowl of cold water for 15–20 minutes.

6 Preheat the oven to 325ºF. Drain the rice, place in a saucepan and add the hot chicken stock or water, together with a little salt. Bring back to a boil, cover and cook for 5–6 minutes.

7 Drain the rice, and pile it in a mound on top of the meat in the casserole. Using the handle of a spoon, make a hole through the rice and meat mixture, to the bottom of the pan. Scatter the fried onions, almonds and golden raisins over the top and dot with butter. Cover the casserole tightly with a double layer of foil and secure with a lid.

8 Cook the biryani in the oven for 30–40 minutes. To serve, spoon the mixture onto a warmed serving plate and garnish with the quartered hard-cooked eggs. Serve with parathas, nan bread or chapatis, if desired.

SPICY LAMB AND APRICOTS WITH PEA RICE

THE SLIGHTLY DRY FLAVOR OF THE SPLIT PEAS AND BASMATI CONTRASTS WELL WITH THE SWEETNESS OF THE LAMB.

SERVES FOUR

INGREDIENTS

1½ pounds lamb leg fillet
1 tablespoon ghee or butter
1 onion, finely chopped
1 teaspoon ground coriander
2 teaspoons ground cumin
1 teaspoon fenugreek
½ teaspoon turmeric
pinch of cayenne pepper
1 cinnamon stick
½ cup chicken stock
6 ounces apricots, halved
  or quartered
salt and freshly ground black pepper
cilantro, to garnish
For the marinade
  ½ cup plain yogurt
  1 tablespoon sunflower oil
  juice of half a lemon
  1-inch piece fresh ginger root,
    grated
For the rice
  ½ cup chana dhal or yellow split peas,
    soaked for 1–2 hours
  generous 1 cup basmati rice, soaked
    and drained
  1 tablespoon sunflower oil
  1 large onion, finely sliced into rings
  1 garlic clove, crushed
  2 teaspoons finely shredded fresh
    ginger root
  4 tablespoons plain yogurt
  1 tablespoon chopped cilantro
  1 tablespoon ghee or butter
  salt

1 Trim the meat and cut into bite-size pieces. Make the marinade by blending together the yogurt, oil, lemon juice and ginger. Add the meat, stir to coat, then cover with plastic wrap and leave in a cool place for 2–4 hours to marinate.

2 Put the chana dhal or yellow split peas in a large pan, cover with boiling water and boil for 20–30 minutes until tender. Drain and set aside. Cook the drained rice in boiling salted water until it is three-quarters cooked and almost tender. Drain and set aside.

3 Heat the oil in a skillet and cook the onion rings until golden. Transfer to a plate. Stir in the garlic and ginger and cook for a few seconds, then add the yogurt and cook for a few minutes, stirring. Add the dhal, coriander and salt. Stir well, then remove from the heat and set aside. Preheat the oven to 350°F.

4 Drain the meat, reserving the marinade. Melt the ghee or butter in a flameproof casserole and cook the onion for 3–4 minutes until soft. Add the coriander, cumin, fenugreek, turmeric, cayenne pepper and cinnamon stick, and cook over a medium heat until the spices are sizzling.

5 Fry the meat until browned, then spoon in the remaining marinade, add the chicken stock and apricots, and season well. Slowly bring to a boil, then cover and cook in the oven for 45–55 minutes until the meat is tender.

6 Meanwhile, finish cooking the rice. Spoon the dhal mixture into a casserole and stir in the rice. Dot the top with ghee or butter and sprinkle with the onion rings. Cover with a double layer of foil, secured with the lid. Place in the oven 30 minutes before the lamb is ready. The rice and dhal should be tender but the grains should be separate. Serve the rice and spiced lamb together, garnished with cilantro.

INDIAN RICE WITH TOMATOES AND SPINACH

THIS TASTY RICE DISH CAN BE SERVED WITH A MEAT CURRY OR AS PART OF A VEGETARIAN MEAL.

SERVES FOUR

INGREDIENTS
    2 tablespoons sunflower oil
    1 tablespoon ghee or butter
    1 onion, chopped
    2 garlic cloves, crushed
    3 tomatoes, peeled, seeded and
        chopped
    generous 1 cup brown basmati
        rice, soaked
    2 teaspoons dhana jeera powder or
        1 teaspoon ground coriander and
        1 teaspoon ground cumin
    2 carrots, coarsely shredded
    3¾ cups vegetable stock
    10 ounces baby spinach leaves,
        washed
    ½ cup unsalted cashews,
        toasted
    salt and freshly ground black
        pepper

1 Heat the oil and ghee or butter in a flameproof casserole and gently cook the onion and garlic for 4–5 minutes until soft. Add the chopped tomatoes and cook for 3–4 minutes, stirring, until slightly thickened.

2 Drain the rice, add it to the casserole and cook gently for 1–2 minutes, stirring, until the rice is coated with the tomato and onion mixture.

COOK'S TIP
If you can't get baby spinach leaves, use larger fresh spinach leaves. Remove any tough stalks and chop the leaves coarsely.

3 Stir in the dhana jeera powder or coriander and cumin, then add the carrots and season with salt and pepper. Pour in the stock and stir well to mix.

4 Bring to a boil, then cover tightly and simmer over very gentle heat for 20–25 minutes until the rice is tender. Lay the spinach on the surface of the rice, cover again and cook for 2–3 minutes until the spinach has wilted. Fold the spinach into the rest of the rice and check the seasoning. Sprinkle with cashews and serve.

SWEET RICE WITH HOT SOUR CHICK-PEAS

MUCH MORE THAN IN THE WEST, INDIANS ENJOY DISHES THAT COMBINE SWEET FLAVORS WITH HOT OR SOUR ONES. HERE, THE RICE IS DISTINCTLY SWEET BUT GOES WELL WITH THE HOT, SOUR TASTE OF THE CHICK-PEAS.

SERVES SIX

INGREDIENTS
   1⅔ cups dried chick-peas,
     soaked overnight
   4 tablespoons vegetable oil
   1 large onion, very finely chopped
   8 ounces tomatoes, peeled and
     finely chopped
   1 tablespoon ground coriander
   1 tablespoon ground cumin
   1 teaspoon ground fenugreek
   1 teaspoon ground cinnamon
   1–2 fresh hot green chilies, seeded
     and finely sliced
   1-inch piece of fresh ginger root,
     shredded
   4 tablespoons lemon juice
   1 tablespoon chopped fresh cilantro
   salt and freshly ground black pepper
For the rice
   3 tablespoons ghee or butter
   4 green cardamom pods
   4 cloves
   2¾ cups boiling water
   1¾ cups basmati rice,
     soaked and drained
   1–2 teaspoons sugar
   5–6 saffron strands, soaked in
     warm water

1 Drain the chick-peas well and place them in a large pan. Pour in water to cover, bring to a boil, then simmer, covered, for 1–1¼ hours until tender, topping up the liquid from time to time. Drain the chick-peas, reserving the cooking liquid.

2 Heat the oil in a pan. Reserve about 2 tablespoons of the chopped onion and add the remainder to the pan. Cook over medium heat for about 5 minutes, stirring frequently.

3 Add the tomatoes. Cook over moderately low heat for 5–6 minutes, until they are very soft, stirring and mashing them frequently.

4 Stir in the coriander, cumin, fenugreek and cinnamon. Cook for about 30 seconds, then add the chick-peas and 1½ cups of the reserved cooking liquid. Season with salt, then cover and simmer gently for 15–20 minutes, stirring occasionally and adding more liquid if the chick-peas begin to dry out.

5 While the chick-peas are cooking, melt the ghee or butter in a pan and cook the cardamom pods and cloves for a few minutes. Remove the pan from the heat, and when the fat has cooled a little, pour in the boiling water and stir in the basmati rice. Cover tightly and cook by the absorption method for 10 minutes.

6 When the rice is cooked, add the sugar and saffron liquid and stir thoroughly. Cover again. The rice will keep warm while you finish cooking the chick-peas.

7 Mix the reserved onion with the sliced chilies, ginger and lemon juice, and stir the mixture into the chick-peas. Add the chopped cilantro, adjust the seasoning and serve with the rice.

SAFFRON RICE <u>WITH</u> CARDAMOMS

THE ADDITION OF AROMATIC GREEN CARDAMOM PODS, CLOVES, MILK AND SAFFRON GIVES THIS DISH BOTH A DELICATE FLAVOR AND COLOR.

2 Add the cardamoms, cloves and salt. Stir, then bring to a boil. Lower heat, cover the pan tightly and simmer for about 10 minutes.

3 Meanwhile, place the milk in a small pan. Add the saffron strands and heat gently, stirring.

4 Drain the rice, return it to the clean pan and pour the saffron milk over the top. Cover with a tight-fitting lid and cook over low heat for 5–6 minutes. Remove from the heat without lifting the lid. Let the rice stand for 5 minutes before serving.

SERVES SIX

INGREDIENTS
- 2⅓ cups basmati rice, soaked
- 3 cups water
- 3 green cardamom pods
- 2 cloves
- 1 teaspoon salt
- 3 tablespoons low-fat milk
- ½ teaspoon saffron strands, crushed

1 Drain the rice and place it in a pan. Pour in the water.

COOK'S TIP
The saffron milk can be heated in the microwave. Mix the milk and saffron strands in a suitable bowl and warm them for 1 minute on Low.

PILAU RICE WITH WHOLE SPICES

THIS FRAGRANT RICE DISH MAKES A PERFECT SIDE DISH FOR ANY INDIAN MEAL.

SERVES FOUR

INGREDIENTS
    generous pinch of saffron strands
    2½ cups hot chicken stock
    ¼ cup butter
    1 onion, chopped
    1 garlic clove, crushed
    ½ cinnamon stick
    6 green cardamom pods
    1 bay leaf
    1⅓ cups basmati rice
    ⅓ cup golden raisins
    1 tablespoon sunflower oil
    ½ cup cashews
    nan bread and tomato and onion
      salad, to serve (optional)

1 Stir the saffron strands into a measuring cup of hot stock and set aside.

2 Heat the butter in a pan and cook the onion and garlic for 5 minutes. Stir in the cinnamon stick, cardamoms and bay leaf and cook for 2 minutes more.

3 Add the rice and cook, stirring, for 2 minutes more. Pour in the saffron-flavored stock and add the golden raisins. Bring to a boil, stir, then lower the heat, cover and cook gently for 15 minutes, or until the rice is tender and the liquid has been absorbed.

4 Meanwhile, heat the oil in a skillet and cook the cashews until browned. Drain on paper towels. Scatter the cashews over the rice. Serve with nan bread and a tomato and onion salad, if desired.

COOK'S TIP
Don't be tempted to use black cardamoms in this dish. They are coarser and more strongly flavored than green cardamoms and are only used in highly spiced dishes that are cooked for a long time.

MUSHROOM PILAU

THIS DISH IS SIMPLICITY ITSELF. SERVE WITH ANY INDIAN DISH OR WITH ROAST LAMB OR CHICKEN.

SERVES FOUR

INGREDIENTS
  2 tablespoons vegetable oil
  2 shallots, finely chopped
  1 garlic clove, crushed
  3 green cardamom pods
  2 tablespoons ghee or butter
  2½ cups white mushrooms, sliced
  generous 1 cup basmati rice,
    soaked
  1 teaspoon shredded fresh ginger
    root
  good pinch of garam masala
  scant 2 cups water
  1 tablespoon chopped cilantro
  salt

1 Heat the oil in a flameproof casserole and cook the shallots, garlic and cardamom pods over medium heat for 3–4 minutes, until the shallots have softened and are beginning to brown.

2 Add the ghee or butter. When it has melted, add the mushrooms and cook for 2–3 minutes more.

3 Add the rice, ginger and garam masala. Stir-fry over low heat for 2–3 minutes, then stir in the water and a little salt. Bring to a boil, then cover tightly and simmer over very low heat for 10 minutes.

4 Remove the casserole from the heat. Let stand, covered, for 5 minutes. Add the chopped cilantro and fork it through the rice. Spoon into a serving bowl and serve immediately.

ASIA

Rice is by far the most important cereal of South-east Asia, yet each country has its own favorite style of cooking rice, and each its own distinguishing rice-based cuisine. Fried Rice from China, Nasi Goreng from Indonesia or Sushi from Japan are just some of the classic Asian rice dishes now enjoyed all over the world.

SUSHI

ONCE BARELY KNOWN OUTSIDE JAPAN, THESE TASTY ROLLS OF FLAVORED RICE AND PAPER-THIN SEAWEED HAVE BECOME VERY POPULAR, PARTLY DUE TO THE PROLIFERATION OF SUSHI BARS THAT HAVE SPRUNG UP IN MANY MAJOR CITIES.

SERVES FOUR TO SIX

INGREDIENTS
For the tuna sushi
   2–3 baby carrots, blanched
   3 sheets nori (paper-thin seaweed),
    cut in half
   4 ounces fresh tuna fillet, cut into
    fingers
   1 teaspoon thin wasabi paste
    (Japanese horseradish mustard)
For the salmon sushi
   2 eggs
   2 teaspoons sugar
   ½ teaspoon salt
   2 teaspoons butter
   3 sheets nori
   5 ounces fresh salmon fillet, cut
    into fingers
   ½ small cucumber, cut into strips
   1 teaspoon thin wasabi paste
For the sushi rice
   4 cups sushi rice, rinsed
   about 2¾ cups water
For the sushi dressing
   4 tablespoons rice vinegar
   1 tablespoon sugar
   ½ teaspoon salt
To serve
   sliced pickled ginger, cut in strips
   wasabi paste, thinned with water
   Japanese sushi soy sauce

1 Put the rice in a heavy pan and add 2¾ cups water or according to the instructions on the packet. Bring to a boil, cover tightly and cook over low heat for 15 minutes. Increase the heat to high for 10 seconds, then remove from the heat and let stand for about 10 minutes. Meanwhile, blend together the rice vinegar, sugar and salt.

2 Stir the sushi dressing into the rice, then cover with a damp cloth and cool. Do not put in the fridge as this will make the rice go hard.

3 To make the tuna sushi, cut the carrots into thin strips. Cut one nori sheet in half and lay one half, shiny side down, on a bamboo sushi mat. Lay strips of tuna across the length of the nori and spread with a little wasabi. Place a line of carrots next to the tuna and, using the mat as a guide, roll up tightly. Repeat with the other half of nori. Set aside any extra tuna or carrot.

4 Place a square of damp waxed paper on the bamboo mat and spread with a little of the cooled sushi rice, leaving a ½-inch edge at the top and bottom.

5 Place the tuna-filled nori roll on top, about 1-inch from the edge of the rice and roll up, using the paper as a guide (and making sure it doesn't get rolled up with the rice). Wrap the roll in waxed paper and chill for 10 minutes. Make another sushi roll using the other tuna-filled nori roll.

6 To make the salmon sushi, beat together the eggs with 2 tablespoons water and the sugar and salt. Melt about one-third of the butter in a small skillet and add one-third of the egg mixture to make an omelet. Repeat until you have three small omelets.

7 Place a nori sheet, shiny side down, on a bamboo mat, cover with an omelet and spread with sushi rice, leaving a ½-inch edge at the top and bottom. Lay strips of salmon across the width and lay cucumber strips next to the salmon. Spread a little wasabi paste over the salmon. Roll the nori around the filling. Wrap in plastic wrap and chill for 10 minutes. Repeat to make three rolls.

8 When the rolls are cool, remove the waxed paper and plastic wrap. Using a wet knife, cut the rolls into six slices. Serve with pickled ginger, wasabi and Japanese sushi soy sauce.

RICE OMELET

RICE OMELETS MAKE A GREAT SUPPER DISH. IN JAPAN, THEY ARE A FAVORITE WITH CHILDREN, WHO USUALLY TOP THEM WITH A LIBERAL HELPING OF TOMATO KETCHUP.

2 Melt a further 2 teaspoons butter in the frying pan, add the rice and stir well. Mix in the fried ingredients, ketchup and pepper. Stir well, adding salt to taste, if necessary. Keep the mixture warm. Beat the eggs with the milk in a bowl. Stir in the measured salt and add pepper to taste.

3 Melt 1 teaspoon of the remaining butter in an omelet pan. Pour in a quarter of the egg mixture and stir it briefly with a fork, then allow it to set for 1 minute. Top with a quarter of the rice mixture.

SERVES FOUR

INGREDIENTS
- 1 skinless, boneless chicken thigh, about 4 ounces, cubed
- 8 teaspoons butter
- 1 small onion, chopped
- ½ carrot, diced
- 2 shiitake mushrooms, stems removed and chopped
- 1 tablespoon finely chopped fresh parsley
- 2 cups cooked long grain white rice
- 2 tablespoons tomato ketchup
- 6 eggs, lightly beaten
- 4 tablespoons milk
- 1 teaspoon salt, plus extra to season
- freshly ground black pepper
- tomato ketchup, to serve

1 Season the chicken with salt and pepper. Melt 2 teaspoons butter in a skillet. Cook the onion for 1 minute, then add the chicken and cook until the cubes are white and completely cooked. Add the carrot and mushrooms, stir-fry over medium heat until soft, then add the parsley. Set this mixture aside. Wipe the skillet with paper towels.

4 Fold the omelet over the rice and slide it to the edge of the pan to shape it into a curve. Slide it onto a warmed plate, cover with a paper towel and press neatly into a rectangular shape. Keep hot while cooking three more omelets from the remaining ingredients. Serve immediately, with tomato ketchup, if desired.

CHICKEN AND MUSHROOM DONBURI

"DONBURI" MEANS A ONE-DISH MEAL THAT IS EATEN FROM A BOWL, AND TAKES ITS NAME FROM THE EPONYMOUS JAPANESE PORCELAIN FOOD BOWL. AS IN MOST JAPANESE DISHES, THE RICE HERE IS COMPLETELY PLAIN BUT IS NEVERTHELESS AN INTEGRAL PART OF THE DISH.

SERVES FOUR

INGREDIENTS
   2 teaspoons groundnut oil
   4 tablespoons butter
   2 garlic cloves, crushed
   1-inch piece of fresh ginger root,
      shredded
   5 scallions, diagonally sliced
   1 green fresh chili, seeded and
      finely sliced
   3 skinless, boneless chicken breasts,
      cut into thin strips
   5 ounces tofu bean curd, cut into
      small cubes
   4 ounces shiitake mushrooms, stalks
      discarded and caps sliced
   1 tablespoon Japanese rice wine
   2 tablespoons light soy sauce
   2 teaspoons sugar
   1⅔ cups chicken stock
For the rice
   generous 1–1½ cups Japanese rice
      or Thai fragrant rice

1 Cook the rice by the absorption method or by following the instructions on the packet.

2 While the rice is cooking, heat the oil and half the butter in a large skillet. Stir-fry the garlic, ginger, scallions and chili for 1–2 minutes until slightly softened. Add the strips of chicken and cook, in batches if necessary, until the pieces are evenly browned.

3 Transfer the chicken mixture to a plate and add the tofu to the pan. Stir-fry for a few minutes, then add the mushrooms. Stir-fry for 2–3 minutes over medium heat until the mushrooms are tender.

4 Stir in the rice wine, soy sauce and sugar and cook over high heat for 1–2 minutes, stirring constantly. Return the chicken to the pan, toss over the heat for about 2 minutes, then pour in the stock. Stir well and cook over a gentle heat for 5–6 minutes until bubbling.

5 Spoon the rice into individual serving bowls and pile the chicken mixture on top, making sure that each portion gets a generous amount of chicken sauce.

COOK'S TIP
Once the rice is cooked, leave it covered until ready to serve. It will stay warm for about 30 minutes. Fork through lightly just before serving.

CHINESE FRIED RICE

THIS DISH, A VARIATION ON SPECIAL FRIED RICE, IS MORE ELABORATE THAN THE MORE FAMILIAR EGG FRIED RICE, AND IS ALMOST A MEAL IN ITSELF.

SERVES FOUR

INGREDIENTS

    2 ounces cooked ham
    2 ounces cooked shrimp, shelled and
      deveined
    3 eggs
    1 teaspoon salt
    2 scallions, finely chopped
    4 tablespoons vegetable oil
    1 cup green peas, thawed
      if frozen
    1 tablespoon light soy sauce
    1 tablespoon Chinese rice wine or
      dry sherry
    4 cups cooked white long grain rice

1 Dice the cooked ham finely. Pat the cooked shrimp dry on kitchen paper.

2 In a bowl, beat the eggs with a pinch of salt and a few scallion pieces.

VARIATIONS
This is a versatile recipe and is ideal for using up leftovers. Use cooked chicken or turkey instead of the ham, doubling the quantity if you omit the shrimp.

3 Heat about half the oil in a wok, stir-fry the peas, shrimp and ham for 1 minute, then add the soy sauce and rice wine or sherry. Transfer to a bowl and keep hot.

4 Heat the remaining oil in the wok and scramble the eggs lightly. Add the rice and stir to make sure that the grains are separate. Add the remaining salt, the remaining scallions and the shrimp mixture. Toss over the heat to mix. Serve hot or cold.

STIR-FRIED RICE AND VEGETABLES

THE GINGER GIVES THIS ORIENTAL DISH A WONDERFUL FLAVOR. SERVE IT AS A VEGETARIAN MAIN COURSE OR AS AN UNUSUAL VEGETABLE SIDE DISH.

SERVES FOUR AS A SIDE DISH

INGREDIENTS
generous ½ cup brown basmati rice,
  rinsed and drained
1½ cups vegetable stock
1-inch piece of fresh ginger root,
  finely sliced
1 garlic clove, halved
2-inch piece of pared lemon rind
1½ cups shiitake mushrooms
1 tablespoon groundnut oil
1 tablespoon ghee or butter
6 ounces baby carrots, trimmed
8 ounces baby zucchini, halved
about 1½ cups broccoli, broken into
  florets
6 scallions, diagonally sliced
1 tablespoon light soy sauce
2 teaspoons toasted sesame oil

1 Put the rice in a pan and pour in the stock. Add the ginger, garlic and lemon rind. Slowly bring to a boil, then cover and cook very gently for 20–25 minutes until the rice is tender. Discard the flavorings and keep the pan covered so that the rice stays warm.

2 Slice the mushrooms, discarding the stems. Heat the oil and ghee or butter in a wok and stir-fry the carrots for 4–5 minutes until partially tender. Add the mushrooms and zucchini, stir-fry for 2–3 minutes, then add the broccoli and scallions and cook for 3 minutes more, by which time all the vegetables should be tender but should still retain a bit of "bite."

3 Add the cooked rice to the vegetables, and toss briefly over the heat to mix and heat through. Toss with the soy sauce and sesame oil. Spoon into a bowl and serve immediately.

CRACKLING RICE PAPER FISH ROLLS

THE RICE IN THIS DISH IS IN THE RICE PAPER WRAPPERS, WHICH MANAGE TO HOLD THEIR SHAPE DURING COOKING, YET ALMOST MAGICALLY DISSOLVE IN YOUR MOUTH WHEN IT COMES TO EATING.

MAKES TWELVE

INGREDIENTS
12 Vietnamese rice paper sheets
  (bahn trang), each about
  8 x 4 inches
3 tablespoons all-purpose flour mixed
  to a paste with 3 tablespoons water
vegetable oil, for deep frying
fresh herbs, to garnish
For the filling
24 young asparagus spears, trimmed
8 ounces shrimp, shelled and
  deveined
1½ tablespoons olive oil
6 scallions, finely chopped
1 garlic clove, crushed
¾-inch piece of fresh ginger root,
  shredded
2 tablespoons chopped cilantro
1 teaspoon five-spice powder
1 teaspoon finely shredded lime or
  lemon rind
salt and freshly ground black pepper

1 Make the filling. Bring a pan of lightly salted water to a boil and cook the asparagus for 3–4 minutes until tender. Drain, refresh under cold water and drain again. Cut the shrimp into ¾-inch pieces.

2 Heat half of the oil in a small skillet or wok and stir-fry the scallions and garlic over low heat for 2–3 minutes until soft. Using a slotted spoon, transfer the vegetables to a bowl and set aside.

3 Heat the remaining oil in the pan and stir-fry the shrimp over a high heat for just a few seconds until they start to go pink. Add to the scallion mixture with the ginger, cilantro, five-spice powder, lime or lemon rind and a little pepper. Stir to mix.

4 To make each roll, brush a sheet of rice paper liberally with water and lay it on a clean surface. Place two asparagus spears and a spoonful of the shrimp mixture just off center. Fold in the sides and roll up to make a fat cigar. Seal the ends with a little of the flour paste.

5 Heat the oil in a wok or deep fryer and fry the rolls in batches until pale golden in color. Drain well, garnish with herbs and serve.

MALACCA FRIED RICE

THERE ARE MANY VERSIONS OF THIS DISH THROUGHOUT ASIA, ALL BASED UPON LEFTOVER COOKED RICE. INGREDIENTS VARY ACCORDING TO WHAT IS AVAILABLE, BUT SHRIMP ARE A POPULAR ADDITION.

SERVES FOUR TO SIX

INGREDIENTS

2 eggs
3 tablespoons vegetable oil
4 shallots or 1 onion, finely chopped
1 teaspoon finely chopped fresh
  ginger root
1 garlic clove, crushed
8 ounces shrimp
1 teaspoon chili sauce (optional)
3 scallions, green part only,
  coarsely chopped
2 cups frozen peas
8 ounces thickly sliced roast pork,
  diced
3 tablespoons light soy sauce
3 cups cooked white long grain
  rice
salt and freshly ground black pepper

1 In a bowl, beat the eggs well with salt and freshly ground black pepper to taste. Heat 1 tablespoon of the oil in a large, non-stick skillet, pour in the eggs and cook until set, without stirring. This will take less than a minute. Roll up the omelet, slide it onto a plate, cut into thin strips and set aside.

COOK'S TIP
You don't have to wait until you have some leftover cooked pork to try this fried rice dish. Most specialty shops sell sliced roast pork.

2 Heat the remaining vegetable oil in a preheated wok, add the shallots or onion, ginger, garlic and shrimp, and cook for 1–2 minutes, taking care that the garlic does not burn.

3 Add the chili sauce, if using, the scallions, peas, pork and soy sauce. Stir to heat through, then add the rice. Fry over medium heat for 6–8 minutes. Spoon into a dish, decorate with the omelet strips and serve immediately.

CHINESE JEWELED RICE

ANOTHER FRIED RICE MEDLEY, THIS TIME WITH CRAB MEAT AND WATER CHESTNUTS, PROVIDING CONTRASTING TEXTURES AND FLAVORS.

SERVES FOUR

INGREDIENTS

    1¾ cups white long grain rice
    3 tablespoons vegetable oil
    1 onion, roughly chopped
    4 dried black Chinese mushrooms,
      soaked for 10 minutes in warm
      water to cover
    4 ounces cooked ham, diced
    6 ounces drained canned white crab
      meat
    ½ cup drained canned water
      chestnuts
    1 cup peas, thawed if frozen
    2 tablespoons oyster sauce
    1 teaspoon sugar
    salt

1 Rinse the rice, then cook for 10–12 minutes in a pan of lightly salted boiling water. Drain the rice, then refresh under cold water, drain again and allow to cool. Heat half the oil in a wok. When the oil is very hot, stir-fry the rice for 3 minutes. Transfer the cooked rice to a bowl and set aside.

2 Heat the remaining oil in the wok and cook the onion until softened but not colored. Drain the mushrooms, cut off and discard the stems, then chop the caps.

3 Add the chopped mushrooms to the wok, with all the remaining ingredients except the rice. Stir-fry for 2 minutes, then add the rice and stir-fry for about 3 minutes more. Serve at once.

COOK'S TIP
When adding the oil to the hot wok, drizzle it in a "necklace" just below the rim. As it runs down, it will coat the inner surface as it heats.

THAI RICE

THIS IS A LOVELY, SOFT, FLUFFY RICE DISH, PERFUMED WITH FRESH LEMONGRASS AND LIMES.

SERVES FOUR

INGREDIENTS
    2 limes
    1 lemongrass stalk
    generous 1 cup brown long grain
        rice
    1 tablespoon olive oil
    1 onion, chopped
    1-inch piece of fresh ginger root,
        peeled and finely chopped
    1½ teaspoons coriander seeds
    1½ teaspoons cumin seeds
    3 cups vegetable stock
    4 tablespoons chopped cilantro
    scallion green, toasted coconut
        strips and lime wedges, to serve

1 Pare the limes using a canelle knife or a fine shredder, taking care to avoid cutting the bitter pith. Set aside the rind. Finely chop the lower portion of the lemongrass stalk and set aside.

2 Rinse the rice in plenty of cold water until the water runs clear. Tip into a strainer and drain thoroughly.

3 Heat the oil in a pan. Add the onion, ginger, spices, lemongrass and lime rind and fry over a low heat for 2–3 minutes.

4 Add the drained rice and cook for 1 minute, then pour in the stock and bring to a boil. Reduce heat to very low and cover the pan. Cook gently for 30 minutes, then check the rice. If it is still crunchy, cover the pan and leave for 3–5 minutes more. Remove from the heat.

5 Stir in the cilantro, fluff up the grains, cover and leave for about 10 minutes. Garnish with scallion green and toasted coconut strips, and serve with lime wedges.

THAI FRIED RICE

THIS SUBSTANTIAL DISH IS BASED ON THAI FRAGRANT RICE, WHICH IS SOMETIMES KNOWN AS JASMINE RICE. CHICKEN, RED BELL PEPPER AND CORN ADD COLOR AND EXTRA FLAVOR.

SERVES FOUR

INGREDIENTS

2 cups water
½ cup coconut milk powder
1¾ cups Thai fragrant rice,
    rinsed
2 tablespoons groundnut oil
2 garlic cloves, chopped
1 small onion, finely chopped
1-inch piece of fresh ginger root,
    shredded
8 ounces skinless, boneless chicken
    breasts, cut into ½-inch dice
1 red bell pepper, seeded and
    sliced
1 cup drained canned corn kernels
1 teaspoon chili oil
1 teaspoon hot curry powder
2 eggs, beaten
salt
scallion shreds, to garnish

3 Push the vegetables to the sides of the wok, add the chicken to the center and stir-fry for 2 minutes. Add the rice and stir-fry over high heat for about 3 minutes more.

4 Stir in the sliced red bell pepper, corn, chili oil and curry powder, with salt to taste. Toss over the heat for 1 minute. Stir in the beaten eggs and cook for 1 minute more. Garnish with scallion shreds and serve.

1 Pour the water into a pan and whisk in the coconut milk powder. Add the rice and bring to a boil. Lower heat, cover and cook for 12 minutes or until the rice is tender and the liquid has been absorbed. Spread the rice on a baking sheet and leave until cold.

2 Heat the oil in a wok, add the garlic, onion and ginger and stir-fry over medium heat for 2 minutes.

COOK'S TIP
It is important that the rice is completely cold before being fried and the oil is very hot, or the rice will absorb too much oil.

EXOTIC FRUIT AND VEGETABLE SALAD

THIS IS A VARIATION ON THE FAMOUS INDONESIAN SALAD KNOWN AS GADO GADO. CHOOSE SOME OR ALL OF THE SUGGESTED FRUITS AND VEGETABLES TO MAKE AN ATTRACTIVE CENTERPIECE FOR AN INDONESIAN OR THAI MEAL.

SERVES SIX TO EIGHT

INGREDIENTS

    4 ounces green beans, trimmed
    2 carrots, cut into thin sticks
    2 cups bean sprouts
    ¼ head napa cabbage, shredded
    ½ small cucumber, cut into thin strips
    8 scallions, sliced diagonally
    6 cherry tomatoes or small tomatoes,
      halved
    12–16 cooked tiger shrimp
    1 small mango
    1 small papaya
    1 quantity Lontong (compressed rice)
    4 hard-cooked eggs, quartered
    fresh cilantro
For the peanut dressing
    8 tablespoons crunchy or smooth
      peanut butter, preferably unsalted
    1 garlic clove, crushed
    1¼ cups coconut milk
    1 tablespoon tamarind water (see
      Cook's Tip) or juice of ½ lemon
    1–2 tablespoons light soy sauce
    hot chili sauce, to taste

1 First, make the peanut dressing. Place all the ingredients except the chili sauce in a pan and heat the mixture, stirring constantly, until it is very hot and smooth. Stir in chili sauce to taste. Keep the dressing warm, or let it cool and reheat it before serving.

2 Cook the beans and carrots in boiling water for 3–4 minutes until just tender but still firm. Drain, then refresh under cold water and drain again. Cook the bean sprouts in boiling water for 2 minutes, then drain and refresh.

3 Arrange the carrots, beans and bean sprouts on a large, attractive platter, with the shredded Chinese leaves, cucumber strips, scallions, tomatoes, and shrimp.

4 Peel the mango and cut the flesh into cubes. Quarter the papaya, remove the skin and seeds, then slice the flesh. Add to the salad platter, with the lontong. Garnish with the egg quarters and fresh cilantro.

5 Reheat the peanut dressing, if necessary. As soon as it is warm, pour it into a serving bowl. Place the bowl in the center of the salad and serve. Guests help themselves to the salad, adding as much dressing as they like.

COOK'S TIP

To make tamarind water, break off a 1-inch cube of tamarind and put it in a bowl. Pour in ⅔ cup warm water. Using your fingers, squeeze the tamarind so that the juices dissolve into the water. Strain, discarding the solid tamarind, and use as directed in the recipe. Any unused tamarind water can be kept in a container in the fridge for up to 1 week.

FESTIVE RICE

This pretty Thai dish is traditionally shaped into a cone and surrounded by a variety of garnishes before being served.

SERVES EIGHT

INGREDIENTS
  2⅓ cups Thai fragrant rice
  4 tablespoons oil
  2 garlic cloves, crushed
  2 onions, finely sliced
  ½ teaspoon ground turmeric
  3 cups water
  1¾ cups coconut milk
  1–2 lemongrass stalks, bruised
For the garnishes
  omelet strips
  2 fresh red chilies, shredded
  cucumber chunks
  tomato wedges
  deep fried onions
  shrimp crackers

1 Put the rice in a strainer and rinse thoroughly under cold water. Drain well.

2 Heat the oil in a skillet which has a lid. Cook the garlic, onions and turmeric over low heat for a few minutes, until the onions are softened but not browned. Add the rice and stir well so that each grain is coated in oil.

3 Pour in the water and coconut milk and add the lemongrass. Bring to a boil, stirring well. Cover the pan and cook gently for 12 minutes, or until all the liquid has been absorbed.

COOK'S TIP
Look out for fresh turmeric at Asian markets or food stores.

4 Remove the pan from the heat and lift the lid. Cover with a clean dish towel, replace the lid and let stand in a warm place for 15 minutes. Remove the lemongrass, mound the rice mixture in a cone on a serving platter and arrange the garnishes around the edge and on the top. Serve immediately.

THAI CRISPY NOODLES WITH BEEF

RICE VERMICELLI ARE VERY FINE, DRY, WHITE NOODLES BUNDLED IN LARGE FRAGILE LOOPS AND SOLD IN PACKETS. THEY ARE DEEP FRIED BEFORE BEING ADDED TO THIS DISH, AND IN THE PROCESS THEY EXPAND TO AT LEAST FOUR TIMES THEIR ORIGINAL SIZE.

SERVES FOUR

INGREDIENTS
about 1 pound rump or sirloin steak
teriyaki sauce, for marinating
6 ounces rice vermicelli
groundnut oil for deep frying and
  stir-frying
8 scallions, diagonally sliced
2 garlic cloves, crushed
4–5 carrots, cut into julienne strips
1–2 fresh red chilies, seeded and
  finely sliced
2 small zucchini, diagonally sliced
1 teaspoon shredded fresh
  ginger root
4 tablespoons white or yellow rice
  vinegar
6 tablespoons light soy sauce
about 2 cups spicy stock

1 Beat out the steak, if necessary, to about 1-inch thick. Place in a shallow dish, brush generously with the teriyaki sauce and set aside for 2–4 hours to marinate.

2 Separate the rice vermicelli into manageable loops and layer several paper towels on a very large plate. Add the oil to a depth of 2-inches in a large wok, and heat until a strand of vermicelli cooks as soon as it is lowered into the oil.

3 Carefully add a loop of vermicelli to the oil. It should immediately expand and become opaque. Turn the noodles over so that the strands cook on both sides, and then transfer the cooked noodles to the plate. Repeat the process until all the noodles are cooked. Transfer the cooked noodles to a separate wok or deep serving bowl and keep them warm while you cook the steak and vegetables.

4 Strain the oil from the wok into a heatproof bowl and set aside. Heat 1 tablespoon groundnut oil in the clean wok. When it sizzles, fry the steak for about 30 seconds on each side until browned. Transfer to a board and cut into thick slices. The meat should be well browned on the outside but still pink inside. Set aside.

5 Add a little extra oil to the wok and stir-fry the scallions, garlic and carrots over medium heat for 5–6 minutes until the carrots are slightly soft and have a glazed appearance. Add the chilies, zucchini and ginger and stir-fry for 1–2 minutes more.

6 Stir in the rice vinegar, soy sauce and stock. Cook for about 4 minutes until the sauce has slightly thickened Add the steak and cook for a further 1–2 minutes (or longer, if you prefer your meat well done).

7 Pour the steak, vegetables and all the mixture over the noodles and toss lightly and carefully to mix. Serve immediately.

COOK'S TIP
As soon as you add the meat mixture to the noodles, they will soften. If you wish to keep a few crispy noodles, stir some to the surface so they do not come into contact with the hot liquid.

RICE NOODLES WITH PORK

RICE NOODLES HAVE LITTLE FLAVOR THEMSELVES BUT THEY HAVE A WONDERFUL ABILITY TO TAKE ON THE FLAVOR OF OTHER INGREDIENTS.

SERVES FOUR TO SIX

INGREDIENTS

   1 pound pork tenderloin
   8 ounces dried rice noodles
   1 cup broccoli florets
   1 red bell pepper, quartered and seeded
   about 3 tablespoons groundnut oil
   2 garlic cloves, crushed
   10 scallions, trimmed and cut into
     2-inch diagonal slices
   1 lemongrass stalk, finely chopped
   1–2 fresh red chilies, seeded and
     finely chopped
   1¼ cups coconut milk
   1 tablespoon tomato paste
   3 kaffir lime leaves (optional)
For the marinade
   3 tablespoons light soy sauce
   1 tablespoon rice wine
   2 tablespoons groundnut oil
   1-inch piece of fresh ginger root

1 Cut the pork into thin strips, about 1-inch long and ½-inch wide. Mix all the marinade ingredients in a bowl, add the pork, stir to coat and let marinate for about 1 hour.

2 Spread out the noodles in a shallow dish, pour over hot water to cover and soak for 20 minutes until soft. Drain. Blanch the broccoli in a small pan of boiling water for 2 minutes, then drain and refresh under cold water. Set aside.

3 Place the pepper pieces under a hot broiler for a few minutes until the skin blackens and blisters. Put in a plastic bag for about 10 minutes and then, when cool enough to handle, peel away the skin and slice the flesh thinly.

4 Drain the pork, reserving the marinade. Heat 2 tablespoons of the oil in a large skillet. Stir-fry the pork, in batches if necessary, for 3–4 minutes until the meat is tender. Transfer to a plate and keep warm.

5 Add a little more oil to the pan if necessary and cook the garlic, scallions, lemongrass and chilies over low to medium heat for 2–3 minutes. Add the broccoli and pepper and stir-fry for a few minutes more.

6 Stir in the reserved marinade, coconut milk and tomato paste, with the kaffir lime leaves, if using. Simmer gently until the broccoli is nearly tender, then add the pork and noodles. Toss over the heat, for 3–4 minutes until completely heated through.

CHICKEN AND BASIL COCONUT RICE

FOR THIS DISH, THE RICE IS PARTIALLY BOILED BEFORE BEING SIMMERED WITH COCONUT SO THAT IT FULLY ABSORBS THE FLAVOR OF THE CHILIES, BASIL AND SPICES.

SERVES FOUR

INGREDIENTS

1¾ cups Thai fragrant rice, rinsed
2–3 tablespoons groundnut oil
1 large onion, finely sliced into rings
1 garlic clove, crushed
1 fresh red chili, seeded and finely sliced
1 fresh green chili, seeded and finely sliced
generous handful of basil leaves
3 skinless, boneless chicken breasts, about 12 ounces, finely sliced
¼-inch piece of lemongrass, pounded or finely chopped
2-ounce piece of creamed coconut dissolved in 2½ cups boiling water
salt and freshly ground black pepper

1 Bring a pan of lightly salted water to a boil. Add the rice to the pan and boil for about 6 minutes, until partially cooked. Drain.

2 Heat the oil in a skillet and cook the onion rings for 5–10 minutes until golden and crisp. Lift out, drain on paper towels and set aside.

3 Cook the garlic and chilies in the oil remaining in the pan for 2–3 minutes, then add the basil leaves and cook briefly until they begin to wilt. Remove a few leaves and set aside for the garnish, then add the chicken slices with the lemongrass and cook for 2–3 minutes until golden.

4 Add the rice. Stir-fry for a few minutes to coat the grains, then pour in the coconut liquid. Cook for 4–5 minutes or until the rice is tender, adding a little more water if necessary. Adjust the seasoning. Pile the rice into a warmed serving dish, scatter with the fried onion rings and basil leaves, and serve immediately.

INDONESIAN PINEAPPLE RICE

THIS WAY OF PRESENTING RICE NOT ONLY LOOKS SPECTACULAR, IT ALSO TASTES SO GOOD THAT IT CAN EASILY BE SERVED SOLO.

SERVES FOUR

INGREDIENTS

¾ cup natural peanuts
1 large pineapple
3 tablespoons groundnut or sunflower oil
1 onion, chopped
1 garlic clove, crushed
2 chicken breasts, about 8 ounces, cut into strips
generous 1 cup Thai fragrant rice, rinsed
2½ cups chicken stock
1 lemongrass stalk, bruised
2 thick slices of ham, cut into julienne strips
1 fresh red chili, seeded and very finely sliced
salt

1 Dry fry the peanuts in a non-stick skillet until golden. When cool, grind one-sixth of them in a spice grinder, and chop the remainder.

2 Cut a lengthwise slice of pineapple, slicing through the crown, then cut out the flesh to leave a neat shell. Chop 4 ounces of the pineapple into cubes, saving the remainder for another dish.

3 Heat the oil in a pan and cook the onion and garlic for 3–4 minutes until soft. Add the chicken strips and stir-fry over medium heat for a few minutes until evenly brown.

4 Add the rice to the pan. Toss with the chicken mixture for a few minutes, then pour in the stock, and add the lemongrass and a little salt. Bring to just below boiling point, then lower the heat, cover the pan and simmer gently for 10–12 minutes until both the rice and the chicken pieces are tender.

5 Stir the chopped peanuts, the pineapple cubes and the ham into the rice, then spoon the mixture into the pineapple shell. Sprinkle the ground peanuts and the sliced chili over the top and serve.

NASI GORENG

One of the most popular and best-known Indonesian dishes, this is a marvelous way to use up leftover rice, chicken and meats such as pork.

SERVES FOUR TO SIX

INGREDIENTS
   1¾ cups basmati rice (dry weight),
      cooked and cooled
   2 eggs
   2 tablespoons water
   7 tablespoons sunflower oil
   8 ounces pork tenderloin or
      tenderloin of beef
   2–3 fresh red chilies, seeded and sliced
   ½-inch cube shrimp paste (blachan)
   2 garlic cloves, crushed
   1 onion, sliced
   4 ounces cooked, shelled shrimp
   8 ounces cooked chicken, chopped
   2 tablespoons dark soy sauce
   salt and freshly ground black pepper
   deep fried onions, to garnish

1 Separate the grains of the cold, cooked rice with a fork. Cover and set aside until needed.

COOK'S TIP
Make the chili, garlic and onion paste using a pestle and mortar, if you prefer.

2 Beat the eggs with the water and a little seasoning. Heat 1 tablespoon of the oil in a skillet, pour in about half the mixture and cook until set, without stirring. Roll up the omelet, slide it on to a plate, cut into strips and set aside. Make another omelet in the same way.

3 Cut the pork or beef tenderloin into neat strips. Finely shred one of the chilies and set aside. Put the shrimp paste into a blender, add the remaining chili, the garlic and the onion. Process to a paste.

4 Heat the remaining oil in a wok. Cook the paste, without browning, until it gives off a spicy aroma. Add the strips of pork or beef and toss the meat over the heat, to seal in the juices. Cook the meat in the wok for about 2 minutes, stirring constantly.

5 Add the shrimp, cook for 2 minutes, then add the chicken, rice, and soy sauce, with salt and pepper to taste, stirring constantly. Serve in individual bowls, garnished with omelet strips, shredded chili and deep fried onions.

INDONESIAN COCONUT RICE

THIS WAY OF COOKING RICE IS VERY POPULAR THROUGHOUT THE WHOLE OF SOUTH-EAST ASIA.
COCONUT RICE GOES PARTICULARLY WELL WITH FISH, CHICKEN AND PORK.

SERVES FOUR TO SIX

INGREDIENTS
    1¾ cups Thai fragrant rice
    1¼ cups coconut milk
    1¼ cups water
    ½ teaspoon ground coriander
    2-inch cinnamon stick
    1 lemongrass stalk, bruised
    1 bay leaf
    salt
    deep fried onions, to garnish

1 Put the rice in a strainer and rinse thoroughly under cold water. Drain well, then put in a pan. Pour in the coconut milk and water. Add the coriander, cinnamon stick, lemongrass and bay leaf. Season with salt. Bring to a boil, then lower heat, cover and simmer for 8–10 minutes.

2 Lift the lid and check that all the liquid has been absorbed, then fork the rice through carefully, removing the cinnamon stick, lemongrass and bay leaf.

3 Cover the pan with a tight-fitting lid and continue to cook over lowest possible heat for 3–5 minutes more.

4 Pile the rice onto a warm serving dish and serve garnished with the crisp, deep fried onions.

COOK'S TIP
When bringing the rice to a boil, stir it frequently to prevent it from settling on the bottom of the pan. Once the rice is nearly tender, continue to cook over very low heat or just let stand for 5 minutes. The important thing is to cover the pan tightly.

LemonGrass <u>and</u> Coconut Rice <u>with</u> Green Chicken Curry

Use one or two fresh green chilies in this dish, according to how hot you like your curry. The mild aromatic flavor of the rice offsets the spiciness of the curry.

SERVES THREE TO FOUR

INGREDIENTS

4 scallions, trimmed and coarsely chopped
1–2 fresh green chilies, seeded and roughly chopped
¾-inch piece of fresh ginger root, peeled
2 garlic cloves
1 teaspoon Thai fish sauce
large bunch of cilantro
small handful of fresh parsley
2–3 tablespoons water
2 tablespoons sunflower oil
4 skinless, boneless chicken breasts, cubed
1 green bell pepper, seeded and finely sliced
3-ounce piece of creamed coconut dissolved in 1⅔ cups boiling water
salt and freshly ground black pepper

For the rice
generous 1 cup Thai fragrant rice, rinsed
3-ounce piece of creamed coconut dissolved in 1⅔ cups boiling water
1 lemongrass stalk, quartered and bruised

1 Put the scallions, chilies, ginger, garlic, fish sauce and fresh herbs in a food processor or blender. Pour in the water and process to a smooth paste.

2 Heat half the oil in large skillet. Cook the chicken cubes until evenly browned. Transfer to a plate.

3 Heat the remaining oil in the pan. Stir-fry the green bell pepper for 3–4 minutes, then add the chili and ginger paste. Fry, stirring, for 3–4 minutes until the mixture becomes fairly thick.

4 Return the chicken to the pan and add the coconut liquid. Season and bring to a boil, then lower heat; half cover the pan and simmer for 8–10 minutes.

5 When the chicken is cooked, transfer it with the peppers to a plate. Boil cooking liquid remaining in the pan for 10–12 minutes until it is well reduced and fairly thick.

6 Meanwhile, put the rice in a large pan. Add the coconut liquid and the bruised pieces of lemongrass. Stir in a little salt, bring to a boil, then lower the heat, cover and simmer gently for 10 minutes, or as recommended on the packet. When the rice is tender, discard the pieces of lemongrass and fork the rice onto a warmed serving plate.

7 Return the chicken and peppers to the green curry sauce, stir well and cook gently for a few minutes to heat through. Spoon the curry over the rice, and serve immediately.

COOK'S TIP
Lemon grass features in many Asian dishes, and makes the perfect partner for coconut, especially when used with chicken. In this recipe, bruise the tough, top end of the lemon grass stem in a pestle and mortar before use.

COCONUT CREAM DESSERT

Use Thai fragrant rice for this dish. Desserts like these are served in countries all over Asia, often with mangoes, pineapple or guavas. Although commercially ground rice can be used for this dish, grinding the rice yourself — in a food processor — gives a much better result.

SERVES FOUR TO SIX

INGREDIENTS
   scant ½ cup Thai fragrant rice,
     soaked overnight in ¾ cup water
   1½ cups coconut milk
   ⅔ cup light cream
   ¼ cup superfine sugar
   fresh raspberries and mint leaves,
     to decorate
For the coulis
   ¾ cup black currants, stems removed
   2 tablespoons superfine sugar
   ½ cup fresh or frozen raspberries

1 Put the rice and its soaking water into a food processor and process for a few minutes until the mixture is soupy.

2 Heat the coconut milk and cream gently in a non-stick pan. When the mixture is on a point of boiling, stir in the rice mixture.

3 Cook over very gentle heat for 10 minutes, stirring constantly, then stir in the sugar and continue cooking for 10–15 minutes more, or until the mixture is thick and creamy.

4 Pour the rice mixture into a rectangular pan that has been lined with non-stick baking parchment. Cool, then chill until the desert is firm.

5 To make the coulis, put the black currants in a bowl and sprinkle with sugar. Set aside for about 30 minutes. Tip into a wire strainer with the raspberries and press the fruit against the sides of the strainer so that the juices collect in a bowl underneath. Taste and add more sugar if necessary.

6 Carefully cut the coconut cream into diamonds. Spoon a little of the coulis onto each dessert plate, arrange the coconut cream diamonds on top and decorate with fresh raspberries and mint leaves.

THAI RICE CAKE

NOT A DRY SNACK FROM THE HEALTH FOOD STORE, BUT A SUMPTUOUS CELEBRATION CAKE, MADE FROM
THAI FRAGRANT RICE, TANGY CREAM AND WITH A FRESH FRUIT TOPPING.

SERVES EIGHT TO TEN

INGREDIENTS
    generous 1 cup Thai fragrant rice,
       rinsed
    4 cups milk
    scant ½ cup superfine sugar
    6 green cardamom pods, crushed
    2 bay leaves
    1¼ cups whipping cream
    6 eggs, separated
    red and white currants, sliced
       star fruit and kiwi fruit,
       to decorate
For the topping
    1 cup heavy cream
    ⅔ cup Quark or low-fat soft
       cheese
    1 teaspoon vanilla extract
    grated rind of 1 lemon
    3 tablespoons superfine sugar

1 Grease and line a 10-inch round, deep cake pan. Cook the rice in a pan of boiling unsalted water for 3 minutes, then drain, return to the pan and pour in the milk. Stir in the superfine sugar, cardamoms and bay leaves. Bring to a boil, then lower the heat and simmer the rice for 20 minutes, stirring occasionally. Allow the mixture to cool, then remove the bay leaves and cardamom husks.

2 Preheat the oven to 350°F. Spoon the rice mixture into a bowl. Beat in the whipping cream and then the egg yolks. Beat the egg whites until they form soft peaks, then fold them into the rice mixture.

3 Spoon into the prepared pan and bake for 45–50 minutes until puffed and golden brown. Chill overnight in the pan. Turn the cake out onto a large serving plate.

4 Whip the cream until stiff, then gently fold in the Quark or soft cheese, vanilla extract, lemon rind and sugar.

5 Cover the top of the cake with the cream mixture, swirling it attractively. Decorate with red and white currants, sliced star fruit and kiwi fruit.

COOK'S TIP
Do not worry if the center of the cake is slightly wobbly when you take it out of the oven. It will firm up as the cake starts to cool.

GREECE, TURKEY AND THE MIDDLE EAST

The people of the Middle East learned about rice from their eastern neighbors and have loved it ever since: rice is almost as much of a staple here as it is in parts of Asia. Rich Arabian spices and luscious Mediterranean produce are the inspiration for the feast of dishes from this region — many of which are now world classics.

AVGOLEMONO

THIS IS A GREAT FAVORITE IN GREECE AND IS A FINE EXAMPLE OF HOW A FEW INGREDIENTS CAN MAKE A MARVELOUS DISH IF CAREFULLY CHOSEN AND COOKED. IT IS ESSENTIAL TO USE A WELL-FLAVORED STOCK. ADD AS LITTLE OR AS MUCH RICE AS YOU LIKE.

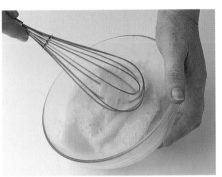

2 Beat the egg yolks in a bowl, then add about 2 tablespoons of the lemon juice, beating constantly until the mixture is smooth and bubbly. Add a ladleful of soup and beat again.

3 Remove the soup from the heat and slowly add the egg mixture, beating all the time. The soup will turn a pretty lemon color and will thicken slightly.

4 Taste and add more lemon juice if necessary. Stir in the parsley. Serve immediately, without reheating, garnished with lemon slices and parsley sprigs.

SERVES FOUR

INGREDIENTS
   3¾ cups chicken stock, preferably
     home-made
   generous ⅓ cup long grain rice
   3 egg yolks
   2–4 tablespoons lemon juice
   2 tablespoons finely chopped fresh
     parsley
   salt and freshly ground black pepper
   lemon slices and parsley sprigs,
     to garnish

1 Pour the stock into a pan, bring to simmering point, then add the drained rice. Half cover and cook for about 12 minutes until the rice is just tender. Season with salt and pepper.

COOK'S TIP
The trick here is to add the egg mixture to the soup without it curdling. Avoid beating the mixture into boiling liquid. It is safest to remove the soup from the heat entirely and then beat in the mixture in a slow but steady stream. Do not reheat as curdling would be almost inevitable.

DOLMADES

NOW POPULAR THE WORLD OVER, THESE STUFFED VINE LEAVES ORIGINATED IN GREECE. IF YOU CAN'T LOCATE FRESH VINE LEAVES, USE A PACKET OR CAN OF BRINED VINE LEAVES. SOAK THE LEAVES IN HOT WATER FOR 20 MINUTES, THEN RINSE AND DRY WELL ON PAPER TOWELS BEFORE USE.

MAKES 20 TO 24

INGREDIENTS
24–28 fresh young vine leaves, soaked
2 tablespoons olive oil
1 large onion, finely chopped
1 garlic clove, crushed
2 cups cooked long grain rice, or mixed white and wild rice
about 3 tablespoons pine nuts
1 tablespoon slivered almonds
¼ cup golden raisins
1 tablespoon chopped fresh chives
1 tablespoon finely chopped fresh mint
juice of ½ lemon
⅔ cup white wine
hot vegetable stock
salt and freshly ground black pepper
fresh mint sprig, to garnish
garlic yogurt and pita bread, to serve (optional)

1 Bring a large pan of water to a boil and cook the vine leaves for about 2–3 minutes. They will darken and go limp after about 1 minute, and simmering for a further minute or so will ensure they are pliable. If using leaves from a packet or can, place them in a large bowl, cover with boiling water and leave for a few minutes until the leaves can be easily separated. Rinse them under cold water and drain on kitchen paper.

2 Heat the oil in a small skillet and fry the onion and garlic for 3–4 minutes over gentle heat until soft. Spoon the mixture into a large bowl and add the cooked rice.

3 Stir in 2 tablespoons of the pine nuts, the almonds, golden raisins, chives and mint. Squeeze in the lemon juice. Add salt and pepper to taste and mix well.

4 Set aside four large vine leaves. Lay a vine leaf on a clean counter, veined side uppermost. Place a spoonful of filling near the stem, fold the lower part of the vine leaf over it and roll up, folding in the sides as you go. Stuff the rest of the vine leaves in the same way.

5 Line the base of a deep skillet with the reserved vine leaves. Place the dolmades close together in the pan, seam side down, in a single layer. Pour over the wine and enough stock to just cover. Anchor the dolmades by placing a plate on top of them, then cover the pan and simmer gently for 30 minutes.

6 Transfer the dolmades to a plate. Cool, chill, then garnish with the remaining pine nuts and the mint. Serve with a little garlic yogurt and pita bread, if you like.

COOK'S TIP
Check the pan frequently when cooking the dolmades, to make sure that the pan does not boil dry.

GREEK PICNIC PIE

EGGPLANT LAYERED WITH SPINACH, FETA CHEESE AND RICE MAKE A MARVELOUS FILLING FOR A PIE THAT IS PERFECT FOR PICNICS. IT CAN BE SERVED WARM OR COLD, AND MAKES A GOOD VEGETARIAN DISH FOR A BUFFET LUNCH.

SERVES SIX

INGREDIENTS

13 ounces unsweetened pastry, thawed if frozen
3–4 tablespoons olive oil
1 eggplant, sliced into circles
1 onion, chopped
1 garlic clove, crushed
6 ounces spinach, washed
4 eggs
½ cup crumbled feta cheese
½ cup freshly shredded Parmesan cheese
4 tablespoons plain yogurt
6 tablespoons whole milk
2 cups cooked white or brown long grain rice
salt and freshly ground black pepper

2 Heat 2–3 tablespoons of the oil in a skillet and cook the eggplant slices for 6–8 minutes on each side until golden. You may need to add a little more oil at first, but this will be released as the flesh softens. Lift out and drain on paper towels.

3 Add the onion and garlic to the oil remaining in the pan and cook over gentle heat for 4–5 minutes until soft, adding a little extra oil if necessary.

4 Chop the spinach finely, by hand or in a food processor. Beat the eggs in a large mixing bowl, then add the spinach, feta, Parmesan, yogurt, milk and the onion mixture. Season well with salt and pepper and stir thoroughly to mix.

5 Spread the rice in an even layer over the bottom of the part-baked pie. Reserve a few eggplant slices for the top, and arrange the rest in an even layer over the rice.

6 Spoon the spinach and feta mixture over the eggplant and place the remaining slices on top. Bake in the oven for 30–40 minutes until lightly browned. Serve the pie warm, or cool completely before transferring to a serving plate or wrapping and packing for a picnic.

1 Preheat the oven to 350°F. Roll out the pastry thinly and line a 10-inch tart pan. Prick the base all over and bake in the oven for 10–12 minutes until the pastry is pale golden. (Alternatively, bake blind, having lined the pastry with parchment paper and weighted it with a handful of baking beans.)

COOK'S TIP
If making your own pastry, add 1 teaspoon dried basil to the flour before rubbing in the butter, margarine or shortening.

VARIATION
Zucchini could be used in place of eggplant, if you prefer. Fry the sliced zucchini in a little oil for 3–4 minutes until golden. You will need three to four medium-size zucchini, or use baby zucchini and slice them horizontally: these would look particularly attractive on top of the pie.

TURKISH LAMB ON A BED OF RICE

IN TURKEY, THE TRADITIONAL WAY OF COOKING MEAT — OVER HOT CHARCOAL OR IN A WOOD-BURNING STOVE — RESULTS IN A CRUSTY, ALMOST CHARRED EXTERIOR ENCLOSING BEAUTIFULLY MOIST, TENDER MEAT. IN THIS RECIPE, THE MEAT JUICES FLAVOR THE RICE BENEATH.

SERVES SIX

INGREDIENTS
  half leg of lamb, about
    3–3½ pounds, boned
  bunch of fresh parsley
  small bunch of cilantro
  ½ cup cashews
  2 garlic cloves
  1 tablespoon sunflower oil
  1 small onion, finely chopped
  1¾ cups cooked white long
    grain rice
  scant ½ cup dried apricots, finely
    chopped
  salt and freshly ground black pepper
  fresh parsley or cilantro sprigs, to
    garnish
  tzatziki, black olives and pita bread,
    to serve (optional)

1 Preheat the oven to 400°F. Remove the excess fat from the lamb, then trim the joint, if necessary, so that it lies flat. (If the leg has been tunnel boned, you will need to cut the meat before it will lie flat.)

2 Put the parsley and cilantro in a food processor or blender and process until finely chopped. Add the cashews and pulse until coarsely chopped.

3 Crush 1 of the garlic cloves. Heat the oil in a skillet and cook the onion and crushed garlic for 3–4 minutes until softened but not browned.

4 Put the rice in a bowl. Using a spatula, scrape all the parsley and cashew mixture into the rice. Add the fried onion mixture and the chopped apricots. Season with salt and pepper, stir well, then spoon into the bottom of a roasting pan, which is just large enough to hold the lamb.

COOK'S TIP
In Turkey, the meat would be cooked until very well done, but it can also be served slightly pink, in the French style. For a doner kebab, split warmed pita breads (preferably home-made) and stuff with meat, plain yogurt and a spicy tomato sauce. Alternatively, serve this dish with rice and a fava bean salad.

5 Cut the remaining garlic clove in half and rub the cut sides over the meat. Season with pepper, then lay the meat on top of the rice, tucking all the rice under the meat, so that no rice is visible.

6 Roast the lamb for 30 minutes, then lower the oven temperature to 350°F. Cook for 35–45 minutes more, or until the meat is cooked to your taste.

7 Cover the lamb and rice with foil and let rest for 5 minutes, then lift the lamb onto a board and slice it thickly. Spoon the rice mixture onto a platter, arrange the meat slices on top and garnish with fresh parsley or cilantro. Serve immediately, with a bowl of tzatziki, black olives and pita bread, if liked.

YOGURT CHICKEN AND RICE CAKE

THIS MIDDLE EASTERN SPECIALTY IS TRADITIONALLY FLAVORED WITH SMALL, DRIED BERRIES CALLED ZERESHK, BUT IS JUST AS DELICIOUS WITH FRESH CRANBERRIES.

SERVES SIX

INGREDIENTS

    3 tablespoons butter
    3–3½ pounds, broiler-fryer
      chicken pieces
    1 large onion, chopped
    1 cup chicken stock
    2 eggs, beaten
    2 cups plain yogurt
    2–3 saffron strands, dissolved in
      1 tablespoon warm water
    1 teaspoon ground cinnamon
    2⅓ cups basmati rice, soaked
    4 cups boiling water
    ¾ cup cranberries or zereshk (see
      Cook's Tip)
    ½ cup slivered almonds
    salt and freshly ground black pepper
    herb and radicchio salad,
      to serve

1 Melt two-thirds of the butter in a flameproof casserole. Cook the chicken pieces with the onion for 4–5 minutes, until the onion is softened and the chicken has browned. Add the stock and season with salt and pepper. Bring to a boil, lower heat and simmer for 45 minutes, or until the chicken is cooked and the stock has reduced by half.

2 Drain the chicken, reserving the stock. Cut the flesh into large pieces, discarding the skin and bones, and place in a large bowl. In a separate bowl, mix the eggs with the yogurt. Add the saffron water and cinnamon. Season lightly. Pour over the chicken and stir to coat. Cover and let marinate for up to 2 hours.

3 Preheat the oven to 325ºF. Grease a large casserole or souffle dish, about 4-inch deep. Drain the rice and put it in a saucepan. Add the boiling water and a little salt, bring back to a boil and then lower the heat and simmer gently for 10 minutes. Drain, rinse thoroughly in warm water and drain once more.

4 Using a slotted spoon, lift the chicken pieces out of the yogurt marinade and put them on a plate. Mix half the rice into the marinade. Spread the mixture on the bottom of the baking dish. Arrange the chicken pieces in a single layer on top, then cover evenly with about half the plain rice. Sprinkle over the cranberries or zereshk, then cover with the rest of the rice.

COOK'S TIP
If you are lucky enough to locate zereshk, wash them thoroughly before use. Heat the berries before layering them with the rice.

5 Pour the reserved chicken stock over the rice. Sprinkle with the almonds and dot with the remaining butter. Cover tightly with foil and bake in the oven for 35–45 minutes

6 Let cool for a few minutes. Place on a cold, damp dish towel (this will help to lift the rice from the bottom of the dish), then run a knife around the inside rim of the casserole or dish. Invert a large, flat plate over the casserole or dish and turn out the rice "cake." Cut into wedges and serve hot, with the herb and radicchio salad.

STUFFED VEGETABLES

COLORFUL, EASY TO PREPARE AND UTTERLY DELICIOUS, THIS MAKES A POPULAR SUPPER DISH, AND WITH A CHOICE OF VEGETABLES INCLUDED IN THE RECIPE, THERE'S BOUND TO BE SOMETHING TO APPEAL TO EVERY MEMBER OF THE FAMILY.

SERVES FOUR

INGREDIENTS
1 eggplant
1 green bell pepper
2 beefsteak tomatoes
3 tablespoons olive oil
1 onion, chopped
2 garlic cloves, crushed
1–1½ cups white mushrooms, chopped
1 carrot, grated
2 cups cooked white long grain rice
1 tablespoon chopped fresh dill weed
scant ½ cup feta cheese, crumbled
¾ cup pine nuts, lightly toasted
2 tablespoons currants
salt and freshly ground black pepper

1 Preheat the oven to 375ºF. Lightly grease a shallow baking dish. Cut the eggplant in half, through the stem, and scoop out the flesh from each half to leave two hollow "boats." Dice the eggplant flesh. Cut the bell pepper in half lengthwise and remove the cores and seeds.

2 Cut off the tops from the tomatoes and hollow out the centers with a spoon. Chop the flesh and add it to the diced eggplant. Place the tomatoes upside down on paper towels to drain.

3 Bring a pan of water to a boil, add the eggplant halves and blanch for 3 minutes. Add the bell pepper halves to boiling water and blanch for 3 minutes more. Drain the vegetables, then place, hollow up, in the baking dish.

4 Heat 2 tablespoons oil in a pan and cook the onion and garlic for about 5 minutes. Stir in the diced eggplant and tomato mixture with the mushrooms and carrot. Cover, cook for 5 minutes until softened, then mix in the rice, dill weed, feta, pine nuts and currants. Season to taste.

5 Divide the mixture among the vegetable shells, sprinkle with the remaining olive oil and bake for 20 minutes until the topping has browned. Serve hot or cold.

PERSIAN RICE WITH A TAHDEEG

PERSIAN OR IRANIAN CUISINE IS EXOTIC AND DELICIOUS, AND THE FLAVORS ARE INTENSE. A TAHDEEG IS THE GLORIOUS, GOLDEN RICE CRUST OR "DIG" THAT FORMS ON THE BOTTOM OF THE SAUCEPAN AS THE RICE COOKS.

SERVES SIX TO EIGHT

INGREDIENTS

2⅓ cups basmati rice, soaked
⅔ cup sunflower oil
2 garlic cloves, crushed
2 onions, 1 chopped, 1 finely sliced
⅔ cup green lentils, soaked
2½ cups stock
⅓ cup raisins
2 teaspoons ground coriander
3 tablespoons tomato paste
a few saffron strands
1 egg yolk, beaten
2 teaspoons plain yogurt
6 tablespoons melted ghee or
    clarified butter
salt and freshly ground black
    pepper

1 Drain the rice, then cook it in plenty of boiling salted water for 3 minutes. Drain again.

2 Heat 2 tablespoons of the oil in a large pan and cook the garlic and the chopped onion for 5 minutes. Stir in the lentils, stock, raisins, ground coriander and tomato paste, with salt and pepper to taste. Bring to a boil, then lower the heat, cover and simmer for 20 minutes.

3 Soak the saffron strands in a little hot water. Mix the egg yolk and yogurt in a bowl. Spoon in about ½ cup of the cooked rice and mix thoroughly. Season well.

4 Heat about two-thirds of the remaining oil in a large pan. Sprinkle the egg and yogurt rice evenly over the bottom of the pan.

COOK'S TIP
In Iran, aromatic white basmati rice would traditionally be used for this dish, but you could use any long grain rice, or a brown rice, if you prefer.

5 Sprinkle the remaining rice into the pan, alternating it with the lentil mixture. Build up in a pyramid shape away from the sides of the pan, finishing with a layer of plain rice. With a long wooden spoon handle, make three holes down to the bottom of the pan; drizzle over the melted ghee or butter. Bring to a high heat, then wrap the pan lid in a clean, wet dish towel and place firmly on top. When a good head of steam appears, turn the heat down to low. Cook slowly for about 30 minutes.

6 Meanwhile, cook the onion slices in the remaining oil until browned and crisp. Drain well. Remove the rice pan from the heat, keeping it covered, and plunge the base briefly into a sink of cold water to loosen the rice on the bottom. Strain the saffron water into a bowl and stir in a few spoons of the white rice.

7 Toss the rice and lentils together in the pan and spoon out onto a serving dish, mounding the mixture. Sprinkle the saffron rice on top. Break up the rice crust on the bottom of the pan and place pieces of it around the mound. Sprinkle over the crispy fried onions and serve.

ROASTED SQUASH

ACORN SQUASH HAS A SWEET, SUBTLE FLAVOR THAT CONTRASTS WELL WITH OLIVES AND SUN-DRIED TOMATOES IN THIS RECIPE. THE RICE ADDS SUBSTANCE WITHOUT CHANGING ANY OF THE FLAVORS.

2 Mix the rice, tomatoes, olives, cheese, half the olive oil and basil in a bowl.

3 Oil a shallow baking dish with the remaining oil, just large enough to hold the squash side by side. Divide the rice mixture among the squash and place them in the dish.

SERVES FOUR AS AN APPETIZER

INGREDIENTS
    4 whole acorn squashes
    2 cups cooked white long
        grain rice
    1½ cups sun-dried tomatoes,
        chopped
    ½ cup pitted black olives,
        chopped
    4 tablespoons soft goat cheese
    2 tablespoons olive oil
    1 tablespoon chopped fresh basil
        leaves, plus basil sprigs, to serve
    plain yogurt and mint dressing or
        green salad, to serve (optional)

1 Preheat the oven to 350ºF. Trim away the base of each squash, slice off the top and scoop out and discard the seeds.

4 Cover with foil and bake for 45–50 minutes until the squash is tender when pierced with a skewer. Garnish with basil sprigs and serve with a yogurt and mint dressing or with a green salad.

EGGPLANT ROLLS

AS WELL AS MAKING AN ORIGINAL APPETIZER, THESE LITTLE ROLLS OF EGGPLANT WRAPPED AROUND A FILLING OF RICOTTA AND RICE ARE TASTY SERVED AS PART OF A BUFFET OR FOR A TURKISH-STYLE MEZE.

SERVES FOUR

INGREDIENTS
  2 eggplants
  olive oil, for shallow frying
  scant ½ cup ricotta cheese
  scant ½ cup soft goat cheese
  2 cups cooked white long
    grain rice
  1 tablespoon chopped fresh basil
  1 teaspoon chopped fresh mint,
    plus mint sprigs, to garnish
  salt and freshly ground black pepper
For the tomato sauce
  1 tablespoon olive oil
  1 red onion, finely chopped
  1 garlic clove, crushed
  14 ounce can chopped tomatoes
  ½ cup chicken stock or white wine
    or a mixture
  1 tablespoon chopped fresh
    parsley

2 Meanwhile, cut the eggplants lengthwise into four or five slices. Heat the oil in a large skillet and cook the eggplant slices in batches until they are golden brown on both sides. Drain on paper towels. Mix the ricotta, goat cheese, rice, basil and mint in a bowl. Season well with salt and pepper.

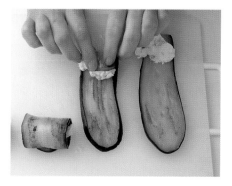

3 Place a generous spoonful of the cheese and rice mixture at one end of each eggplant slice and roll up. Arrange the rolls side by side in a shallow baking dish. Pour the tomato sauce over the top and bake for 10–15 minutes until heated through. Garnish with the mint sprigs and serve.

1 Preheat the oven to 375°F. Make the tomato sauce. Heat the oil in a small pan and cook the onion and garlic for 3–4 minutes until softened. Add the tomatoes, chicken stock and wine, if using, and sprinkle in the parsley. Season with salt and pepper. Bring to a boil, then lower heat and simmer for 10–12 minutes until slightly thickened, stirring.

COOK'S TIP
Cut off and discard the skin on the two outer slices of eggplant. If you prefer to use less oil for the eggplants, brush each slice with a little oil, then broil until evenly browned.

RICE WITH DILL AND FAVA BEANS

THIS IS A FAVORITE RICE DISH IN IRAN, WHERE IT IS CALLED BAGHALI POLO. THE COMBINATION OF FAVA BEANS, DILL WEED AND WARM SPICES WORKS VERY WELL, AND THE SAFFRON RICE ADDS A SPLASH OF BRIGHT COLOR.

SERVES FOUR

INGREDIENTS

1½ cups basmati rice, soaked
3 cups water
3 tablespoons melted butter
1½ cups frozen baby fava beans,
  thawed and peeled
6 tablespoons finely chopped fresh
  dill weed, plus 1 fresh dill weed
  sprig, to garnish
1 teaspoon ground cinnamon
1 teaspoon ground cumin
2–3 saffron strands, soaked in
  1 tablespoon boiling water
salt

1 Drain the rice, turn it into a pan and pour in the water. Add a little salt. Bring to a boil, then lower the heat and simmer very gently for 5 minutes. Drain, rinse well in warm water and drain once again.

2 Melt the butter in a non-stick pan. Pour two-thirds of the melted butter into a small measure and set aside. Spoon enough rice into the pan to cover the bottom. Add a quarter of the beans and a little dill weed. Spread over another layer of rice, then a layer of beans and dill weed. Repeat the layers until all the beans and dill weed have been used up, ending with a layer of rice. Cook over gentle heat for 8 minutes until nearly tender.

3 Pour the reserved melted butter over the rice. Sprinkle with the ground cinnamon and cumin. Cover the pan with a clean dish towel and a tight-fitting lid, lifting the corners of the cloth back over the lid. Cook over low heat for 25–30 minutes.

4 Spoon about 3 tablespoons of the cooked rice into the bowl of saffron water; mix well. Mound the remaining rice mixture on a large serving plate and spoon the saffron rice on one side to decorate. Serve immediately, garnished with the sprig of dill weed.

SWEET AND SOUR RICE

THIS POPULAR MIDDLE EASTERN DISH IS FLAVORED WITH FRUIT AND SPICES. IT IS OFTEN SERVED WITH LAMB OR CHICKEN.

SERVES FOUR

INGREDIENTS
　½ cup zereshk (see Cook's
　　Tip)
　3 tablespoons butter
　⅓ cup raisins
　¼ cup sugar
　1 teaspoon ground cinnamon
　1 teaspoon ground cumin
　1¾ cups basmati rice,
　　soaked
　2–3 saffron strands, soaked in
　　1 tablespoon boiling water
　pinch of salt

1 Thoroughly wash the zereshk in cold water at least four or five times to rinse off any bits of grit. Drain well.

2 Melt 1 tablespoon of the butter in a skillet and cook the raisins for about 1–2 minutes.

3 Add the zereshk, cook for a few seconds, and then add the sugar, with half of the cinnamon and cumin. Cook briefly and then set aside.

4 Drain the rice, then put it in a pan with plenty of boiling, lightly salted water. Bring back to a boil, then reduce the heat and simmer for 4 minutes. Drain and rinse once again, if liked.

COOK'S TIP
Zereshk are small dried berries. Look for them in Middle Eastern markets and shops. If you cannot locate them, use semi-dried cranberries instead.

5 Melt half the remaining butter in the clean pan, add 1 tablespoon water and stir in half the cooked rice. Sprinkle with half the raisin and zereshk mixture and top with all but 3 tablespoons of the rice. Sprinkle over the remaining raisin and zereshk mixture.

6 Mix the remaining cinnamon and cumin with the reserved rice, and sprinkle this mixture evenly over the layered mixture. Melt the remaining butter, drizzle it over the surface, then cover the pan with a clean dish towel. Cover with a tight-fitting lid, lifting the corners of the cloth back over the lid. Steam the rice over very low heat for about 20–30 minutes.

7 Just before serving, mix 3 tablespoons of the rice with the saffron water. Spoon the sweet and sour rice onto a large, flat serving dish and sprinkle the saffron rice over the top, to garnish.

SWEET RICE

IN IRAN, SWEET RICE IS A TRADITIONAL DISH WHICH IS SERVED AT WEDDING BANQUETS AND ON OTHER SPECIAL FEASTING OCCASIONS. IT CAN BE SERVED SOLO OR TO ACCOMPANY A MEAT DISH.

3 Melt 1 tablespoon of the butter in a pan and cook the carrots for 2–3 minutes. Add the remaining sugar and 4 tablespoons water. Simmer for 10 minutes, shaking the pan frequently, until most of the liquid has evaporated.

4 Stir the carrots and half of the nuts into the orange rind and set aside. Drain the rice, boil in salted water for 5 minutes, then reduce heat and simmer gently for 10 minutes until half-cooked. Drain and rinse.

SERVES FOUR TO SIX

INGREDIENTS
  2 oranges
  3 tablespoons sugar
  3 tablespoons butter
  3 carrots, cut into julienne strips
  ½ cup mixed chopped pistachios,
    almonds and pine nuts
  1¾ cups basmati rice, soaked
  2–3 saffron strands, soaked in
    1 tablespoon warm water
  salt, to taste

1 Pare the rind from the oranges in wide strips, using a vegetable peeler. Cut the rind into thin shreds. Place in a pan with enough water to cover and bring to a boil. Simmer for a few minutes, then drain. Repeat until the rind no longer tastes bitter.

2 Return the orange rind to the pan. Add half the sugar, then pour in 4 tablespoons water. Bring to a boil, then simmer until the syrup is reduced by half. Set aside.

5 Melt half the remaining butter in the clean pan. Add 3 tablespoons water. Fork a little of the rice into the pan and spoon on some of the carrot mixture. Repeat these layers until all the mixture has been used up. Cook gently for 10 minutes. Melt the remaining butter, pour it over the sweet rice and cover the pan with a clean dish towel and a tight-fitting lid. Steam for 30–45 minutes. Mound on plates, garnish with the remaining nuts, drizzle with the saffron water, and serve.

ALMA-ATA

THIS DISH COMES FROM CENTRAL ASIA AND IS A SPECTACULAR COMBINATION OF THE FRUITS AND NUTS FROM THAT REGION.

SERVES FOUR

INGREDIENTS
¾ cup blanched almonds
4 tablespoons sunflower oil
8 ounces carrots, cut into julienne
  strips
2 onions, chopped
½ cup dried apricots,
  chopped
⅓ cup raisins
1¾ cups basmati rice,
  soaked
2½ cups vegetable stock
⅔ cup orange juice
grated rind of 1 orange
⅓ cup pine nuts
1 red eating apple, chopped
salt and freshly ground black pepper

3 Pour in the vegetable stock and orange juice, stirring constantly, then stir in the orange rind. Reserve a few toasted almonds for the garnish and stir in the remainder with the pine nuts. Cover the pan with a double piece of foil and fit the casserole lid securely. Transfer to the oven and bake for 30–35 minutes, until the rice is tender and all the liquid has been absorbed.

4 Remove from the oven, season to taste and stir in the chopped apple. Serve from the casserole or spoon into a warmed serving dish. Garnish with the reserved almonds.

1 Preheat the oven to 325°F. Toast the almonds in a dry skillet for about 4–5 minutes until golden.

2 Heat the oil in a heavy, flameproof casserole and cook the carrots and onions over moderately high heat for 6–8 minutes until slightly glazed. Add the apricots, raisins and drained rice and cook over medium heat for a few minutes, stirring constantly, until the grains of rice are coated in the oil.

VARIATION
For a one-dish meal, add 1 pound lamb, cut into cubes. Brown in the casserole in a little oil, then transfer to a dish while you cook the onion and carrots. Stir the meat back into the casserole when you add the stock and orange juice.

SWEET BASMATI DESSERT

YOU WILL FIND VARIATIONS ON THIS SWEET AND CREAMY DESSERT IN TURKEY, EGYPT, LEBANON AND SYRIA. THE BASMATI AROMA IS DISTINCTIVE WITHOUT BEING INTRUSIVE.

SERVES SIX TO EIGHT

INGREDIENTS
   1½ cups basmati rice, soaked
   5 cups milk
   pinch of saffron strands, dissolved in
     warm milk or water
   about ½ teaspoon ground
     cardamom seeds
   ½ cup sugar
   14 ounce can evaporated milk
To serve
   1 papaya
   ½–¾ cup slivered almonds (optional)

1 Drain the rice and cook it in plenty of water, using a non-stick pan.

2 Drain the rice again, return to the pan and pour in the milk. Heat very gently until barely simmering and cook for 30–45 minutes, stirring occasionally.

3 Stir in the saffron milk or water, the ground cardamom seeds and the sugar. Cook for 3–4 minutes more, then stir in the evaporated milk.

4 Cut the papaya in half, remove the skin and scoop out the seeds. Slice the flesh and arrange it on a platter. Spoon the sweet basmati rice into individual bowls, sprinkle with almonds and top each portion with two small slices of papaya. Serve at once.

COOK'S TIP
If you cook the dessert on the stovetop, it is essential to use a non-stick pan. If you haven't got one, bake the pudding instead. Spoon the cooked rice into a baking dish. Bring the milk to a boil, pour it over the rice, stir and cover tightly. Bake at 300°F for 45 minutes, then stir in the remaining ingredients and bake for 15 minutes more. Cool slightly before serving.

FRUITED RICE RING

THIS UNUSUAL RICE DESSERT LOOKS BEAUTIFUL TURNED OUT OF A RING MOLD, BUT IF YOU PREFER, YOU CAN STIR THE FRUIT INTO THE RICE AND SERVE IN INDIVIDUAL DISHES.

SERVES FOUR

INGREDIENTS
⅓ cup short grain dessert rice
3¾ cups low-fat milk
2-inch cinnamon stick
1½ cups dried fruit salad
¾ cup orange juice
3 tablespoons sugar
finely shredded rind of 1 small
   orange
sunflower oil, for greasing

1 Mix the rice and milk in a pan. Add the cinnamon stick and bring to a boil. Lower heat, cover the pan and simmer gently, stirring occasionally, for about 1½ hours, until all the liquid has been absorbed.

2 Meanwhile, put the dried fruit salad in a separate pan, pour over the orange juice and bring to a boil. Lower heat, cover and simmer very gently for about 1 hour, until the fruit is tender and no liquid remains.

3 Remove the cinnamon stick from the rice and gently stir in the sugar and shredded orange rind.

COOK'S TIP
When spooning the dried fruit into the tin, bear in mind that this will be the topping when the ring is turned out. Try to balance colors and varieties of fruit.

4 Lightly oil a 6¼ cup ring mold. Spoon in the fruit so that it covers the bottom of the tin evenly. Top with the rice, smooth it down firmly, then chill until firm.

5 Run a knife around the edge of the ring mold, then invert a serving plate on top. Turn mold and plate over together, then lift off the mold. Serve in slices.

SPAIN AND PORTUGAL

Spain is one of Europe's most
important rice-growing countries,
and has grown rice for over 1000
years. It is not surprising, then, to
find in Spain and neighboring
Portugal a wealth of superb rice
recipes, most famously the noble
paella. Other traditional dishes
include Moors and Christians,
which dates back over 1200 years.

FLAMENCO EGGS

THIS ADAPTATION OF A CLASSIC SPANISH RECIPE WORKS VERY WELL WITH CAMARGUE RED RICE, ALTHOUGH ANY LONG GRAIN RICE — BROWN OR WHITE — COULD BE USED.

SERVES FOUR

INGREDIENTS

    scant 1 cup Camargue red rice
    chicken or vegetable stock
      or water
    3 tablespoons olive oil
    1 Spanish onion, chopped
    1 garlic clove, crushed
    12 ounces lean ground beef
    3 ounces chorizo sausage, cut into
      small cubes
    1 teaspoon paprika, plus extra for
      dusting
    2 teaspoons tomato paste
    1–2 tablespoons chopped fresh
      parsley
    2 red bell peppers, seeded and
      sliced
    3 tomatoes, peeled, seeded and
      chopped
    ½ cup passata or tomato juice
    4 eggs
    8 teaspoons light cream
    salt and freshly ground black pepper

3 Heat the remaining oil in a pan and cook the peppers until they begin to sizzle. Cover and cook over moderate heat, shaking the pan occasionally, for 4–5 minutes until the bell peppers are singed in places. Add the tomatoes and continue cooking for 3–4 minutes until they are very soft. Remove the pan from the heat, stir in the passata or tomato juice and add salt to taste.

4 Drain the rice, and divide it among four shallow ovenproof gratin dishes. Spread the meat mixture over the rice and top with the bell peppers and tomatoes. Make a hole in the center of each portion and break in an egg. Spoon 2 teaspoons of cream over each egg yolk, dust with paprika, and bake for 12–15 minutes until the whites of the eggs are set. Serve at once.

1 Preheat the oven to 350ºF. Cook the rice in stock or water, following the instructions on the packet. Heat 2 tablespoons of oil and cook the onion and garlic for 5 minutes until the onion is tinged with brown, stirring occasionally.

2 Add the ground beef and cook, stirring occasionally, until browned. Stir in the chorizo and paprika and continue cooking over low heat for 4–5 minutes. Stir in the tomato paste and parsley and season with salt and pepper.

Orange Chicken Salad

WITH THEIR TANGY FLAVOR, ORANGE SEGMENTS ARE THE PERFECT PARTNER FOR TENDER CHICKEN IN THIS TASTY RICE SALAD. TO APPRECIATE ALL THE FLAVORS FULLY, SERVE IT AT ROOM TEMPERATURE.

SERVES FOUR

INGREDIENTS
    3 large seedless oranges
    scant 1 cup white long grain
      rice
    2 cups water
    2 teaspoons Dijon mustard
    ½ teaspoon sugar
    ¾ cup vinaigrette dressing (see
      Cook's Tip)
    1 pound cooked chicken, diced
    3 tablespoons chopped fresh chives
    ¾ cup cashews, toasted
    salt and freshly ground black pepper
    mixed salad leaves, to serve

1 Pare 1 of the oranges thinly, taking care to remove only the colored part of the rind and avoiding the bitter pith.

2 Put the pieces of orange rind in a pan and add the rice. Pour in the water, add a pinch of salt and bring to a boil. Cover and steam over very low heat for about 15 minutes, or until the rice is tender and all the water has been absorbed.

3 Meanwhile, peel all the oranges. Working over a plate to catch the juices, cut them into segments. Add the orange juice, mustard and sugar to the vinaigrette dressing and beat to combine well. Taste and add more salt and pepper if needed.

4 When the rice is cooked, remove it from the heat and discard the orange rind. Spoon the rice into a bowl, let it cool slightly, then add half the dressing. Toss well and cool completely.

5 Add the chicken, chives, cashews and orange segments to the rice in the bowl. Add the remaining dressing and toss gently. Serve on a bed of mixed salad leaves.

COOK'S TIP
To make the dressing, beat 3 tablespoons red wine vinegar with salt and pepper to taste. Gradually beat in 6 tablespoons corn oil and 4 tablespoons olive oil.

MOORS AND CHRISTIANS

THIS DISH IS THE TRADITIONAL CENTERPIECE OF THE MOYOS E CRISTIANOS FESTIVAL, WHICH IS HELD IN SPAIN EVERY YEAR TO REMEMBER THE CONQUEST OF THE CHRISTIANS OVER THE MOORS. THE BLACK BEANS REPRESENT THE DARK-SKINNED MOORS, AND THE WHITE RICE THE WHITE CHRISTIANS.

SERVES SIX

INGREDIENTS
   2 cups black or turtle beans, soaked
      overnight
   1 onion, quartered
   1 carrot, sliced
   1 stalk celery, sliced
   1 garlic clove, crushed
   1 bay leaf
   1 teaspoon paprika
   3 tablespoons olive oil
   juice of 1 orange
   1¾ cups long grain rice
   salt and cayenne pepper
For the garnish
   chopped fresh parsley, sliced orange,
      sliced red onion, 2 hard-cooked
      eggs, cut into wedges

1 Put the beans in a pan with the onion, carrot, celery, garlic and bay leaf and 7½ cups water. Bring to a boil and cook rapidly for 10 minutes, then reduce the heat and simmer for about 1 hour, topping up the water if necessary. When the beans are almost tender, drain, discarding the vegetables. Return the beans to a clean pan.

2 Blend together the paprika, oil and cayenne pepper and stir into the beans with the orange juice. Top up with a little extra water, if necessary. Heat gently until barely simmering, then cover and cook for 10–15 minutes until the beans are completely tender. Remove from the heat and let stand in the liquid for 15 minutes. Add salt to taste.

3 Meanwhile, cook the rice until tender, either by boiling or by the absorption method. Drain, then pack into a buttered bowl and let stand for 10 minutes.

4 Unmold the rice onto a serving plate, placing the black beans around the edge of the plate. Garnish with chopped parsley, orange slices, red onion and egg wedges.

ALICANTE OMELET RICE

THIS IS A REALLY UNUSUAL DISH, FLAVORED WITH GARLICKY SPANISH SAUSAGE AND TOPPED WITH BEATEN EGG SO THAT THE EFFECT SUGGESTS AN OMELET OR EVEN A SOUFFLE. IF YOU CANNOT GET BUTIFARRA, USE CHORIZO OR ANY SIMILAR SPANISH SAUSAGE INSTEAD.

SERVES SIX

INGREDIENTS
   3 tablespoons sunflower oil
   7 ounces butifarra or other Spanish
      sausage, sliced
   2 tomatoes, peeled, seeded and
      chopped
   6 ounces lean pork, cut into bite-size
      pieces
   6 ounces skinless, boneless chicken
      breast or rabbit, cut into chunks
   1¾ cups Spanish rice or
      risotto rice
   3¾–4 cups hot chicken stock
   pinch of saffron strands, crushed
   ⅔ cup cooked chick-peas
   6 eggs
   salt and freshly ground black pepper

1 Preheat the oven to 375°F. Heat the oil in a flameproof casserole and cook the sausage for a few minutes. Transfer to a plate.

2 Add the tomatoes and cook for a few minutes until slightly thickened. Stir in the pork and chicken or rabbit pieces and cook for 2–3 minutes until the meat has browned lightly, stirring frequently. Add the rice, stir over the heat for about a minute, then pour in the hot stock. Add the saffron, with salt and pepper to taste, and stir well.

3 Bring to a boil, then lower the heat and add the sausage and chick-peas. Cover tightly with the lid and cook over low heat for about 15 minutes until the rice is tender.

4 Beat the eggs with a little water and a pinch of salt and pour over the rice. Place the casserole, uncovered, in the oven and cook for about 10 minutes, until the eggs have set and browned slightly on top.

BAKED TROUT WITH RICE, SUN-DRIED TOMATOES AND NUTS

TROUT IS VERY POPULAR IN SPAIN, PARTICULARLY IN THE NORTH. IF YOU FILLET THE TROUT BEFORE YOU COOK IT, IT COOKS MORE EVENLY, AND IS EASIER TO SERVE BECAUSE THERE ARE NO BONES TO GET IN THE WAY OF THE STUFFING.

SERVES FOUR

INGREDIENTS

2 fresh trout, each about 1¼ pounds
¾ cup mixed unsalted cashews, pine nuts, almonds or hazelnuts
1½ tablespoons olive oil, plus extra for drizzling
1 small onion, finely chopped
2 teaspoons shredded fresh ginger root
1½ cups cooked white long grain rice
4 tomatoes, peeled and very finely chopped
4 sun-dried tomatoes in oil, drained and chopped
2 tablespoons chopped fresh tarragon
2 tarragon sprigs
salt and freshly ground black pepper
dressed green leaves, to serve

1 Unless the fishmonger has already filleted the trout, use a sharp knife to do so, leaving as little flesh on the bones as possible. Check the cavity for any tiny bones remaining and remove these with tweezers.

2 Preheat the oven to 375ºF. Spread out the nuts in a shallow baking pan and bake for 3–4 minutes until golden, shaking the tin occasionally. Chop the nuts coarsely.

3 Heat the oil in a small skillet and cook the onion for 3–4 minutes until soft. Stir in the ginger, cook for 1 minute more, then spoon into a mixing bowl.

4 Stir in the rice, chopped tomatoes, sun-dried tomatoes, toasted nuts and tarragon. Season the stuffing well.

5 Place each of the two trout in turn on a large piece of oiled foil and spoon the stuffing into the cavity. Add a sprig of tarragon and a drizzle of olive oil.

6 Fold the foil over to enclose each trout completely, and put the parcels in a large roasting pan. Bake for 20–25 minutes until the fish is just tender. Cut the fish into thick slices. Serve with dressed green leaves.

SEVILLE CHICKEN

ORANGES AND ALMONDS ARE A FAVORITE INGREDIENT IN SOUTHERN SPAIN, ESPECIALLY AROUND SEVILLE, WHERE THE ORANGE AND ALMOND TREES ARE A FAMILIAR AND WONDERFUL SIGHT.

SERVES FOUR

INGREDIENTS

1 orange
8 chicken thighs
all-purpose flour, seasoned with salt and pepper
3 tablespoons olive oil
1 large Spanish onion, coarsely chopped
2 garlic cloves, crushed
1 red bell pepper, seeded and sliced
1 yellow bell pepper, seeded and sliced
4 ounces chorizo sausage, sliced
½ cup slivered almonds
generous 1 cup brown basmati rice
about 2½ cups chicken stock
14 ounce can chopped tomatoes
¾ cup white wine
generous pinch of dried thyme
salt and freshly ground black pepper
fresh thyme sprigs, to garnish

1 Pare a thin strip of peel from the orange and set it aside. Peel the orange, then cut it into segments, working over a bowl to catch the juice. Dust the chicken thighs with seasoned flour.

2 Heat the oil in a large skillet and cook the chicken pieces on both sides until nicely brown. Transfer to a plate. Add the onion and garlic to the pan and cook for 4–5 minutes until the onion begins to brown. Add the red and yellow bell peppers and cook, stirring occasionally, until softened.

3 Add the chorizo, stir-fry for a few minutes, then sprinkle over the almonds and rice. Cook, stirring, for 1–2 minutes.

4 Pour in the chicken stock, tomatoes and wine and add the orange strip and thyme. Season well. Bring to simmering point, stirring, then return the chicken pieces to the pan.

5 Cover tightly and cook over very low heat for 1–1¼ hours until the rice and chicken are tender. Just before serving, add the orange segments and allow to cook briefly to heat through. Garnish with fresh thyme and serve.

COOK'S TIP
Cooking times for this dish will depend largely on the heat. If the rice seems to be drying out too quickly, add a little more stock or wine and reduce the heat. If, after 40 minutes or so, the rice is still barely cooked, increase the heat a little. Make sure the rice is kept below the liquid (the chicken can lie on the surface) and stir the rice occasionally if it seems to be cooking unevenly.

CELEBRATION PAELLA

THIS PAELLA IS A MARVELOUS MIXTURE OF SOME OF THE FINEST SPANISH INGREDIENTS. CHICKEN AND RABBIT, SEAFOOD AND VEGETABLES ARE MIXED WITH RICE TO MAKE A COLORFUL PARTY DISH.

SERVES SIX TO EIGHT

INGREDIENTS

1 pound fresh mussels
6 tablespoons white wine
5 ounces green beans, cut into
    1-inch lengths
1 cup frozen fava beans
6 small skinless, boneless chicken
    breasts, cut into large pieces
2 tablespoons all-purpose flour,
    seasoned with salt and pepper
about 6 tablespoons olive oil
6–8 large shrimp, tailed and
    deveined, or 12 smaller shrimp
5 ounces pork tenderloin, cut into
    bite-size pieces
2 onions, chopped
2–3 garlic cloves, crushed
1 red bell pepper, seeded and sliced
2 ripe tomatoes, peeled, seeded and
    chopped
3¾ cups well-flavored chicken stock
good pinch of saffron, dissolved in
    2 tablespoons hot water
1¾ cups Spanish rice or risotto rice
8 ounces chorizo sausage, thickly
    sliced
1 cup frozen peas
6–8 stuffed green olives, thickly
    sliced

COOK'S TIP
Ideally, you need to use a paella pan
for this dish and, strictly speaking, the
paella shouldn't be stirred during
cooking. You may find, though, that –
because of the distribution of heat – the
rice cooks in the center but not around
the outside. (This doesn't happen if
paella is cooked traditionally – outdoors,
on a large wood fire.) To make sure your
paella cooks evenly, you could break the
rule and stir occasionally, or cook the
paella on the sole of a hot 375°F oven
for about 15–18 minutes. The result
should be practically identical, but in
Spain this would be termed an *arroz* –
a rice – rather than paella.

1 Scrub the mussels, discarding any
that do not close when sharply tapped.
Place in a large pan with the wine,
bring to a boil, then cover the pan
tightly and cook for 3–4 minutes until
all the mussels have opened, shaking
the pan occasionally. Drain, reserving
the liquid and discarding any mussels
that have not opened.

2 Briefly cook the green beans and
fava beans in separate pans of boiling
water for 2–3 minutes. Drain. As soon
as the fava beans are cool enough to
handle, pop them out of their skins.

3 Dust the chicken with the seasoned
flour. Heat half the oil in a paella pan or
deep skillet and cook the chicken until
evenly browned. Transfer to a plate.
Cook the shrimp briefly, adding more oil
if needed, then use a slotted spoon to
transfer them to a plate. Heat a further
2 tablespoons of the oil in the pan and
brown the pork evenly. Transfer to a
separate plate.

4 Heat the remaining oil and cook the
onions and garlic for 3–4 minutes until
golden brown. Add the red bell pepper,
cook for 2–3 minutes, then add the
chopped tomatoes and cook until the
mixture is fairly thick.

5 Stir in the chicken stock, the
reserved mussel liquid and the saffron
liquid. Season well with salt and pepper
and bring to a boil. When the liquid is
bubbling, throw in all the rice. Stir once,
then add the chicken pieces, pork,
shrimp, beans, chorizo and peas.
Cook over moderately high heat for
12 minutes, then lower the heat and let
cook for 8–10 minutes more, until all
the liquid has been absorbed.

6 Add the mussels and olives and
continue cooking for a further 3–4
minutes to heat through. Remove the
pan from the heat, cover with a clean,
damp dish towel and let stand for
10 minutes before serving from the pan.

SEAFOOD PAELLA

THIS IS A GREAT DISH TO SERVE TO GUESTS ON A SPECIAL OCCASION BECAUSE IT LOOKS SPECTACULAR.
BRING THE PAELLA PAN TO THE TABLE AND LET EVERYONE HELP THEMSELVES.

SERVES FOUR

INGREDIENTS
  4 tablespoons olive oil
  8 ounces monkfish or cod fillets,
    skinned and cut into chunks
  3 prepared baby squid, body cut into
    rings and tentacles chopped
  1 red mullet, filleted, skinned and
    cut into chunks (optional)
  1 onion, chopped
  3 garlic cloves, finely chopped
  1 red bell pepper, seeded and sliced
  4 tomatoes, peeled and coarsely
    chopped
  generous 1 cup risotto rice
  scant 2 cups fish stock
  ⅔ cup white wine
  4–5 saffron strands soaked in
    2 tablespoons hot water
  4 ounces cooked, shelled shrimp,
    thawed if frozen
  ¾ cup frozen peas
  8 fresh mussels, scrubbed
  salt and freshly ground black pepper
  4 jumbo shrimp, in the shell, and
    fresh parsley sprigs, to garnish
  lemon wedges, to serve

1 Heat half the oil in paella pan or a large skillet and add the monkfish or cod, the squid and the red mullet, if using. Stir-fry for 2 minutes, then tip the contents of the pan into a bowl and set aside.

2 Heat the remaining oil in the pan and add the onion, garlic and bell pepper. Cook for 6–7 minutes, stirring frequently, until softened.

3 Stir in the tomatoes and cook for 2 minutes, then add the rice. Stir to coat the grains with oil, then cook for 2–3 minutes. Pour over the fish stock, wine and saffron water. Season with salt and freshly ground black pepper, and mix well.

COOK'S TIP
Before adding the mussels to the rice mixture, check that they are all closed. Any that are open should close when sharply tapped; any that fail to do this must be discarded.

4 Gently stir in the reserved cooked fish (with all the juices), then the shelled shrimp and the peas. Push the mussels into the rice. Cover and cook over gentle heat for about 30 minutes, or until the stock has been absorbed but the rice mixture is still relatively moist. All the mussels should have opened; discard any that remain closed.

5 Remove from heat, and leave the paella to stand, covered, for 5 minutes. Arrange the whole shrimp on top. Sprinkle the paella with parsley and serve with the lemon wedges.

CHICKEN PIRI-PIRI

THIS IS A CLASSIC PORTUGUESE DISH, BASED ON A HOT SAUCE MADE FROM ANGOLAN CHILIES. IT IS POPULAR WHEREVER THERE ARE PORTUGUESE COMMUNITIES, AND IS OFTEN SERVED IN SOUTH AFRICA.

SERVES FOUR

INGREDIENTS

4 chicken breast portions
2–3 tablespoons olive oil
1 large onion, finely sliced
2 carrots, cut into thin strips
1 large parsnip or 2 small parsnips, cut into thin strips
1 red bell pepper, seeded and sliced
1 yellow bell pepper, seeded and sliced
4 cups chicken stock
3 tomatoes, peeled, seeded and chopped
generous dash of piri-piri sauce
1 tablespoon tomato paste
½ cinnamon stick
1 fresh thyme sprig, plus extra fresh thyme, to garnish
1 bay leaf
1½ cups white long grain rice
1 tablespoon lime or lemon juice
salt and freshly ground black pepper

3 Pour in the chicken stock, then add the tomatoes, piri-piri sauce, tomato paste and cinnamon stick. Stir in the thyme and bay leaf. Season to taste and bring to a boil. Using a ladle, spoon off 1¼ cups of the liquid and set aside in a small pan.

4 Put the rice in the bottom of a casserole. Using a slotted spoon, scoop the vegetables out of the pan and spread them over the rice. Arrange the chicken pieces on top. Pour over the spicy chicken stock from the pan, cover the casserole tightly and cook in the oven for about 45 minutes, until both the rice and chicken are completely tender.

5 Meanwhile, heat the reserved chicken stock, adding a few more drops of piri-piri sauce and the lime or lemon juice.

6 To serve, spoon the piri-piri chicken and rice onto warmed serving plates. Serve the remaining sauce separately or poured over the chicken.

1 Preheat the oven to 350°F. Rub the chicken skin with a little salt and pepper. Heat 2 tablespoons of the oil in a large skillet and brown the chicken portions on all sides. Transfer to a plate.

2 Add some more oil if necessary and cook the onion for 2–3 minutes until slightly softened. Add the carrots, parsnip and bell peppers, stir-fry for a few minutes and then cover and sweat for 4–5 minutes until quite soft.

SPANISH RICE SALAD

RICE AND A CHOICE OF CHOPPED SALAD VEGETABLES ARE SERVED IN A WELL-FLAVORED DRESSING.

SERVES SIX

INGREDIENTS

 1½ cups white long grain rice
 1 bunch scallions, finely sliced
 1 green bell pepper, seeded and
  finely diced
 1 yellow bell pepper, seeded and
  finely diced
 8 ounces tomatoes, peeled, seeded
  and chopped
 2 tablespoons chopped cilantro
For the dressing
 5 tablespoons mixed sunflower and
  olive oil
 1 tablespoon rice vinegar
 1 teaspoon Dijon mustard
 salt and freshly ground black pepper

COOK'S TIP
Cooked garden peas, cooked diced carrot
and drained, canned corn can be added
to this versatile salad.

1 Cook the rice in plenty of boiling
water for 10–12 minutes until tender
but still *al dente*. Do not overcook.
Drain, rinse under cold water and drain
again. Let cool completely.

2 Place the rice in a large serving
bowl. Add the scallions, bell peppers,
tomatoes and cilantro.

3 Make the dressing. Mix all the
ingredients in a jar with a tight-fitting lid
and shake vigorously until well mixed.
Stir 4–5 tablespoons of the dressing into
the rice and adjust the seasoning.

4 Cover and chill for about 1 hour
before serving. Offer the remaining
dressing separately.

SHRIMP, MELON AND CHORIZO SALAD

THIS IS A RICH AND COLORFUL SALAD. IT TASTES BEST WHEN MADE WITH FRESH SHRIMP.

SERVES FOUR

INGREDIENTS

 4 cups cooked white long grain
  rice
 1 avocado
 1 tablespoon lemon juice
 ½ small melon, cut into wedges
 1 tablespoon butter
 ½ garlic clove
 4 ounces shrimp, shelled and
  deveined
 1 ounce chorizo sausage, finely
  sliced
 Italian parsley, to garnish
For the dressing
 5 tablespoons plain yogurt
 3 tablespoons mayonnaise
 1 tablespoon olive oil
 3 fresh tarragon sprigs
 freshly ground black pepper

1 Put the cooked rice in a large salad
bowl, breaking it up with your fingers if
necessary.

2 Peel the avocado and cut it into
chunks. Place in a mixing bowl and toss
lightly with the lemon juice. Slice the
melon off the rind, cut the flesh into
chunks and add to the avocado.

3 Melt the butter in a small pan and
cook the garlic for 30 seconds. Add the
shrimp and cook for about 3 minutes
until evenly pink. Add the chorizo and
stir-fry for 1 minute more, then tip the
mixture into the bowl with the avocado
and melon chunks. Mix lightly, then
let cool.

4 Make the dressing by whizzing
together all the ingredients in a food
processor or blender. Stir half of the
mixture into the rice and the remainder
into the shrimp and avocado mixture.
Pile the salad on top of the rice. Chill
for about 30 minutes before serving,
garnished with Italian parsley sprigs.

PORTUGUESE RICE DESSERT

THIS IS POPULAR ALL OVER PORTUGAL AND IF YOU VISIT THAT COUNTRY YOU'RE LIKELY TO FIND IT ON MOST MENUS. TRADITIONALLY IT IS SERVED COLD, BUT IS ACTUALLY DELICIOUS WARM AS WELL.

2 Drain well, then return to the clean pan. Add the milk, lemon rind and butter. Bring to a boil over moderately low heat, then cover, reduce the heat to the lowest setting and simmer for about 20 minutes or until the rice is thick and creamy.

3 Remove the pan from the heat and allow the rice to cool a little. Remove and discard the lemon rind, then stir in the sugar and the egg yolks. Mix well.

SERVES FOUR TO SIX

INGREDIENTS
    scant 1 cup short grain dessert rice
    2½ cups whole milk
    2 or 3 strips pared lemon rind
    5 tablespoons butter, in pieces
    ½ cup superfine sugar
    4 egg yolks
    salt
    ground cinnamon, for dusting
    lemon wedges, to serve

1 Cook the rice in plenty of lightly salted water for about 5 minutes, by which time it will have lost its brittleness.

4 Divide among four to six serving bowls and dust with ground cinnamon. Serve cool, with lemon wedges for squeezing.

RICE CONDE SUNDAE

COOKING RICE DESSERT ON THE STOVETOP INSTEAD OF IN THE OVEN GIVES IT A LIGHT, CREAMY TEXTURE, ESPECIALLY IF YOU REMEMBER TO STIR IT FREQUENTLY. IT IS PARTICULARLY GOOD SERVED COLD WITH A TOPPING OF FRUIT AND TOASTED NUTS OR A DRIZZLE OF HOT CHOCOLATE SAUCE.

SERVES FOUR

INGREDIENTS
 generous ¼ cup short grain dessert
  rice
 1 teaspoon vanilla extract
 ½ teaspoons ground cinnamon
 3 tablespoons sugar
 2½ cups milk
For the toppings
 soft berry fruits such as
  strawberries, raspberries and
  cherries
 chocolate sauce and slivered toasted
  almonds (optional)

3 When the grains are soft, remove the pan from the heat. Allow the rice to cool, stirring it occasionally, then chill.

4 Before serving, stir the rice dessert and spoon it into four sundae dishes. Top with fresh fruits, and with chocolate sauce and almonds, if using.

VARIATION
For a special occasion, use light cream instead of milk, and glaze the fruit with a little melted red currant jelly. (Add a splash of port if you like.)

1 Mix the rice, vanilla extract, cinnamon and sugar in a pan. Pour in the milk. Bring to a boil, stirring constantly, then reduce heat so that the mixture barely simmers.

2 Cook the rice over low heat for 30–40 minutes, stirring frequently. Add extra milk to the rice if it begins to dry out.

ITALY

In Italy, especially in the north, rice is more than just a useful side dish for meat and fish. Risottos are one of the few rice dishes that are entirely native to Europe, and, like the rice eaten in the east, the rice here is loved for its own merits. Other ingredients are added for flavor, but the star of the risotto is the rice itself.

FRIED RICE BALLS STUFFED WITH MOZZARELLA

THESE DEEP-FRIED BALLS OF RISOTTO GO BY THE NAME OF SUPPLI AL TELEFONO IN THEIR NATIVE ITALY. STUFFED WITH MOZZARELLA CHEESE, THEY ARE VERY POPULAR SNACKS, WHICH IS HARDLY SURPRISING AS THEY ARE QUITE DELICIOUS.

SERVES FOUR

INGREDIENTS

   1 quantity Risotto with Parmesan
     or Mushroom Risotto
   3 eggs
   bread crumbs and all-purpose flour,
     to coat
   ⅔ cup mozzarella cheese, cut into
     small cubes
   oil, for deep frying
   dressed frisee leaves and cherry
     tomatoes, to serve

1 Put the risotto in a bowl and allow it to cool completely. Beat two of the eggs, and stir them into the cold risotto until well mixed.

2 Use your hands to form the rice mixture into balls the size of a large egg. If the mixture is too moist to hold its shape well, stir in a few tablespoons of bread crumbs. Poke a hole into the center of each ball with your finger, then fill it with a few small cubes of mozzarella, and close the hole over again with the rice mixture.

3 Heat the oil for deep frying until a small piece of bread sizzles as soon as it is dropped in.

4 Spread some flour on a plate. Beat the remaining egg in a shallow bowl. Sprinkle another plate with bread crumbs. Roll the balls in the flour, then in the egg, and finally in the bread crumbs.

5 Fry the balls a few at a time in the hot oil until golden and crisp. Drain on paper towels while the remaining balls are being fried. Serve hot, with a simple salad of dressed frisee leaves and cherry tomatoes.

COOK'S TIP
Rice balls provide the perfect solution as to what to do with leftover risotto, as they are best made with a cold mixture, cooked the day before.

SPINACH AND RICE SOUP

USE VERY YOUNG SPINACH LEAVES TO PREPARE THIS LIGHT AND FRESH-TASTING SOUP.

SERVES FOUR

INGREDIENTS

1½ pounds fresh spinach leaves,
  washed
3 tablespoons extra virgin
  olive oil
1 small onion, finely chopped
2 garlic cloves, finely chopped
1 small fresh red chili, seeded and
  finely chopped
generous 1 cup risotto rice
5 cups vegetable stock
salt and freshly ground black pepper
shavings of pared Parmesan or
  Pecorino cheese, to serve

1 Place the spinach in a large pan with just the water that clings to its leaves after washing. Add a large pinch of salt. Heat gently until the spinach has wilted, then remove from the heat and drain, reserving any liquid.

2 Either chop the spinach finely using a large kitchen knife or place in a food processor and process the leaves to a fairly coarse purée.

COOK'S TIP
Buy Parmesan or Pecorino cheese in the piece from a reputable supplier, and it will be full of flavor and easy to shred or shave with a vegetable peeler.

3 Heat the oil in a large pan and gently cook the onion, garlic and chili for 4–5 minutes until softened. Stir in the rice until well coated, then pour in the stock and reserved spinach liquid. Bring to a boil, lower the heat and simmer gently for 10 minutes.

4 Add the spinach, with salt and pepper to taste. Cook for 5–7 minutes, until the rice is tender. Check the seasoning. Serve in heated bowls, topped with the shavings of cheese.

TROUT AND PROSCIUTTO RISOTTO ROLLS

THIS MAKES A DELICIOUS AND ELEGANT MEAL. THE RISOTTO — MADE WITH PORCINI MUSHROOMS AND SHRIMP — IS A FINE MATCH FOR THE ROBUST FLAVOR OF THE TROUT ROLLS.

SERVES FOUR

INGREDIENTS
   4 trout fillets, skinned
   4 slices prosciutto ham
   caper berries, to garnish
For the risotto
   2 tablespoons olive oil
   8 large shrimp, shelled and deveined
   1 medium onion, chopped
   generous 1 cup risotto
      rice
   about 7 tablespoons white wine
   about 3 cups simmering fish or
      chicken stock
   2 tablespoons dried porcini or
      chanterelle mushrooms, soaked
      for 10 minutes in warm water to
      cover
   salt and freshly ground black pepper

2 Add the chopped onion to the oil remaining in the pan and cook over a gentle heat for 3–4 minutes until soft. Add the rice and stir for 3–4 minutes until the grains are evenly coated in oil. Add 5 tablespoons of the wine and then the stock, a little at a time, stirring over gentle heat and allowing the rice to absorb the liquid before adding more.

4 Remove the pan from the heat and stir in the shrimp. Preheat the oven to 375°F.

1 First make the risotto. Heat the oil in a heavy-based pan or deep skillet and cook the shrimp very briefly until flecked with pink. Lift out on a slotted spoon and transfer to a plate.

5 Take a trout fillet, place a spoonful of risotto at one end and roll up. Wrap each fillet in a slice of prosciutto ham and place in a greased ovenproof dish.

3 Drain the mushrooms, reserving the liquid, and cut the larger ones in half. Towards the end of cooking, stir the mushrooms into the risotto with 1 tablespoon of the reserved mushroom liquid. If the rice is not yet *al dente*, add a little more stock or mushroom liquid and cook for 2–3 minutes more. Season to taste with salt and pepper.

COOK'S TIP
There are no hard and fast rules about which type of risotto to use for this dish. Almost any risotto could be used, although a vegetable or seafood risotto would be particularly suitable.

6 Spoon any remaining risotto around the fish fillets and sprinkle over the rest of the wine. Bake for 15–20 minutes until the fish is tender. Spoon the risotto onto a platter, top with the trout rolls and garnish with fat caper berries. Serve immediately.

STUFFED CHICKEN ROLLS

THESE DELICIOUS CHICKEN ROLLS ARE SIMPLE TO MAKE, BUT SOPHISTICATED ENOUGH TO SERVE AT A DINNER PARTY, ESPECIALLY IF YOU ARRANGE SLICES ON A BED OF TAGLIATELLE TOSSED WITH FRIED WILD MUSHROOMS.

SERVES FOUR

INGREDIENTS
  2 tablespoons butter
  1 garlic clove, chopped
  1¼ cups cooked white long grain
    rice
  3 tablespoons ricotta cheese
  2 teaspoons chopped fresh Italian
    parsley
  1 teaspoon chopped fresh tarragon
  4 skinless, boneless chicken breasts
  3–4 slices prosciutto ham
  1 tablespoon olive oil
  ½ cup white wine
  salt and freshly ground black pepper
  fresh Italian parsley sprigs,
    to garnish
  cooked tagliatelle and sauteed blewit
    mushrooms, to serve (optional)

1 Preheat the oven to 350°F. Melt about 2 teaspoons of the butter in a pan and cook the garlic for a few seconds without browning. Spoon into a bowl.

COOK'S TIP
Risotto rice could be used in place of white long grain in this dish. Risotto rice has a different consistency to long grain, and will make a much denser stuffing for the chicken rolls.

2 Add the rice, ricotta, parsley and tarragon and season with salt and pepper. Stir to mix.

3 Place each chicken breast in turn between two sheets of plastic wrap and flatten by beating lightly, but firmly, with a rolling pin.

4 Lay slices of prosciutto ham over each chicken breast, trimming the ham to fit, if necessary.

5 Place a spoonful of the rice stuffing at the wider end of each ham-topped breast. Roll up carefully and tie in place with cooking string or secure with a toothpick.

6 Heat the oil and the remaining butter in a skillet and lightly cook the chicken rolls until browned on all sides. Place side by side in a shallow baking dish and pour over the white wine.

7 Cover the dish with waxed paper and cook in the oven for 30–35 minutes until the chicken is tender.

8 Cut the rolls into slices and serve on a bed of tagliatelle with sauteed blewit mushrooms and a generous grinding of black pepper, if you like. Garnish with sprigs of Italian parsley.

PUMPKIN AND PISTACHIO RISOTTO

VEGETARIANS TIRED OF THE STANDARD DINNER PARTY FARE WILL LOVE THIS ELEGANT COMBINATION
OF CREAMY, GOLDEN RICE AND ORANGE PUMPKIN, AND SO WILL EVERYONE ELSE. IT WOULD LOOK
PARTICULARLY IMPRESSIVE SERVED IN THE HOLLOWED-OUT PUMPKIN SHELL.

SERVES FOUR

INGREDIENTS
   5 cups vegetable stock or water
   generous pinch of saffron strands
   2 tablespoons olive oil
   1 onion, chopped
   2 garlic cloves, crushed
   2 pound pumpkin, peeled, seeded
      and cut into ¾-inch cubes (about
      7 cups)
   2 cups risotto rice
   scant 1 cup dry white wine
   2 tablespoons freshly shredded
      Parmesan cheese
   ½ cup pistachios, coarsely
      chopped
   3 tablespoons chopped fresh
      marjoram or oregano, plus leaves
      to garnish
   salt, freshly shredded nutmeg and
      freshly ground black pepper

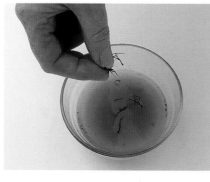

1 Bring the stock or water to a boil and reduce to low simmer. Ladle a little of it into a small bowl. Add the saffron strands and let infuse.

2 Heat the oil in a large, heavy pan or deep skillet. Add the onion and garlic and cook gently for about 5 minutes until softened. Add the pumpkin and rice and stir to coat everything in oil. Cook for a few more minutes until the rice looks transparent.

3 Pour in the wine and allow it to bubble hard. When it has been absorbed, add a quarter of the hot stock or water and the saffron liquid. Stir until all the liquid has been absorbed. Gradually add the remaining stock or water, a little at a time, allowing the rice to absorb the liquid before adding more, and stirring constantly. After 20–30 minutes the rice should be golden yellow, creamy and *al dente*.

4 Stir in the Parmesan cheese, cover the pan and let the risotto stand for 5 minutes. To finish, stir in the pistachios and marjoram or oregano. Season to taste with a little salt, nutmeg and pepper, sprinkle over a few marjoram or oregano leaves and serve.

RISOTTO WITH PARMESAN

THIS TRADITIONAL RISOTTO IS SIMPLY FLAVORED WITH SHREDDED PARMESAN CHEESE AND GOLDEN, FRIED CHOPPED ONION.

SERVES THREE TO FOUR

INGREDIENTS
5 cups beef, chicken or
  vegetable stock
5 tablespoons butter
1 small onion, finely chopped
1½ cups risotto rice
½ cup dry white wine
1 cup freshly shredded Parmesan
  cheese, plus extra to garnish
basil leaves, to garnish
salt and freshly ground black pepper

1 Heat the stock in a pan, and leave to simmer until needed.

2 Melt two-thirds of the butter in a large heavy pan or deep skillet. Stir in the onion, and cook gently until soft and golden.

3 Add the rice and stir to coat the grains with butter. After 1–2 minutes, pour in the white wine. Raise the heat slightly, and cook until the wine evaporates. Add one small ladleful of the hot stock. Cook until the stock has been absorbed, stirring constantly.

4 Gradually add the remaining stock, a little at a time, allowing the rice to absorb the liquid before adding more, and stirring constantly. After 20–30 minutes the rice should be creamy and *al dente*. Season to taste.

5 Remove the pan from the heat. Stir in the remaining butter and the Parmesan cheese. Taste again for seasoning. Allow the risotto to rest for 3–4 minutes before serving, garnished with basil leaves and shavings of Parmesan, if you like.

COOK'S TIP
If you run out of stock when cooking the risotto, use hot water, but do not worry if the rice is done before you have used up all the stock.

RISOTTO WITH RICOTTA AND BASIL

THIS IS A WELL-FLAVORED RISOTTO, WHICH BENEFITS FROM THE DISTINCT PUNGENCY OF BASIL, MELLOWED WITH SMOOTH RICOTTA.

SERVES THREE TO FOUR

INGREDIENTS
    3 tablespoons olive oil
    1 onion, finely chopped
    1½ cups risotto rice
    4 cups hot chicken or
      vegetable stock
    ¾ cup ricotta cheese
    generous 1 cup fresh basil leaves,
      finely chopped, plus extra
      to garnish
    1 cup freshly shredded Parmesan
      cheese
    salt and freshly ground black pepper

1 Heat the oil in a large pan or flameproof casserole and cook the onion over a gentle heat until soft.

2 Turn in the rice. Cook for a few minutes, stirring, until the rice is coated with oil and is slightly translucent.

3 Pour in about a quarter of the stock. Cook, stirring, until all the stock has been absorbed, then add another ladleful. Continue in this manner, adding more stock when the previous ladleful has been absorbed, until the risotto has been cooking for about 20 minutes and the rice is just tender.

4 Spoon the ricotta into a bowl and break it up a little with a fork. Stir into the risotto along with the basil and Parmesan. Taste and adjust the seasoning, then cover and let stand for 2–3 minutes before serving, garnished with basil leaves.

RISOTTO FRITTATA

HALF OMELET, HALF RISOTTO, THIS MAKES A DELIGHTFUL LIGHT LUNCH OR SUPPER DISH.
IF POSSIBLE, COOK EACH FRITTATA SEPARATELY, AND PREFERABLY IN A SMALL, CAST IRON PAN,
SO THAT THE EGGS COOK QUICKLY UNDERNEATH BUT STAY MOIST ON TOP.

SERVES FOUR

INGREDIENTS

2–3 tablespoons olive oil
1 small onion, finely chopped
1 garlic clove, crushed
1 large red bell pepper, seeded and
  cut into thin strips
¾ cup risotto rice
1⅔–2 cups simmering chicken
  stock
2–3 tablespoons butter
2½ cups white mushrooms, finely
  sliced
4 tablespoons freshly shredded
  Parmesan cheese
6–8 eggs
salt and freshly ground black pepper

1 Heat 1 tablespoon oil in a large skillet and cook the onion and garlic over a gentle heat for 2–3 minutes until the onion begins to soften but does not brown. Add the bell pepper and cook, stirring, for 4–5 minutes, until soft.

2 Stir in the rice and cook gently for 2–3 minutes, stirring all the time, until the grains are evenly coated with oil.

3 Add a quarter of the chicken stock and season. Stir over low heat until the stock has been absorbed. Continue to add more stock, a little at a time, allowing the rice to absorb the liquid before adding more. Continue cooking in this way until the rice is *al dente*.

4 In a separate small pan, heat a little of the remaining oil and some butter and quickly cook the mushrooms until golden. Transfer to a plate.

5 When the rice is tender, remove from the heat and stir in the mushrooms and Parmesan cheese.

6 Beat together the eggs with 8 teaspoons cold water and season well. Heat the remaining oil and butter in an omelet pan and add the risotto mixture. Spread the mixture out in the pan, then immediately add the beaten egg, tilting the pan so that the omelet cooks evenly. Fry over moderately high heat for 1–2 minutes, then transfer to a warmed plate and serve.

COOK'S TIP
This will make a more substantial dish for two, using five or six eggs. If preferred, the frittata could be cooked as individual portions.

PORCINI AND PARMESAN RISOTTO

THE SUCCESS OF A GOOD RISOTTO DEPENDS ON BOTH THE QUALITY OF THE RICE USED AND THE TECHNIQUE. ADD THE STOCK GRADUALLY AND STIR CONSTANTLY TO COAX A CREAMY TEXTURE FROM THE STARCH GRAINS. THIS VARIATION ON THE CLASSIC RISOTTO ALLA MILANESE INCLUDES SAFFRON, PORCINI MUSHROOMS AND PARMESAN.

SERVES FOUR

INGREDIENTS

2 tablespoons dried porcini
  mushrooms
⅔ cup warm water
4 cups vegetable stock
generous pinch of saffron strands
2 tablespoons olive oil
1 onion, finely chopped
1 garlic clove, crushed
1¾ cups Arborio or Carnaroli
  rice
⅔ cup dry white wine
2 tablespoons butter
⅔ cup freshly shredded Parmesan
  cheese
salt and freshly ground black pepper
pink and yellow oyster mushrooms,
  to serve (optional)

1 Put the dried porcini in a bowl and pour over the warm water. Leave the mushrooms to soak for 20 minutes, then lift out with a slotted spoon. Filter the soaking water through a layer of paper towels in a strainer, then place it in a pan with the stock. Bring the liquid to a gentle simmer.

2 Spoon about 3 tablespoons of the hot stock into a cup and stir in the saffron strands. Set aside. Finely chop the porcini. Heat the oil in a separate pan and lightly saute the onion, garlic and mushrooms for 5 minutes. Gradually add the rice, stirring to coat the grains in oil. Cook for 2 minutes, stirring constantly. Season with salt and pepper.

3 Pour in the white wine. Cook, stirring, until it has been absorbed, then ladle in a quarter of the stock. Cook, stirring, until the stock has been absorbed. Gradually add the remaining stock, a little at a time, allowing the rice to absorb the liquid before adding more, and stirring constantly.

4 After about 20 minutes, when all the stock has been absorbed and the rice is cooked but still has a "bite," stir in the butter, saffron water (with the strands) and half the Parmesan. Serve, sprinkled with the remaining Parmesan. Garnish with pink and yellow oyster mushrooms, if desired.

VARIATIONS

There are endless variations on this delectable dish. The proportion of stock to rice, onions, garlic and butter must remain constant but you can ring the changes with the flavorings and cheese.

RISOTTO WITH FOUR VEGETABLES

THIS IS ONE OF THE PRETTIEST RISOTTOS, ESPECIALLY WHEN MADE WITH ACORN SQUASH.

SERVES THREE TO FOUR

INGREDIENTS
   1 cup shelled fresh peas
   1 cup green beans, cut into short
     lengths
   2 tablespoons olive oil
   6 tablespoons butter
   1 acorn squash, skin and seeds
     removed, flesh cut into short thin
     sticks
   1 onion, finely chopped
   1½ cups risotto rice
   ½ cup Italian dry white vermouth
   4 cups boiling chicken stock
   1 cup freshly shredded Parmesan
     cheese
   salt and freshly ground black pepper

1 Bring a pan of lightly salted water to a boil, add the peas and beans and cook for 2–3 minutes, until the vegetables are just tender. Drain, refresh under cold running water, drain again and set aside.

2 Heat the oil with 2 tablespoons of the butter in a medium pan until foaming. Add the squash and cook gently for 2–3 minutes or until just softened. Remove with a slotted spoon and set aside. Add the onion to the pan and cook gently for about 3 minutes, stirring frequently, until softened.

3 Stir in the rice until the grains start to swell and burst, then add the vermouth. Stir until the vermouth stops sizzling and most of it has been absorbed by the rice, then add a few ladlefuls of the stock, with salt and pepper to taste. Stir over low heat until the stock has been absorbed.

4 Gradually add the remaining stock, a few ladlefuls at a time, allowing the rice to absorb the liquid before adding more, and stirring constantly.

VARIATIONS
Shelled fava beans can be used instead of the peas, and asparagus tips instead of the green beans. Use zucchini if acorn squash is not available.

5 After about 20 minutes, when all the stock has been absorbed and the rice is cooked and creamy but still has a "bite," gently stir in the vegetables, the remaining butter and about half the shredded Parmesan. Heat through, then taste for seasoning and serve with the remaining shredded Parmesan served separately.

GREEN RISOTTO

YOU COULD USE SPINACH-FLAVORED RISOTTO RICE TO GIVE THIS STUNNING DISH EVEN GREATER DRAMATIC IMPACT. HOWEVER, WHITE RISOTTO RICE MAKES A PRETTY CONTRAST TO THE SPINACH.

SERVES THREE TO FOUR

INGREDIENTS
  2 tablespoons olive oil
  1 onion, finely chopped
  1½ cups risotto rice
  4 cups hot chicken stock
  5 tablespoons white wine
  about 14 ounces tender baby spinach
    leaves
  1 tablespoon chopped fresh basil
  1 teaspoon chopped fresh mint
  4 tablespoons freshly shredded
    Parmesan cheese
  salt and freshly ground black pepper
  knob of butter or more shredded
    Parmesan cheese, to serve

1 Heat the oil and cook the onion for 3–4 minutes until soft. Add the rice and stir to coat each grain. Pour in the stock and wine, a little at a time, stirring constantly over a gentle heat until all the liquid has been absorbed.

2 Stir in the spinach leaves and herbs with the last of the liquid, and add a little seasoning. Continue cooking until the rice is tender and the spinach leaves have wilted. Stir in the Parmesan cheese, with a knob of butter, if you like, or serve with extra Parmesan.

COOK'S TIP
The secret with risotto is to add the hot liquid gradually, about a ladleful at a time, and to stir constantly until the liquid has been absorbed before adding more.

RISOTTO WITH BACON, BABY ZUCCHINI AND BELL PEPPERS

THIS WOULD MAKE THE PERFECT DISH TO COME HOME TO AFTER AN EARLY SHOW AT THE THEATER. CREAMY RISOTTO TOPPED WITH VEGETABLES AND CRISP BACON IS IRRESISTIBLE AND EASY TO MAKE.

SERVES FOUR

INGREDIENTS
  2 tablespoons olive oil
  4 ounces rindless lean bacon strips,
    cut into thick strips
  1¾ cups risotto rice
  5 cups hot vegetable or chicken stock
  2 tablespoons single cream
  3 tablespoons dry sherry
  ⅔ cup freshly shredded Parmesan
    cheese
  ⅔ cup chopped fresh parsley
  salt and freshly ground black pepper
For the vegetables
  1 small red bell pepper, seeded
  1 small green bell pepper, seeded
  2 tablespoons butter
  1 cup wild or portobello mushrooms,
    sliced
  8 ounces baby zucchini, halved
  1 onion, halved and sliced
  1 garlic clove, crushed

1 Heat half the oil in a skillet. Add the bacon and heat gently until the fat runs. Increase the heat and cook until crisp, then drain on paper towels and set aside.

2 Heat the remaining oil in a heavy-based pan. Add the rice, stir to coat the grains, then ladle in a little of the hot stock. Stir until it has been absorbed. Gradually add the rest of the stock, stirring constantly.

3 Cut the bell peppers into chunks. Melt the butter in a separate pan and cook the bell peppers, mushrooms, zucchini, onion and garlic until the onion is just tender. Season well, then stir in the bacon.

4 When all the stock has been absorbed by the rice, stir in the cream, sherry, Parmesan, parsley and seasoning. Spoon the risotto onto individual plates and top each portion with fried vegetables and bacon. Serve immediately.

RISOTTO WITH ASPARAGUS

FRESH FARM ASPARAGUS ONLY HAS A SHORT SEASON, SO IT IS SENSIBLE TO MAKE THE MOST OF IT. THIS ELEGANT RISOTTO IS ABSOLUTELY DELICIOUS.

SERVES THREE TO FOUR

INGREDIENTS
    8 ounces fresh asparagus
    3 cups vegetable or chicken
      stock
    5 tablespoons butter
    1 small onion, finely chopped
    1½ cups risotto rice, such as
      Arborio or Carnaroli
    1 cup freshly shredded Parmesan
      cheese
    salt and freshly ground black pepper

1 Bring a pan of water to a boil. Cut off any woody pieces on the butts of the asparagus stalks, peel the lower portions, then cook in the water for 5 minutes. Drain the asparagus, reserving the cooking water, refresh under cold water and drain again. Cut the asparagus diagonally into 1½-inch pieces. Keep the bud and next-highest sections separate from the stalks.

2 Place the stock in a pan and add scant 2 cups of the asparagus cooking water. Heat to simmering point, and keep it hot.

3 Melt two-thirds of the butter in a large, heavy pan or deep skillet. Add the onion and cook until it is soft and golden. Stir in all the asparagus except the top two sections. Cook for 2–3 minutes. Add the rice and cook for 1–2 minutes, mixing well to coat it with butter. Stir in a ladleful of the hot liquid. Using a wooden spoon, stir until the stock has been absorbed.

4 Gradually add the remaining stock, a little at a time, allowing the rice to absorb the liquid before adding more, and stirring constantly.

5 After 10 minutes, add the remaining asparagus sections. Continue to cook as before, for about 15 minutes, until the rice is *al dente* and the risotto is creamy. Off the heat, stir in the remaining butter and the Parmesan. Grind in a little black pepper, and taste again for salt. Serve immediately.

RISOTTO WITH FOUR CHEESES

THIS IS A VERY RICH DISH. SERVE IT FOR A SPECIAL DINNER-PARTY FIRST COURSE, WITH A LIGHT, DRY SPARKLING WHITE WINE.

SERVES FOUR

INGREDIENTS
    3 tablespoons butter
    1 small onion, finely chopped
    5 cups chicken stock, preferably
      home-made
    1¾ cups risotto rice
    scant 1 cup dry white wine
    ½ cup shredded Gruyère cheese
    ½ cup diced taleggio or dolcelatte
      cheese
    ½ cup diced Gorgonzola cheese
    ⅔ cup freshly shredded Parmesan
      cheese
    salt and freshly ground black pepper
    chopped fresh Italian parsley,
      to garnish

1 Melt the butter in a large, heavy-based pan or deep skillet and cook the onion over a gentle heat for about 4–5 minutes, stirring frequently, until softened and lightly browned. Pour the stock into another pan and heat it to simmering point.

2 Add the rice to the onion mixture, stir until the grains start to swell and burst, then add the wine. Stir until it stops sizzling and most of it has been absorbed by the rice, then pour in a little of the hot stock. Add salt and pepper to taste. Stir over low heat until the stock has been absorbed.

3 Gradually add the remaining stock, a little at a time, allowing the rice to absorb the liquid before adding more, and stirring constantly. After 20–25 minutes the rice will be *al dente* and the risotto creamy.

4 Turn off the heat under the pan, then add the Gruyère, taleggio, Gorgonzola and 2 tablespoons of the Parmesan cheese. Stir gently until the cheeses have melted, then taste for seasoning. Spoon into a serving bowl and garnish with parsley. Serve the remaining Parmesan separately.

TIMBALLO OF RICE WITH PEAS

THE TIMBALLO GETS ITS NAME FROM THE FACT THAT IT LOOKS LIKE AN INVERTED KETTLE-DRUM (TIMBALLO OR TIMPANO). IT IS MADE LIKE A RISOTTO, BUT IS GIVEN A FINAL BAKING IN THE OVEN.

SERVES FOUR

INGREDIENTS

6 tablespoons butter
2 tablespoons olive oil
1 small onion, finely chopped
2 ounces cooked ham, cut into small dice
3 tablespoons finely chopped fresh parsley, plus a few sprigs to garnish
2 garlic cloves, very finely chopped
2 cups shelled peas, thawed if frozen
4 tablespoons water
5½ cups chicken or vegetable stock
1½ cups risotto rice, preferably Arborio
1 cup freshly shredded Parmesan cheese
6 ounces fontina cheese, very thinly sliced
salt and freshly ground black pepper

1 Preheat the oven to 350°F. Heat half the butter and all the oil in a large, heavy skillet. Cook the onion until soft, then add the ham and stir over a medium heat for 3–4 minutes. Stir in the parsley and garlic. Cook for 2 minutes. Add the peas, then season and add the water.

2 Cover the pan, and cook for about 8 minutes for fresh peas, or 4 minutes for frozen peas. Remove the lid and cook until the liquid has evaporated. Spoon half the mixture into a dish. Heat the stock and keep it simmering. Butter a flat-based baking dish and line with non-stick baking parchment.

3 Stir the rice into the pea mixture in the pan. Heat through, then add a ladleful of stock. Cook until this has been absorbed, stirring constantly. Add the remaining stock in the same way, adding more liquid only when the previous quantity has been absorbed.

4 After about 20 minutes, when the rice is just tender, remove it from the heat. Season and mix in most of the remaining butter and half the Parmesan.

5 Assemble the timballo. Sprinkle the bottom of the dish with Parmesan, and spoon in half the rice. Add a layer of fontina slices and spoon over the reserved pea and ham mixture. Smooth level, and sprinkle with Parmesan.

6 Cover with the remaining fontina slices and end with the remaining rice. Sprinkle with the last of the Parmesan, and dot with butter. Bake for 10–15 minutes. Remove from the oven, and let stand for 10 minutes.

7 To unmold, slip a knife around the timballo between the rice and the dish. Place a serving plate upside down on top. Wearing oven mitts, turn over dish and plate together. Peel off the lining paper. Serve by cutting into wedges.

LEMON AND HERB RISOTTO CAKE

THIS UNUSUAL DISH CAN BE SERVED AS A MAIN COURSE WITH SALAD OR AS A SATISFYING SIDE DISH. IT IS ALSO GOOD SERVED COLD, AND PACKS WELL FOR PICNICS.

SERVES FOUR

INGREDIENTS

1 small leek, finely sliced
2½ cups chicken stock
generous 1 cup risotto rice
finely shredded rind of 1 lemon
2 tablespoons chopped fresh chives
2 tablespoons chopped fresh parsley
¾ cup shredded mozzarella cheese
salt and freshly ground black pepper

1 Preheat the oven to 400°F. Lightly oil a 8½-inch round loose-based cake pan.

2 Put the leek in a large pan with 3 tablespoons of the stock. Cook over a medium heat, stirring occasionally, until softened. Stir in the rice, then add the remaining stock.

3 Bring to a boil. Lower heat, cover the pan and simmer gently, stirring occasionally, for about 20 minutes, or until all the liquid has been absorbed.

4 Stir in the lemon rind, herbs, cheese, and seasoning. Spoon the mixture into the pan, cover with foil and bake for 30–35 minutes or until lightly browned. Let stand for 5 minutes, then turn out. Serve hot or cold, in slices.

COOK'S TIP
This risotto uses less liquid than normal and therefore has a drier consistency.

RISOTTO WITH SHRIMP

THIS SHRIMP RISOTTO IS GIVEN A SOFT PINK COLOR BY THE ADDITION OF A LITTLE TOMATO PASTE.

<u>SERVES THREE TO FOUR</u>

INGREDIENTS
  12 ounces jumbo shrimp, in
    the shells
  5 cups water
  1 bay leaf
  1–2 fresh parsley sprigs
  1 teaspoon whole peppercorns
  2 garlic cloves, peeled and left whole
  5 tablespoons butter
  2 shallots, finely chopped
  1½ cups risotto rice
  1 tablespoon tomato paste softened
    in ½ cup dry white wine
  salt and freshly ground black pepper

1 Put the shrimp in a large pan and add the water, herbs, peppercorns and garlic. Bring to a boil over a medium heat. As soon as the shrimp turn pink, lift them out, shell them and return the shells to the pan. Boil the stock with the shells for 10 minutes more, then strain. Return the stock to the clean pan, and simmer gently until needed.

2 Slice the shrimp in half lengthways, removing the dark vein along the back. Set four halves aside for the garnish, and coarsely chop the rest.

3 Heat two-thirds of the butter in a flameproof casserole and cook the shallots until golden. Add the rice, mixing well to coat it with butter. Pour in the tomato paste and wine and cook until it has been absorbed. Add the simmering stock, a ladleful at a time, allowing it to be absorbed before adding more.

4 When all the stock has been absorbed and the rice is creamy, stir in the chopped shrimp, the remaining butter and seasoning. Cover and let the risotto rest for 3–4 minutes. Spoon into a bowl, garnish with the reserved shrimp and serve.

MUSHROOM RISOTTO

MUSHROOM RISOTTO IS EASY TO MAKE AND APPEALS TO ALMOST EVERYONE. WILD MUSHROOMS WILL GIVE A MORE INTENSE FLAVOR, BUT YOU CAN USE WHATEVER MUSHROOMS ARE AVAILABLE.

<u>SERVES THREE TO FOUR</u>

INGREDIENTS
  ⅓ cup dried wild mushrooms,
    preferably porcini
  1½ cups warm water
  3¾ cups beef or chicken stock
  1½–2 cups white mushrooms,
    sliced
  juice of ½ lemon
  6 tablespoons butter
  2 tablespoons finely chopped fresh
    parsley
  2 tablespoons olive oil
  1 small onion, finely chopped
  1½ cups risotto rice
  ½ cup dry white wine
  3 tablespoons freshly shredded
    Parmesan cheese
  salt and freshly ground black pepper
  fresh herbs, to garnish

1 Put the dried mushrooms in a bowl with the warm water. Soak them for at least 40 minutes, then lift them out and rinse them thoroughly. Filter the soaking water through a strainer lined with paper towels, and pour into a pan. Add the stock to the pan and bring to simmering point.

2 Toss the mushrooms with the lemon juice in a bowl. Melt a third of the butter in a pan and cook the mushrooms until they give up their juices and begin to brown. Stir in the parsley, cook for 30 seconds more, then transfer to a bowl.

3 Heat the olive oil and half the remaining butter in the pan and cook the onion until soft. Add the rice, stirring so that the grains are evenly coated in oil.

4 Stir in all of the mushrooms, add the wine, and cook over medium heat until it has been absorbed. Add the stock, a ladleful at a time, making sure each is absorbed before adding more. When all the liquid has been absorbed, remove the pan from the heat, stir in the remaining butter, the Parmesan and seasoning. Cover the pan and allow to rest for 3–4 minutes before serving.

RISOTTO ALLA MILANESE

THIS CLASSIC RISOTTO IS ALWAYS SERVED WITH THE HEARTY BEEF STEW, OSSO BUCO, BUT ALSO MAKES A DELICIOUS FIRST COURSE OR LIGHT SUPPER DISH IN ITS OWN RIGHT.

SERVES THREE TO FOUR

INGREDIENTS

about 5 cups beef or chicken
   stock
good pinch of saffron strands
6 tablespoons butter
1 onion, finely chopped
1½ cups risotto rice
1 cup freshly shredded Parmesan
   cheese
salt and freshly ground black pepper

1 Bring the stock to a boil, then reduce to a low simmer. Ladle a little stock into a small bowl. Add the saffron strands and let infuse.

2 Melt 4 tablespoons of the butter in a large pan until foaming. Add the onion and cook gently for 3 minutes, stirring frequently, until softened but not browned.

3 Add the rice. Stir until the grains start to swell and burst, then add a few ladlefuls of the stock, with the saffron liquid and salt and pepper to taste. Stir over low heat until the stock has been absorbed. Add the remaining stock, a few ladlefuls at a time, allowing the rice to absorb all the liquid before adding more, and stirring constantly. After 20–25 minutes, the rice should be just tender and the risotto golden yellow, moist and creamy.

4 Gently stir in about two-thirds of the shredded Parmesan and the remaining butter. Heat through until the butter has melted, then taste for seasoning. Transfer the risotto to a warmed serving bowl or platter and serve hot, with the remaining shredded Parmesan served separately.

RISI E BISI

A classic pea and ham risotto from the Veneto. Although this is traditionally served as a starter in Italy, it also makes an excellent supper dish with hot, crusty bread.

SERVES FOUR

INGREDIENTS

6 tablespoons butter
1 small onion, finely chopped
about 4 cups simmering chicken
  stock
1½ cups risotto rice
⅔ cup dry white wine
2 cups frozen petits pois, thawed
4 ounces cooked ham, diced
salt and freshly ground black pepper
⅔ cup freshly shredded Parmesan
  cheese, to serve

1 Melt 4 tablespoons of the butter in a pan until foaming. Add the onion and cook gently for about 3 minutes, stirring frequently, until softened. Have the hot stock ready in an adjacent pan.

2 Add the rice to the onion mixture. Stir until the grains start to swell, then pour in the wine. Stir until it stops sizzling and most of it has been absorbed, then pour in a little hot stock, with salt and pepper to taste. Stir continuously, over low heat, until all the stock has been absorbed.

3 Add the remaining stock, a little at a time, allowing the rice to absorb all the liquid before adding more, and stirring constantly. Add the peas after about 20 minutes. After 25–30 minutes, the rice should be *al dente* and the risotto moist and creamy.

4 Gently stir in the diced cooked ham and the remaining butter. Heat through until the butter has melted, then taste for seasoning. Transfer to a warmed serving bowl. Shave a little Parmesan over the top and serve the rest separately.

COOK'S TIP
Always use fresh Parmesan cheese, shredded off a block. It has a far superior flavor to the ready-shredded Parmesan.

RISOTTO-STUFFED EGGPLANTS
WITH SPICY TOMATO SAUCE

*EGGPLANTS ARE A CHALLENGE TO THE CREATIVE COOK AND ALLOW FOR SOME UNUSUAL RECIPE IDEAS.
HERE, THEY ARE FILLED WITH A RICE STUFFING AND BAKED WITH A CHEESE AND PINE NUT TOPPING.*

SERVES FOUR

INGREDIENTS
  4 small eggplants
  7 tablespoons olive oil
  1 small onion, chopped
  scant 1 cup risotto rice
  3 cups hot vegetable stock
  1 tablespoon white wine vinegar
  ⅓ cup freshly shredded Parmesan
    cheese
  2 tablespoons pine nuts
For the tomato sauce
  1¼ cups thick passata or puréed
    tomatoes
  1 teaspoon mild curry paste
  pinch of salt

1 Preheat the oven to 400°F. Cut the
eggplant in half lengthwise, and
remove the flesh with a small knife.
Brush the shells with 2 tablespoons
of the oil and bake on a baking sheet,
supported by crumpled foil, for
6–8 minutes.

2 Chop the eggplant flesh. Heat the
remaining oil in a medium pan. Add
the eggplant flesh and the onion, and
cook over gentle heat for 3–4 minutes
until soft. Add the rice and stock, and
let simmer, uncovered, for 15 minutes.
Add the vinegar.

COOK'S TIP
If the eggplant shells do not stand level,
cut a thin slice from the bottom.

3 Increase the oven temperature to
450°F. Spoon the rice mixture into the
eggplant, top with the cheese and pine
nuts, return to the oven and brown for
5 minutes.

4 To make the sauce, mix the passata
or puréed tomatoes with the curry paste
in a small pan. Heat through and add
salt to taste. Spoon the sauce onto four
individual serving plates and arrange
two eggplant halves on each one.

LEEK, MUSHROOM AND LEMON RISOTTO

LEEKS AND LEMON GO TOGETHER BEAUTIFULLY IN THIS LIGHT RISOTTO, WHILE MUSHROOMS ADD TEXTURE AND EXTRA FLAVOR.

SERVES FOUR

INGREDIENTS
    8 ounces trimmed leeks
    2–3 cups brown mushrooms
    2 tablespoons olive oil
    3 garlic cloves, crushed
    6 tablespoons butter
    1 large onion, roughly chopped
    1¾ cups risotto rice
    4 cups simmering vegetable stock
    grated rind of 1 lemon
    3 tablespoons lemon juice
    ⅔ cup freshly shredded Parmesan
        cheese
    4 tablespoons mixed chopped fresh
        chives and Italian parsley
    salt and freshly ground black pepper

1 Slice the leeks in half lengthwise, wash them well and then slice them evenly. Wipe the mushrooms with a paper towel and chop them coarsely.

2 Heat the oil in a large pan and cook the garlic for 1 minute. Add the leeks, mushrooms and plenty of seasoning and cook over medium heat for about 10 minutes, or until the leeks have softened and browned. Spoon into a bowl and set aside.

3 Add 2 tablespoons of the butter to the pan. As soon as it has melted, add the onion and cook over medium heat for 5 minutes until it has softened and is golden.

4 Stir in the rice and cook for about 1 minute until the grains begin to look translucent and are coated in the fat. Add a ladleful of stock and cook gently, stirring occasionally, until the liquid has been absorbed.

5 Continue to add stock, a ladleful at a time, until all of it has been absorbed, and stirring constantly. This should take about 25–30 minutes. The risotto will turn thick and creamy and the rice should be tender but not sticky.

6 Just before serving, add the leeks and mushrooms, with the remaining butter. Stir in the lemon rind and juice. Add the shredded Parmesan cheese and the herbs. Adjust the seasoning and serve immediately.

RISOTTO <u>WITH</u> CHICKEN

THIS IS A CLASSIC COMBINATION OF CHICKEN AND RICE, COOKED WITH PROSCIUTTO HAM, WHITE WINE AND PARMESAN CHEESE.

<u>SERVES SIX</u>

INGREDIENTS

2 tablespoons olive oil
8 ounces skinless, boneless chicken
  breasts, cut into 1-inch cubes
1 onion, finely chopped
1 garlic clove, finely chopped
2⅓ cups risotto rice
½ cup dry white wine
¼ teaspoons saffron strands
7½ cups simmering chicken
  stock
2 ounces prosciutto ham, cut
  into thin strips
2 tablespoons butter, cubed
⅓ cup freshly shredded Parmesan
  cheese, plus extra to serve
salt and freshly ground black pepper
flat leaf parsley, to garnish

1 Heat the olive oil in a skillet over moderately high heat. Add the chicken cubes and cook, stirring, until they start to turn white.

2 Reduce the heat to low and add the onion and garlic. Cook, stirring, until the onion is soft. Stir in the rice. Saute for 1–2 minutes, stirring constantly, until all the rice grains are coated in oil.

3 Add the wine and cook, stirring, until the wine has been absorbed. Stir the saffron into the simmering stock, then add ladlefuls of stock to the rice, allowing each ladleful to be absorbed before adding the next.

4 When the rice is three-quarters cooked, add the prosciutto ham and continue cooking until the rice is just tender and the risotto creamy.

5 Add the butter and the Parmesan and stir in well. Season with salt and pepper to taste. Serve the risotto hot, sprinkled with a little more Parmesan, and garnish with parsley.

RISOTTO WITH SMOKED BACON AND TOMATO

A CLASSIC RISOTTO, WITH PLENTY OF ONIONS, SMOKED BACON AND SUN-DRIED TOMATOES. YOU'LL WANT TO KEEP GOING BACK FOR MORE!

SERVES FOUR TO SIX

INGREDIENTS

8 sun-dried tomatoes in olive oil
10 ounces good-quality rindless
  smoked lean bacon
6 tablespoons butter
1 pound onions, coarsely chopped
2 garlic cloves, crushed
1¾ cups risotto rice
1¼ cups dry white wine
3¾ cups simmering vegetable
  stock
⅔ cup freshly shredded Parmesan
  cheese
3 tablespoons mixed chopped fresh
  chives and Italian parsley
salt and freshly ground black pepper

1 Drain the sun-dried tomatoes and reserve 1 tablespoon of the oil. Coarsely chop the tomatoes and set aside. Cut the bacon into 1-inch pieces.

2 Heat the oil from the sun-dried tomatoes in a large skillet. Cook the bacon until golden, then remove with a slotted spoon and drain well on paper towels.

3 Heat 2 tablespoons of the butter in a pan and fry the onions and garlic over medium heat for 10 minutes, until soft and golden brown.

4 Stir in the rice. Cook for 1 minute, until the grains turn translucent. Stir the wine into the stock. Add a ladleful of the mixture to the rice and cook gently until the liquid has been absorbed.

5 Stir in another ladleful of the stock and wine mixture and allow it to be absorbed. Repeat this process until all the liquid has been used up. This should take 25–30 minutes. The risotto will turn thick and creamy, and the rice should be tender but not sticky.

6 Just before serving, stir in the bacon, sun-dried tomatoes, Parmesan, half the herbs and the remaining butter. Adjust the seasoning (remember that the bacon may be quite salty) and serve sprinkled with the remaining herbs.

SHELLFISH RISOTTO <u>WITH</u> MIXED MUSHROOMS

THIS IS A QUICK AND EASY RISOTTO, WHERE ALL THE LIQUID IS ADDED IN ONE GO. THE METHOD IS WELL-SUITED TO THIS SHELLFISH DISH, AS IT MEANS EVERYTHING COOKS TOGETHER UNDISTURBED.

<u>SERVES SIX</u>

INGREDIENTS
  8 ounces live mussels
  8 ounces live Venus or carpet
    shell clams
  3 tablespoons olive oil
  1 onion, chopped
  2⅓ cups risotto rice
  7½ cups simmering chicken or
    vegetable stock
  ⅔ cup white wine
  2–3 cups assorted wild and
    cultivated mushrooms, trimmed
    and sliced
  4 ounces shelled shrimp,
    deveined
  1 medium or 2 small squid,
    cleaned, trimmed and sliced
  3 drops truffle oil (optional)
  5 tablespoons chopped mixed fresh
    parsley and chervil
  celery salt and cayenne pepper

1 Scrub the mussels and clams clean and discard any that are open and do not close when tapped with a knife. Set aside. Heat the oil in a large skillet and cook the onion for 6–8 minutes until soft but not browned.

2 Add the rice, stirring to coat the grains in oil, then pour in the stock and wine and cook for 5 minutes. Add the mushrooms and cook for 5 minutes more, stirring occasionally.

3 Add the shrimp, squid, mussels and clams and stir into the rice. Cover the pan and simmer over low heat for 15 minutes until the shrimp have turned pink and the mussels and clams have opened. Discard any of the shellfish that remain closed.

4 Switch off the heat. Add the truffle oil, if using, and stir in the herbs. Cover tightly and let stand for 5–10 minutes to allow all the flavors to blend. Season to taste with celery salt and a pinch of cayenne, pile into a warmed dish, and serve immediately.

SALMON RISOTTO <u>WITH</u> CUCUMBER <u>AND</u> TARRAGON

THIS SIMPLE RISOTTO IS COOKED ALL IN ONE GO, AND IS THEREFORE SIMPLER THAN THE USUAL RISOTTO. IF YOU PREFER TO COOK THE TRADITIONAL WAY, ADD THE LIQUID GRADUALLY, ADDING THE SALMON ABOUT TWO-THIRDS OF THE WAY THROUGH COOKING.

SERVES FOUR

INGREDIENTS

2 tablespoons butter
small bunch of scallions, white parts
  only, chopped
½ cucumber, peeled, seeded and
  chopped
1¾ cups risotto rice
5 cups hot chicken or fish stock
⅔ cup dry white wine
1 pound salmon fillet, skinned and
  diced
3 tablespoons chopped fresh tarragon
salt and freshly ground black pepper

1 Heat the butter in a large pan and add the scallions and cucumber. Cook for 2–3 minutes without letting the scallions color.

2 Stir in the rice, then pour in the stock and wine. Bring to a boil, then lower the heat and simmer, uncovered, for 10 minutes, stirring occasionally.

3 Stir in the diced salmon and season to taste with salt and freshly ground black pepper. Continue cooking for a further 5 minutes, stirring occasionally, then switch off the heat. Cover and let stand for 5 minutes.

4 Remove the lid, add the chopped tarragon and mix lightly. Spoon into a warmed bowl and serve.

VARIATION
Carnaroli risotto rice would be excellent in this risotto, although if it is not available, use Arborio instead.

TRUFFLE AND LOBSTER RISOTTO

TO CAPTURE THE PRECIOUS QUALITIES OF THE FRESH TRUFFLE, PARTNER IT WITH LOBSTER AND SERVE IN A SILKY SMOOTH RISOTTO. BOTH TRUFFLE SHAVINGS AND TRUFFLE OIL ARE ADDED TOWARDS THE END OF COOKING TO PRESERVE THEIR FLAVOR.

SERVES FOUR

INGREDIENTS

4 tablespoons unsalted butter
1 medium onion, chopped
1¾ cups risotto rice, preferably Carnaroli
1 fresh thyme sprig
⅔ cup dry white wine
5 cups simmering chicken stock
1 freshly cooked lobster
3 tablespoons chopped mixed fresh parsley and chervil
3–4 drops truffle oil
2 hard-cooked eggs
1 fresh black or white truffle
salt and freshly ground black pepper

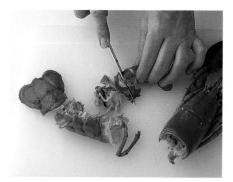

1 Melt the butter, add the onion and cook until soft. Add the rice and stir well to coat with fat. Add the thyme, then the wine, and cook until it has been absorbed. Add the chicken stock a little at a time, stirring. Let each ladleful be absorbed before adding the next.

2 Twist off the lobster tail, cut the underside with scissors and remove the white tail meat. Carefully break open the claws with a small kitchen hammer and remove the flesh. Cut half the meat into big chunks, then roughly chop the remainder.

3 Remove the rice from the heat and stir in the chopped lobster meat, half the chopped herbs and the truffle oil. Cover and let stand for 5 minutes.

4 Divide among warmed plates and center the lobster chunks on top. Cut the hard-cooked eggs into wedges and arrange them around the lobster meat. Finally, shave fresh truffle over each portion and sprinkle with the remaining herbs. Serve immediately.

COOK'S TIP
To make the most of the aromatic truffle scent, keep the tuber in the rice jar for a few days before use.

PANCETTA AND FAVA BEAN RISOTTO

THIS DELICIOUS RISOTTO MAKES A HEALTHY AND FILLING MEAL, SERVED WITH COOKED FRESH SEASONAL VEGETABLES OR A MIXED GREEN SALAD.

SERVES FOUR

INGREDIENTS

    1 tablespoon olive oil
    1 onion, chopped
    2 garlic cloves, finely chopped
    6 ounces smoked pancetta,
      diced
    1¾ cups risotto rice
    6¼ cups simmering chicken
      stock
    2 cups frozen baby fava beans
    2 tablespoons chopped fresh mixed
      herbs, such as parsley, thyme and
      oregano
    salt and freshly ground black pepper
    shavings of Parmesan cheese, to
      serve

1 Heat the oil in a large pan. Add the onion, garlic and pancetta and cook gently for about 5 minutes, stirring occasionally. Do not allow the onion and garlic to brown.

2 Add the rice to the pan and cook for 1 minute, stirring. Add a ladleful of stock and cook, stirring all the time, until the liquid has been absorbed.

3 Continue adding the stock, a ladleful at a time, until the rice is tender, and almost all the liquid has been absorbed. This will take 30–35 minutes.

4 Meanwhile, cook the fava beans in a pan of lightly salted, boiling water for about 3 minutes until tender. Drain well and stir into the risotto, with the mixed herbs. Add salt and pepper to taste. Spoon into a bowl and serve, sprinkled with shavings of fresh Parmesan cheese.

COOK'S TIP
If the fava beans are large, or if you prefer skinned beans, remove the outer skin after cooking.

BROWN RICE RISOTTO WITH MUSHROOMS AND PARMESAN

A CLASSIC RISOTTO OF MIXED MUSHROOMS, HERBS AND FRESH PARMESAN CHEESE, BUT MADE USING BROWN LONG GRAIN RICE. SERVE SIMPLY, WITH A MIXED LEAF SALAD TOSSED IN A LIGHT DRESSING.

SERVES FOUR

INGREDIENTS

1 tablespoon olive oil
4 shallots, finely chopped
2 garlic cloves, crushed
2 tablespoons dried porcini
  mushrooms, soaked in ⅔ cup hot
  water for 20 minutes
1⅓ cups brown long grain rice
3¾ cups well-flavored vegetable
  stock
6 cups mixed mushrooms,
  such as white, brown and
  portobello mushrooms, sliced
  if large
2–3 tablespoons chopped fresh
  Italian parsley
⅔ cup freshly shredded Parmesan
  cheese
salt and freshly ground black
  pepper

1 Heat the oil in a large pan, add the shallots and garlic and cook gently for 5 minutes, stirring. Drain the porcini, reserving their liquid, and chop coarsely. Add the brown rice to the shallot mixture and stir to coat the grains in oil.

2 Stir the vegetable stock and the porcini soaking liquid into the rice mixture in the saucepan. Bring to a boil, lower the heat and simmer, uncovered, for about 20 minutes or until most of the liquid has been absorbed, stirring frequently.

3 Add all the mushrooms, stir well, and cook the risotto for 10–15 minutes more until the liquid has been absorbed.

4 Season with salt and pepper to taste, stir in the chopped parsley and shredded Parmesan and serve at once.

CRAB RISOTTO

*THIS IS A FRESH-FLAVORED RISOTTO WHICH MAKES A WONDERFUL MAIN COURSE OR APPETIZER.
YOU WILL NEED TWO CRABS FOR THIS RECIPE, AND IT IS THEREFORE A GOOD DISH TO FOLLOW
A TRIP TO THE COAST, WHERE CRABS ARE CHEAP AND PLENTIFUL.*

SERVES THREE TO FOUR

INGREDIENTS

2 large cooked crabs
1 tablespoon olive oil
2 tablespoons butter
2 shallots, finely chopped
1½ cups risotto rice, preferably
   Carnaroli
5 tablespoons Marsala or brandy
4 cups simmering fish stock
1 teaspoon chopped fresh tarragon
1 teaspoon chopped fresh parsley
4 tablespoons heavy cream
salt and freshly ground black pepper

1 First remove the crab meat from each of the shells in turn. Hold the crab firmly in one hand and hit the back underside firmly with the heel of your hand. This should loosen the shell from the body. Using your thumbs, push against the body and pull away from the shell. From the inside of the shell, remove and discard the intestines.

2 Discard the gray gills (dead man's fingers). Break off the claws and legs from the body, then use a small hammer or crackers to break them open. Using a pick, remove the meat from the claws and legs. Place the meat on a plate.

3 Using a pick or a skewer, pick out the white meat from the body cavities and place on the plate with the meat from the claws and legs, reserving some white meat to garnish. Scoop out the brown meat from inside the shell and set aside with the white meat on the plate.

4 Heat the oil and butter in a pan and gently cook the shallots until soft but not browned. Add the rice. Cook for a few minutes, stirring, until the rice is slightly translucent, then add the Marsala or brandy, bring to a boil, and cook, stirring, until the liquid has evaporated.

5 Add a ladleful of hot stock and cook, stirring, until all the stock has been absorbed. Continue cooking in this way until about two-thirds of the stock has been added, then carefully stir in all the crab meat and the herbs.

6 Continue to cook the risotto, adding the remaining stock. When the rice is almost cooked but still has a slight "bite," remove it from the heat, stir in the cream and adjust the seasoning. Cover and let stand for 3 minutes to finish cooking. Serve garnished with the reserved white crab meat.

MONKFISH RISOTTO

MONKFISH IS A VERSATILE, FIRM-TEXTURED FISH WITH A SUPERB FLAVOR, WHICH IS ACCENTUATED
WITH LEMONGRASS IN THIS SOPHISTICATED RISOTTO.

SERVES THREE TO FOUR

INGREDIENTS
   seasoned flour
   about 1 pound monkfish, cut into
     cubes
   2 tablespoons olive oil
   3 tablespoons butter
   2 shallots, finely chopped
   1 lemongrass stalk, finely chopped
   1½ cups risotto rice, preferably
     Carnaroli
   ¾ cup dry white wine
   4 cups simmering fish stock
   2 tablespoons chopped fresh
     parsley
   salt and white pepper
   dressed salad leaves, to serve

4 Add the rice. Cook for 2–3 minutes, stirring, until the rice is coated with oil and is slightly translucent. Gradually add the wine and the hot stock, stirring and waiting until each ladleful has been absorbed before adding the next.

5 When the rice is about three-quarters cooked, stir in the monkfish. Continue to cook the risotto, adding the remaining stock and stirring constantly until the grains of rice are tender, but still retain a bit of "bite." Season with salt and white pepper.

6 Remove the pan from the heat, stir in the parsley and cover with the lid. Let the risotto stand for a few minutes before serving with a garnish of dressed salad leaves.

COOK'S TIP
Lemongrass adds a subtle flavor to this dish. Remove the tough outer skin and chop the inner flesh finely.

1 Spoon the seasoned flour over the monkfish cubes in a bowl. Toss the monkfish until coated.

2 Heat 1 tablespoon of the oil with half the butter in a skillet. Cook the monkfish cubes over a medium to high heat for 3–4 minutes until cooked, turning occasionally. Transfer to a plate and set aside.

3 Heat the remaining oil and butter in a pan and cook the shallots over a low heat for about 4 minutes until soft but not brown. Add the lemongrass and cook for 1–2 minutes more.

SCALLOP RISOTTO

TRY TO BUY FRESH SCALLOPS FOR THIS DISH, WHICH TASTE MUCH BETTER THAN FROZEN ONES.
FRESH SCALLOPS COME WITH THE CORAL ATTACHED, WHICH ADDS FLAVOR, TEXTURE AND COLOR.

SERVES FOUR

INGREDIENTS
    about 12 scallops, with their corals
    4 tablespoons butter
    1 tablespoon olive oil
    2 tablespoons Pernod
    2 shallots, finely chopped
    1½ cups risotto rice
    4 cups simmering fish stock
    generous pinch of saffron strands,
        dissolved in 1 tablespoon warm
        milk
    2 tablespoons chopped fresh parsley
    4 tablespoons heavy cream
    salt and freshly ground black pepper

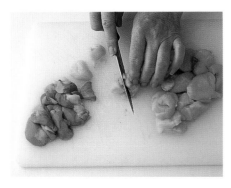

1 Separate the scallops from their corals. Cut the white flesh in half or into ¾-inch slices.

2 Melt half the butter with 1 teaspoon oil. Cook the white parts of the scallops for 2–3 minutes. Pour over the Pernod, heat for a few seconds, then ignite and allow to flame for a few seconds. When the flames have died down, remove the pan from the heat.

3 Heat the remaining butter and olive oil in a pan and cook the shallots for about 3–4 minutes, until soft but not browned. Add the rice and cook for a few minutes, stirring, until the rice is coated with oil and is beginning to turn translucent around the edges.

4 Gradually add the hot stock, a ladleful at a time, stirring constantly and waiting for each ladleful of stock to be absorbed before adding the next.

5 When the rice is very nearly cooked, add the scallops and all the juices from the pan, together with the corals, the saffron milk, parsley and seasoning. Stir well to mix. Continue cooking, adding the remaining stock and stirring occasionally, until the risotto is thick and creamy.

6 Remove the pan from the heat, stir in the heavy cream and cover. Let the risotto rest for about 3 minutes to complete the cooking, then pile it into a warmed bowl and serve.

SQUID RISOTTO WITH CHILI AND CILANTRO

SQUID NEEDS TO BE COOKED EITHER VERY QUICKLY OR VERY SLOWLY. HERE THE SQUID IS MARINATED IN LIME AND KIWI FRUIT — A POPULAR METHOD IN NEW ZEALAND FOR TENDERIZING SQUID.

SERVES FOUR

INGREDIENTS
    about 1 pound squid
    about 3 tablespoons olive oil
    1 tablespoon butter
    1 onion, finely chopped
    2 garlic cloves, crushed
    1 fresh red chili, seeded and finely
        sliced
    1½ cups risotto rice
    ¾ cup dry white wine
    4 cups simmering fish stock
    2 tablespoons chopped cilantro
    salt and freshly ground black pepper
For the marinade
    2 ripe kiwi fruit, chopped and
        mashed
    1 fresh red chili, seeded and finely
        sliced
    2 tablespoons fresh lime juice

1 If not already cleaned, prepare the squid by cutting off the tentacles at the base and pulling to remove the quill. Discard the quill and intestines, if necessary, and pull away the thin outer skin. Rinse the body and cut into thin strips: cut the tentacles into short pieces, discarding the beak and eyes.

2 Mash the kiwi fruit for the marinade in a bowl, then stir in the chili and lime juice. Add the squid, stirring to coat all the strips in the mixture. Season with salt and freshly ground black pepper, cover with plastic wrap and set aside in the fridge for 4 hours or overnight.

3 Drain the squid. Heat 1 tablespoon of the olive oil in a skillet and cook the strips, in batches if necessary, for about 30–60 seconds over high heat. It is important that the squid cooks very quickly. Transfer the cooked squid to a plate and set aside. Don't worry if some of the marinade clings to the squid, but if too much juice accumulates in the pan, pour this into a measuring cup and add more olive oil when cooking the next batch, so that the squid fries rather than simmers. Reserve all of the accumulated juices.

4 Heat the remaining oil with the butter in a pan and gently cook the onion and garlic for 5–6 minutes until soft and golden. Add the sliced chilli to the pan and cook for 1 minute more.

5 Add the rice. Cook for a few minutes, stirring, until the rice is coated with oil and is slightly translucent, then stir in the wine until it has been absorbed.

6 Gradually add the hot stock and the reserved cooking liquid from the squid, a ladleful at a time, stirring the rice constantly and waiting until each quantity of stock has been absorbed before adding the next.

7 When the rice is about three-quarters cooked, stir in the squid and continue cooking the risotto until all the stock has been absorbed and the rice is tender, but retains a bit of "bite." Stir in the chopped cilantro, cover with the lid or a dish towel, and let rest for a few minutes before serving.

COOK'S TIP
Although fish stock underlines the flavor of the squid, a light chicken or vegetable stock would also work well in this recipe.

MUSSEL RISOTTO

FRESH GINGER ROOT AND CILANTRO ADD A DISTINCTIVE FLAVOR TO THIS DISH, WHILE THE GREEN CHILLIES GIVE IT A LITTLE HEAT. THE CHILIES COULD BE OMITTED FOR A MILDER DISH.

SERVES THREE TO FOUR

INGREDIENTS

    2 pounds fresh mussels
    about 1 cup dry white wine
    2 tablespoons olive oil
    1 onion, chopped
    2 garlic cloves, crushed
    1–2 fresh green chilies, seeded and
      finely sliced
    1-inch piece of fresh ginger root,
      shredded
    1½ cups risotto rice
    3¾ cups simmering fish stock
    2 tablespoons chopped cilantro
    2 tablespoons heavy cream
    salt and freshly ground black
      pepper

3 Add the rice and cook over medium heat for 2 minutes, stirring, until the rice is coated in oil and becomes translucent.

4 Stir in the reserved cooking liquid from the mussels. When this has been absorbed, add the remaining wine and cook, stirring, until this has been absorbed. Now add the hot fish stock, a little at a time, making sure each addition has been absorbed before adding the next.

5 When the rice is about three-quarters cooked, stir in the mussels. Add the cilantro and season with salt and pepper. Continue adding stock to the risotto until it is creamy and the rice is tender but slightly firm in the center.

6 Remove the risotto from the heat, stir in the cream, cover and let rest for a few minutes. Spoon into a warmed serving dish, decorate with the reserved mussels in their shells, and serve immediately.

1 Scrub the mussels, discarding any that do not close when sharply tapped. Place in a large pan. Add ½ cup of the white wine and bring to a boil. Cover the pan and cook the mussels for 4–5 minutes until they have opened, shaking the pan occasionally. Drain, reserving the liquid and discarding any mussels that have not opened. Remove most of the mussels from their shells, reserving a few in their shells for decoration. Strain the mussel liquid.

2 Heat the oil and cook the onion and garlic for 3–4 minutes until beginning to soften. Add the chilies. Continue to cook over low heat for 1–2 minutes, stirring frequently, then stir in the shredded ginger root and cook gently for 1 minute more.

SEAFOOD RISOTTO

YOU CAN USE ANY SHELLFISH OR SEAFOOD FOR THIS RISOTTO, AS LONG AS THE TOTAL WEIGHT IS SIMILAR TO THAT USED HERE. THE RISOTTO WOULD ALSO MAKE A VERY GOOD APPETIZER FOR EIGHT.

SERVES FOUR TO SIX

INGREDIENTS

1 pound fresh mussels
about 1 cup dry white wine
8 ounces sea bass fillet, skinned and
  cut into pieces
seasoned all-purpose flour
4 tablespoons olive oil
8 scallops with corals separated,
  white parts halved or sliced, if large
8 ounces squid, cleaned and cut
  into rings
12 jumbo shrimp, heads removed
2 shallots, finely chopped
1 garlic clove, crushed
2 cups risotto rice, preferably
  Carnaroli
3 tomatoes, peeled, seeded and
  chopped
6¼ cups simmering fish stock
2 tablespoons chopped fresh
  parsley
2 tablespoons heavy cream
salt and freshly ground black pepper

1 Scrub the mussels, discarding any that do not close when sharply tapped. Place them in a large pan and add 6 tablespoons of the wine. Bring to a boil, cover the pan and cook for 3–4 minutes until all the mussels have opened, shaking the pan occasionally. Drain, reserving the liquid and discarding any mussels that have not opened. Set aside a few mussels in their shells for garnishing; remove the others from their shells. Strain the cooking liquid.

2 Dust the pieces of sea bass in seasoned flour. Heat 2 tablespoons of the olive oil in a skillet and cook the fish for 3–4 minutes until cooked. Transfer to a plate. Add a little more oil to the pan and cook the white parts of the scallops for 1–2 minutes on both sides until tender. Transfer to a plate.

3 Cook the squid for 3–4 minutes in the same pan, adding a little more oil if necessary, then set aside. Lastly, add the shrimp and cook for a further 3–4 minutes until pink, turning frequently. Towards the end of cooking, add a splash of wine – about 2 tablespoons – and continue cooking so that the shrimp become tender, but do not burn. Remove the shrimp from the pan. As soon as they are cool enough to handle, remove the shells and legs, leaving the tails intact.

4 In a large pan, heat the remaining olive oil and cook the shallots and garlic for 3–4 minutes over gentle heat until the shallots are soft but not brown. Add the rice and cook for a few minutes, stirring, until the rice is coated with oil and the grains are slightly translucent. Stir in the tomatoes, with the reserved liquid from the mussels.

5 When all the free liquid has been absorbed, add the remaining wine, stirring constantly. When it has also been absorbed, gradually add the hot stock, one ladleful at a time, continuing to stir the rice constantly and waiting until each quantity of stock has been absorbed before adding the next.

6 When the risotto is three-quarters cooked, carefully stir in all the seafood, except the mussels reserved for the garnish. Continue to cook until all the stock has been absorbed and the rice is tender but still has a bit of "bite."

7 Stir in the parsley and cream and adjust the seasoning. Cover the pan and let the risotto stand for 2–3 minutes. Serve in individual bowls, garnished with the reserved mussels in their shells.

CHAMPAGNE RISOTTO

THIS MAY SEEM RATHER EXTRAVAGANT, BUT IT MAKES A REALLY BEAUTIFULLY FLAVORED RISOTTO, PERFECT FOR THAT SPECIAL ANNIVERSARY DINNER.

SERVES FOUR

INGREDIENTS

2 tablespoons butter
2 shallots, finely chopped
1½ cups risotto rice, preferably
  Carnaroli
½ bottle or 1¼ cups champagne
3 cups simmering light vegetable or
  chicken stock
⅔ cup heavy cream
½ cup freshly shredded Parmesan
  cheese
2 teaspoons very finely chopped
  fresh chervil
salt and freshly ground
  black pepper
black truffle shavings, to garnish
  (optional)

1 Melt the butter in a pan and cook the shallots for 2–3 minutes until softened. Add the rice and cook, stirring all the time, until the grains are evenly coated in butter and are beginning to look translucent around the edges.

2 Pour in about two-thirds of the champagne and cook over a high heat so that the liquid bubbles fiercely. Cook, stirring, until all the liquid has been absorbed before beginning to add the hot stock.

3 Add the stock, a ladleful at a time, making sure that each addition has been completely absorbed before adding the next. The risotto should gradually become creamy and velvety and all the stock should be absorbed.

4 When the rice is tender but retains a bit of "bite," stir in the remaining champagne and the heavy cream and Parmesan. Adjust the seasoning. Remove from the heat, cover and leave to stand for a few minutes. Stir in the chervil. Garnish with a few truffle shavings if desired.

ROASTED BELL PEPPER RISOTTO

THIS MAKES AN EXCELLENT VEGETARIAN SUPPER DISH, OR AN APPETIZER FOR SIX.

SERVES THREE TO FOUR

INGREDIENTS
1 red bell pepper
1 yellow bell pepper
1 tablespoon olive oil
2 tablespoons butter
1 onion, chopped
2 garlic cloves, crushed
1½ cups risotto rice
4 cups simmering vegetable stock
⅔ cup freshly shredded Parmesan
 cheese
salt and freshly ground black pepper
freshly shredded Parmesan cheese,
 to serve (optional)

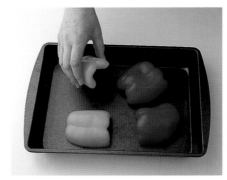

1 Preheat the broiler to high. Cut the bell peppers in half, remove the seeds and pith and arrange, cut side down, on a baking sheet. Place under the broiler for 5–6 minutes until the skin is charred. Put the bell peppers in a plastic bag, tie and leave for 4 minutes.

2 Peel the bell peppers when cool enough to handle and the steam has loosened the skin. Cut into thin strips,

3 Heat the oil and butter in a pan and cook the onion and garlic for 4–5 minutes over low heat until the onion begins to soften. Add the bell peppers and cook the mixture for 3–4 minutes more, stirring occasionally.

4 Stir in the rice. Cook over medium heat for 3–4 minutes, stirring all the time, until the rice is evenly coated in oil and the outer part of each grain has become translucent.

5 Add a ladleful of stock. Cook, stirring, until all the liquid has been absorbed. Continue to add the stock, a ladleful at a time, making sure each quantity has been absorbed before adding the next.

6 When the rice is tender but retains a bit of "bite," stir in the Parmesan, and add seasoning to taste. Cover and leave to stand for 3–4 minutes, then serve, with extra Parmesan, if using.

Two Cheese Risotto

This undeniably rich and creamy risotto is just the thing to serve on cold winter evenings when everyone needs warming up.

SERVES THREE TO FOUR

INGREDIENTS
1½ teaspoons olive oil
4 tablespoons butter
1 onion, finely chopped
1 garlic clove, crushed
1½ cups risotto rice, preferably
  Vialone Nano
¾ cup dry white wine
4 cups simmering vegetable or
  chicken stock
¾ cup fontina cheese, cubed
⅔ cup freshly grated Parmesan
  cheese, plus extra, to serve
salt and freshly ground black pepper

1 Heat the olive oil with half the butter in a pan and gently fry the onion and garlic for 5–6 minutes until soft. Add the rice and cook, stirring all the time, until the grains are coated in fat and have become slightly translucent around the edges.

2 Stir in the wine. Cook, stirring, until the liquid has been absorbed, then add a ladleful of hot stock. Stir until the stock has been absorbed, then add the remaining stock in the same way, waiting for each quantity of stock to be absorbed before adding more.

3 When the rice is half cooked, stir in the fontina cheese, and continue cooking and adding stock. Keep stirring the rice all the time.

4 When the risotto is creamy and the grains are tender but still have a bit of "bite," stir in the remaining butter and the Parmesan. Season, then remove the pan from the heat, cover and leave to rest for 3–4 minutes before serving.

Quick Risotto

This is rather a cheat's risotto as it defies all the rules that insist the stock is added gradually. Instead, the rice is cooked quickly in a conventional way, and the other ingredients are simply thrown in at the last minute. It tastes good for all that.

SERVES THREE TO FOUR

INGREDIENTS
1½ cups risotto rice
4 cups simmering chicken stock
1 cup mozzarella cheese, cut into
  small cubes
2 egg yolks
2 tablespoons freshly shredded
  Parmesan cheese
3 ounces cooked ham, cut into small
  cubes
2 tablespoons chopped fresh parsley
salt and freshly ground black pepper
fresh parsley sprigs, to garnish
freshly shredded Parmesan cheese,
  to serve

1 Put the rice in a pan. Pour in the stock, bring to a boil and then cover and simmer for about 18–20 minutes until the rice is tender.

2 Remove the pan from the heat and quickly stir in the mozzarella, egg yolks, Parmesan, ham and parsley. Season well with salt and pepper.

3 Cover the pan with a dish towel and leave to stand for 2–3 minutes to allow the cheese to melt, then stir again. Pile the risotto into warmed serving bowls and serve immediately, with extra Parmesan cheese.

PESTO RISOTTO

IF YOU BUY THE PESTO — AND THERE ARE SOME GOOD VARIETIES AVAILABLE NOWADAYS — THIS IS JUST ABOUT AS EASY AS A RISOTTO GETS.

SERVES THREE TO FOUR

INGREDIENTS
    2 tablespoons olive oil
    2 shallots, finely chopped
    1 garlic clove, crushed
    1½ cups risotto rice
    ¾ cup dry white wine
    4 cups simmering vegetable stock
    3 tablespoons pesto
    ⅓ cup freshly shredded Parmesan
        cheese, plus extra, to serve
        (optional)
    salt and freshly ground black pepper

1 Heat the olive oil in a pan and cook the shallots and garlic for 4–5 minutes until the shallots are soft but not browned.

2 Add the rice and cook over medium heat, stirring constantly, until the grains of rice are coated in oil and the outer part of the grain is translucent and the inner part opaque.

3 Pour in the wine. Cook, stirring, until all of it has been absorbed, then start adding the hot stock, a ladleful at a time, stirring constantly and waiting until each addition of stock has been absorbed before adding the next.

4 After about 20 minutes, when all the stock has been absorbed and the rice is creamy and tender, stir in the pesto and Parmesan. Taste and adjust seasoning and then cover and rest for 3–4 minutes. Spoon into a bowl and serve, with extra Parmesan, if desired.

PUMPKIN AND APPLE RISOTTO

PUMPKIN AND OTHER WINTER SQUASH ARE VERY POPULAR IN ITALY AND APPEAR IN MANY CLASSIC RECIPES. IF PUMPKINS ARE OUT OF SEASON, USE BUTTERNUT OR ONION SQUASH — THE FLAVORS WILL BE SLIGHTLY DIFFERENT, BUT THEY BOTH WORK WELL.

SERVES THREE TO FOUR

INGREDIENTS
    8 ounces butternut squash or
        pumpkin flesh
    1 cooking apple
    ½ cup water
    2 tablespoons butter
    1½ tablespoons olive oil
    1 onion, finely chopped
    1 garlic clove, crushed
    1½ cups risotto rice, such as
        Vialone Nano
    ¾ cup fruity white wine
    3¾–4 cups simmering vegetable
        stock
    1 cup freshly shredded Parmesan
        cheese
    salt and freshly ground black pepper

1 Cut the squash into small pieces. Peel, core and coarsely chop the apple. Place in a pan and pour in the water. Bring to a boil, then simmer for about 15–20 minutes until the squash is very tender. Drain, return the squash mixture to the pan and add half the butter. Mash the mixture coarsely with a fork to break up any large pieces, but leave the mixture chunky.

2 Heat the oil and remaining butter in a pan and cook the onion and garlic until the onion is soft. Add the rice. Cook, stirring constantly, over medium heat for 2 minutes until it is coated in oil and the grains are slightly translucent.

3 Add the wine and stir into the rice. When all the liquid has been absorbed, begin to add the stock a ladleful at a time, making sure each addition has been absorbed before adding the next. This should take about 20 minutes.

4 When about two ladlefuls of stock are left, add the squash and apple mixture together with another addition of stock. Continue to cook, stirring well and adding the rest of the stock, until the risotto is very creamy. Stir in the Parmesan cheese, adjust the seasoning and serve immediately.

ROSEMARY RISOTTO <u>WITH</u> BORLOTTI BEANS

*THIS IS A CLASSIC RISOTTO WITH A SUBTLE AND COMPLEX TASTE, FROM THE HEADY FLAVORS OF
ROSEMARY TO THE SAVORY BEANS AND THE FRUITY-SWEET FLAVORS OF MASCARPONE AND PARMESAN.*

<u>SERVES THREE TO FOUR</u>

INGREDIENTS
    14 ounce can borlotti beans
    2 tablespoons olive oil
    1 onion, chopped
    2 garlic cloves, crushed
    1½ cups risotto rice
    ¾ cup dry white wine
    3¾–4 cups simmering vegetable or
      chicken stock
    4 tablespoons mascarpone cheese
    scant 1 cup freshly shredded
      Parmesan cheese, plus extra,
      to serve (optional)
    1 teaspoon chopped fresh rosemary
    salt and freshly ground black pepper

1 Drain the beans, rinse under cold water and drain again. Purée about two-thirds of the beans fairly coarsely in a food processor or blender. Set the remaining beans aside.

2 Heat the olive oil in a large pan and gently cook the onion and garlic for 6–8 minutes until very soft. Add the rice and cook over medium heat for a few minutes, stirring constantly, until the grains are thoroughly coated in oil and are slightly translucent.

VARIATION
Fresh thyme or marjoram could be used for this risotto instead of rosemary, if preferred. One of the great virtues of risotto is that it lends itself well to variation—experiment with your recipes.

3 Pour in the wine. Cook over medium heat for 2–3 minutes, stirring all the time, until the wine has been absorbed. Add the stock gradually, a ladleful at a time, waiting for each quantity to be absorbed before adding more, and continuing to stir.

4 When the rice is three-quarters cooked, stir in the bean purée. Continue to cook the risotto, adding the remaining stock, until it is creamy and the rice is tender but still has a bit of "bite." Add the reserved beans, with the mascarpone, Parmesan and rosemary, then season to taste. Stir thoroughly, then cover and let stand for about 5 minutes so that the risotto absorbs the flavors fully and the rice completes cooking. Serve with extra Parmesan, if desired.

JERUSALEM ARTICHOKE RISOTTO

THIS IS A SIMPLE AND WARMING RISOTTO, WHICH BENEFITS FROM THE DELICIOUS AND DISTINCTIVE FLAVOR OF JERUSALEM ARTICHOKES.

SERVES THREE TO FOUR

INGREDIENTS

14 ounces Jerusalem artichokes
3 tablespoons butter
1 tablespoon olive oil
1 onion, finely chopped
1 garlic clove, crushed
1½ cups risotto rice
½ cup fruity white wine
4 cups simmering vegetable stock
2 teaspoons chopped fresh thyme
½ cup freshly shredded Parmesan
  cheese, plus extra, to serve
salt and freshly ground black pepper
fresh thyme sprigs, to garnish

1 Peel the artichokes, cut them into pieces and immediately add them to a pan of lightly salted water. Simmer them until tender, then drain and mash with 1 tablespoon of the butter. Add a little more salt, if needed.

2 Heat the oil and the remaining butter in a pan and cook the onion and garlic for 5–6 minutes until soft. Add the rice and cook over medium heat for about 2 minutes until the grains are translucent around the edges.

3 Pour in the wine, stir until it has been absorbed, then start adding the simmering stock, a ladleful at a time, making sure each quantity has been absorbed before adding more.

4 When you have just one last ladleful of stock to add, stir in the mashed artichokes and the chopped thyme. Season with salt and pepper. Continue cooking until the risotto is creamy and the artichokes are hot. Stir in the Parmesan. Remove from heat, cover the pan and let risotto stand for a few minutes. Spoon into a serving dish, garnish with thyme, and serve with Parmesan cheese.

DUCK RISOTTO

THIS MAKES AN EXCELLENT FIRST COURSE FOR SIX OR COULD BE SERVED FOR HALF THAT NUMBER AS A LUNCH DISH. ADD A GREEN SALAD, OR SERVE WITH SNOW PEAS AND SAUTEED RED BELL PEPPER SLICES.

SERVES THREE TO FOUR

INGREDIENTS
2 duck breasts
2 tablespoons brandy
2 tablespoons orange juice
1 tablespoon olive oil (optional)
1 onion, finely chopped
1 garlic clove, crushed
1½ cups risotto rice
4–5 cups simmering duck, turkey or
    chicken stock
1 teaspoon chopped fresh thyme
1 teaspoon chopped fresh mint
2 teaspoons shredded orange rind
½ cup freshly shredded Parmesan
    cheese
salt and freshly ground black pepper
strips of thinly pared orange rind,
    to garnish

1 Score the fatty side of the duck breasts and rub them with salt. Put them, fat side down, in a heavy skillet and dry fry over a medium heat for 6–8 minutes to render the fat. Transfer the breasts to a plate and then pull away and discard the fat. Cut the flesh into strips about ¾-inch wide.

2 Pour all but 1 tablespoon of the rendered duck fat from the pan into a cup, then reheat the fat in the pan. Cook the duck slices for 2–3 minutes over medium high heat until evenly brown but not overcooked. Add the brandy, heat to simmering point and then ignite, either by tilting the pan or using a taper. When the flames have died down, add the orange juice and season with salt and pepper. Remove from the heat and set aside.

3 In a pan, heat either 1 tablespoon of the remaining duck fat or use olive oil. Cook the onion and garlic over a gentle heat until the onion is soft but not browned. Add the rice and cook, stirring all the time, until the grains are coated in oil and have become slightly translucent around the edges.

4 Add the stock, a ladleful at a time, waiting for each quantity of stock to be absorbed completely before adding the next. Just before adding the final ladleful of stock, stir in the duck, with the thyme and mint. Continue cooking until the risotto is creamy and the rice is tender but still has a bit of "bite."

5 Add the orange rind and Parmesan. Taste and adjust the seasoning, then remove from heat, cover the pan and let stand for a few minutes. Serve on individual plates, garnished with the pared orange rind.

CHICKEN LIVER RISOTTO

THE COMBINATION OF CHICKEN LIVERS, BACON, PARSLEY AND THYME GIVES THIS RISOTTO A WONDERFULLY RICH FLAVOR. SERVE IT AS AN APPETIZER FOR FOUR OR A LUNCH FOR TWO OR THREE.

SERVES TWO TO FOUR

INGREDIENTS
    6 ounces chicken livers
    about 1 tablespoon olive oil
    about 2 tablespoons butter
    about 1½ ounces speck or 3 rindless
       lean bacon strips, finely chopped
    2 shallots, finely chopped
    1 garlic clove, crushed
    1 celery stalk, finely sliced
    1½ cups risotto rice
    ¾ cup dry white wine
    3¾–4 cups simmering chicken
       stock
    1 teaspoon chopped fresh thyme
    1 tablespoon chopped fresh
       parsley
salt and freshly ground black pepper
parsley and thyme sprigs to garnish

1 Clean the chicken livers carefully, removing any fat or membrane. Rinse well, pat dry with paper towels and cut into small, even pieces.

2 Heat the oil and butter in a skillet and cook the speck or bacon for 2–3 minutes. Add the shallots, garlic and celery and continue cooking for 3–4 minutes over a low heat until the vegetables are slightly softened. Increase the heat and add the chicken livers, stir-frying for a few minutes until they are brown all over.

3 Add the rice. Cook, stirring, for a few minutes, then pour over the wine. Allow to boil so that the alcohol is driven off. Stir frequently, taking care not to break up the chicken livers. When all the wine has been absorbed, add the hot stock, a ladleful at a time, stirring constantly.

4 About halfway through cooking, add the thyme and season with salt and pepper. Continue to add the stock as before, making sure that each quantity has been absorbed before adding more.

5 When the risotto is creamy and the rice is tender but still has a bit of "bite," stir in the parsley. Taste and adjust the seasoning. Remove the pan from the heat, cover and let rest for a few minutes before serving, garnished with parsley and thyme.

LEEK AND HAM RISOTTO

ANOTHER SIMPLE RISOTTO THAT MAKES AN EASY SUPPER, YET IS SPECIAL ENOUGH FOR A DINNER PARTY.

SERVES THREE TO FOUR

INGREDIENTS
  1½ teaspoons olive oil
  3 tablespoons butter
  2 leeks, cut in slices
  6 ounces prosciutto, torn into pieces
  generous 1 cup white mushrooms,
    sliced
  1½ cups risotto rice
  4 cups simmering chicken stock
  3 tablespoons chopped fresh Italian
    parsley
  ½ cup freshly shredded Parmesan
    cheese
  salt and freshly ground black pepper

1 Heat the oil and butter in a pan and cook the leeks until soft. Set aside a few strips of prosciutto for the garnish and add the rest to the pan. Cook for 1 minute, then add the mushrooms and stir-fry for 2–3 minutes until lightly browned.

2 Add the rice. Cook, stirring, for 1–2 minutes until the grains are evenly coated in oil and have become translucent around the edges. Add a ladleful of hot stock. Stir until this has been absorbed completely, then add the next ladleful. Continue in this way until all the stock has been absorbed.

3 When the risotto is creamy and the rice is tender but still has a bit of "bite," stir in the parsley and Parmesan. Adjust the seasoning, remove from the heat and cover. Allow to rest for a few minutes. Spoon into a bowl, garnish with the reserved prosciutto and serve.

RABBIT AND LEMONGRASS RISOTTO

THE LEMONGRASS ADDS A PLEASANT TANG TO THIS RISOTTO. IF RABBIT ISN'T AVAILABLE, USE CHICKEN OR TURKEY INSTEAD.

SERVES THREE TO FOUR

INGREDIENTS
  8 ounces rabbit meat or chicken
    breast fillet, cut into strips
  seasoned all-purpose flour
  ¼ cup butter
  1 tablespoon olive oil
  3 tablespoons dry sherry
  1 onion, finely chopped
  1 garlic clove, crushed
  1 lemongrass stalk, peeled and very
    finely sliced
  1½ cups risotto rice, preferably
    Carnaroli
  4 cups simmering chicken stock
  2 teaspoons chopped fresh thyme
  3 tablespoons heavy cream
  ⅓ cup freshly shredded Parmesan
    cheese
  salt and freshly ground black pepper

1 Coat the rabbit strips in the seasoned flour. Heat half the butter and oil in a skillet and cook the rabbit quickly until evenly browned. Add the sherry, and allow to boil briefly to burn off the alcohol. Season with salt and pepper to taste and set aside.

2 Heat the remaining oil and butter in a large pan and cook the onion and garlic over low heat for 4–5 minutes until the onion is soft. Add the lemongrass and cook for a few more minutes.

3 Add the rice and stir to coat in the oil. Add a ladleful of stock and cook, stirring, until the liquid has been absorbed. Continue adding the stock, stirring constantly. When the rice is almost cooked, stir in three-quarters of the rabbit strips, with the pan juices. Add the thyme and seasoning.

4 Continue cooking until the rice is tender but still has a "bite." Stir in the cream and Parmesan, remove from the heat and cover. Let rest before serving, garnished with rabbit strips.

APPLE AND LEMON RISOTTO WITH POACHED PLUMS

*ALTHOUGH IT'S ENTIRELY POSSIBLE TO COOK THIS BY THE CONVENTIONAL RISOTTO METHOD —
BY ADDING THE LIQUID SLOWLY — IT MAKES MORE SENSE TO COOK THE RICE WITH THE MILK,
IN THE SAME WAY AS FOR A TRADITIONAL ENGLISH RICE PUDDING.*

SERVES FOUR

INGREDIENTS
  1 stove cooking apple
  1 tablespoon butter
  scant 1 cup risotto rice
  2½ cups whole milk
  about ¼ cup sugar
  ¼ teaspoons ground cinnamon
  2 tablespoons lemon juice
  3 tablespoons heavy cream
  grated rind of 1 lemon,
    to decorate
For the poached plums
  ¼ cup light brown sugar
  scant 1 cup apple juice
  3 star anise
  cinnamon stick
  6 plums, halved and sliced

1 Peel and core the apple. Cut it into large chunks. Put these in a large, non-stick pan and add the butter. Heat gently until the butter melts.

2 Add the rice and milk and stir well. Bring to a boil over medium heat, then simmer very gently for 20–25 minutes, stirring occasionally.

COOK'S TIP
If the apple is very sharp (acidic) the milk may curdle. There is no need to worry about this – it won't affect the look or taste of the sauce.

3 To make the poached plums, dissolve the sugar in ⅔ cup apple juice in a pan. Add the spices and bring to a boil. Boil for 2 minutes. Add the plums and simmer for 2 minutes. Set aside until ready to serve.

4 Stir the sugar, cinnamon and lemon juice into the risotto. Cook for 2 minutes, stirring all the time, then stir in the cream. Taste and add more sugar, if necessary. Decorate with the lemon rind and serve with the poached plums.

CHOCOLATE RISOTTO

IF YOU'VE NEVER TASTED A SWEET RISOTTO, THERE'S A TREAT IN STORE. CHOCOLATE RISOTTO IS DELECTABLE, AND CHILDREN OF ALL AGES LOVE IT.

SERVES FOUR TO SIX

INGREDIENTS
   scant 1 cup risotto rice
   2½ cups whole milk
   3 ounces semi-sweet chocolate,
     broken into pieces
   2 tablespoons butter
   about ¼ cup sugar
   pinch of ground cinnamon
   4 tablespoons heavy cream
   fresh raspberries and chocolate
     caraque, to decorate
   chocolate sauce, to serve

3 Remove the pan from the heat and stir in the ground cinnamon and heavy cream. Cover the pan and let stand for a few minutes.

4 Spoon the risotto into individual dishes or dessert plates, and decorate with fresh raspberries and chocolate caraque. Serve with chocolate sauce.

1 Put the rice in a non-stick pan. Pour in the milk and bring to a boil over low to medium heat. Reduce the heat to the lowest setting and simmer very gently for about 20 minutes, stirring occasionally, until the rice is very soft.

2 Stir in the chocolate, butter and sugar. Cook, stirring all the time over very gentle heat for 1–2 minutes, until the chocolate has melted.

FRANCE

There are many wonderful rice recipes from France, which was quick to assimilate the variety of rice dishes discovered from colonial adventures abroad. Pilafs and rice stuffings have been favorites for years. More recently, the red rice from the Camargue region, with its unique nutty flavor, has become very popular.

PROVENÇAL FISH SOUP

THE RICE MAKES THIS A SUBSTANTIAL MAIN MEAL SOUP. BASMATI OR THAI RICE HAS THE BEST FLAVOR, BUT ANY LONG GRAIN RICE COULD BE USED. IF USING A QUICK-COOK RICE, COOK THE VEGETABLES FOR LONGER BEFORE ADDING THE RICE.

SERVES FOUR TO SIX

INGREDIENTS
1 pound fresh mussels
about 1 cup white wine
1½–2 pounds mixed white fish
    fillets such as monkfish, flounder
    or cod
6 large scallops
2 tablespoons olive oil
3 leeks, chopped
1 garlic clove, crushed
1 red bell pepper, seeded and cut
    into 1-inch pieces
1 yellow bell pepper, seeded and cut
    into 1-inch pieces
6 ounces fennel, cut into 1½-inch
    pieces
14 ounce can chopped tomatoes
about 5 cups well-flavored fish
    stock
generous pinch of saffron strands,
    soaked in 1 tablespoon hot water
scant 1 cup basmati rice, soaked
8 jumbo shrimp, shelled and
    deveined
salt and freshly ground black pepper
2–3 tablespoons fresh dill weed,
    to garnish
crusty bread, to serve (optional)

1 Clean the mussels, discarding any that do not close when tapped with a knife. Place them in a heavy-based pan. Add 6 tablespoons of the wine, cover, bring to a boil over a high heat and cook for about 3 minutes or until all the mussels have opened. Strain, reserving the liquid. Set aside half the mussels in their shells for the garnish; shell the rest and put them in a bowl. Discard any mussels that have not opened.

2 Cut the fish into 1-inch cubes. Detach the corals from the scallops and slice the white flesh into three or four pieces. Add the scallops to the fish and the corals to the mussels.

3 Heat the olive oil in a pan and cook the leeks and garlic for 3–4 minutes until soft. Add the bell peppers and fennel and cook for 2 minutes more.

4 Add the tomatoes, stock, saffron water, reserved mussel liquid and the remaining wine. Season well and cook for 5 minutes. Drain the rice, stir it into the mixture, cover and simmer for 10 minutes until it is just tender.

5 Carefully stir in the white fish and cook over low heat for 5 minutes. Add the shrimp, cook for 2 minutes then add the scallop corals and mussels and cook for 2–3 minutes more, until all the fish is tender. If the soup seems dry, add a little extra white wine or stock, or a little of both. Spoon into warmed soup dishes, top with the mussels in their shells and sprinkle with the dill weed. Serve with fresh crusty bread, if desired.

COOK'S TIP
To make your own fish stock, place about 1 pound white fish trimmings – bones, heads, but not gills – in a large pan. Add a chopped onion, carrot, bay leaf, parsley sprig, 6 peppercorns and a 2-inch piece of pared lemon rind. Pour in 5 cups water, bring to a boil, then simmer gently for 25–30 minutes. Strain through cheesecloth.

SALMON AND RICE GRATIN

THIS ALL-IN-ONE SUPPER DISH IS IDEAL FOR INFORMAL ENTERTAINING AS IT CAN BE MADE AHEAD OF TIME AND REHEATED FOR ABOUT HALF AN HOUR BEFORE BEING SERVED WITH A TOSSED SALAD.

SERVES SIX

INGREDIENTS
- 1½ pounds fresh salmon fillet, skinned
- 1 bay leaf
- a few parsley stems
- 4 cups water
- 2 cups basmati rice, soaked and drained
- 2–3 tablespoons chopped fresh parsley, plus extra to garnish
- 1½ cups Cheddar cheese, shredded
- 3 hard-cooked eggs, chopped
- salt and freshly ground black pepper

For the sauce
- 4 cups milk
- ⅓ cup all-purpose flour
- 3 tablespoons butter
- 1 teaspoon mild curry paste or French mustard

1 Put the salmon in a wide, shallow pan. Add the bay leaf and parsley stems, with salt and pepper. Pour in the water and bring to simmering point. Poach the fish for about 12 minutes until just tender.

2 Lift the fish out of the pan using a slotted spoon, then strain the liquid into a pan. Leave the fish to cool, then remove any visible bones and flake the flesh gently with a fork.

3 Add the rice to the pan containing the fish-poaching liquid. Bring to a boil, then lower heat, cover and simmer for 10 minutes without lifting the lid.

4 Remove the pan from the heat and, without lifting the lid, let the rice stand undisturbed for 5 minutes.

5 Meanwhile, make the sauce. Mix the milk, flour and butter in a pan. Bring to a boil over a low heat, beating constantly until the sauce is smooth and thick. Stir in the curry paste or mustard, with salt and pepper to taste. Simmer for 2 minutes.

6 Preheat the broiler. Remove the sauce from the heat and stir in the chopped parsley and rice, with half the cheese. Using a large metal spoon, fold in the flaked fish and eggs. Spoon into a shallow gratin dish and sprinkle with the rest of the cheese. Heat under the broiler until the topping is golden brown and bubbling. Serve in individual dishes, garnished with chopped parsley.

VARIATIONS
Shrimp could be substituted for the salmon, and other hard cheeses, such as Monterey Jack, could be used instead of the Cheddar.

RED RICE SALAD NIÇOISE

RED RICE, WITH ITS SWEET NUTTINESS, GOES WELL IN THIS CLASSIC SALAD. THE TUNA OR SWORDFISH COULD BE BARBECUED OR PAN-FRIED BUT TAKE CARE THAT IT DOES NOT OVERCOOK.

SERVES SIX

INGREDIENTS
  about 1½ pounds fresh tuna or
    swordfish, sliced into ¾-inch thick
    steaks
  1¾ cups Camargue red rice
  fish or vegetable stock or water
  1 pound green beans
  1 pound fava beans, shelled
  1 cos lettuce
  1 pound cherry tomatoes, halved
    unless very tiny
  2 tablespoons coarsely chopped
    cilantro
  3 hard-cooked eggs
  1½ cups pitted black olives
  olive oil, for brushing
For the marinade
  1 red onion, coarsely chopped
  2 garlic cloves
  ½ bunch fresh parsley
  ½ bunch cilantro
  2 teaspoons paprika
  3 tablespoons olive oil
  3 tablespoons water
  2 tablespoons white wine vinegar
  1 tablespoon fresh lime or lemon
    juice
  salt and freshly ground black pepper
For the dressing
  2 tablespoons fresh lime or lemon
    juice
  1 teaspoon Dijon mustard
  ½ garlic clove, crushed (optional)
  4 tablespoons olive oil
  4 tablespoons sunflower oil

COOK'S TIP
A good salad Niçoise is a feast for the eyes as well as the palate. Arrange the ingredients with care, either on a large serving dish or individual salad plates.

1 Make the marinade by mixing all the ingredients in a food processor and processing them for 30–40 seconds until the vegetables and herbs are finely chopped.

2 Prick the tuna or swordfish steaks all over with a fork, lay them side by side in a shallow dish and pour over the marinade, turning the fish to coat each piece. Cover with plastic wrap and leave in a cool place for 2–4 hours.

3 Cook the rice in stock or water, following the instructions on the packet, then drain, turn into a bowl and set aside.

4 Make the dressing. Mix the citrus juice, mustard and garlic (if using) in a bowl. Whisk in the oils, then add salt and freshly ground black pepper to taste. Stir 4 tablespoons of the dressing into the rice, then spoon the rice into the center of a large serving dish.

5 Cook the green beans and fava beans in boiling salted water until tender. Drain, refresh under cold water and drain again. Remove the outer shell from the fava beans and add them to the rice.

6 Discard the outer leaves from the lettuce and tear the inner leaves into pieces. Add to the salad with the tomatoes and cilantro. Shell the hard-cooked eggs and cut them into sixths. Preheat the broiler.

7 Arrange the tuna or swordfish steaks on a broiler pan. Brush with the marinade and a little extra olive oil. Cook for 3–4 minutes on each side, until the fish is tender and flakes easily when tested with the tip of a sharp knife. Brush with marinade and more olive oil when turning the fish over.

8 Allow the fish to cool a little, then break the steaks into large pieces. Toss into the salad with the olives and the remaining dressing. Garnish with the eggs and serve.

BEEF IN PASTRY WITH WILD MUSHROOMS AND RICE

A TASTY LAYER OF RICE AND JUICY WILD MUSHROOMS TOPS EACH BEEF TENDERLOIN BEFORE IT IS WRAPPED IN PUFF PASTRY. THIS COOKS TO CRISP AND FLAKY PERFECTION, THE PERFECT FOIL FOR THE FILLING.

SERVES FOUR

INGREDIENTS

   2¼ cup dried wild mushrooms,
     soaked for 10 minutes in warm
     water to cover
   1½–1¾ cups morel mushrooms
   about 3 tablespoons olive oil
   4 shallots, finely chopped
   1 garlic clove, crushed
   1½ tablespoons butter
   1½ cups cooked white long grain
     rice
   2 teaspoons chopped fresh marjoram
   1 tablespoon finely chopped fresh
     parsley
   10 ounces puff pastry, thawed if
     frozen
   4 beef tenderloins, each about
     3½ ounces and 1-inch thick
   2 teaspoons Dijon mustard
   1 egg, beaten with 1 tablespoon
     water
   salt and freshly ground black pepper
   roast potatoes and patty pan squash,
     to serve (optional)

1 Preheat the oven to 425ºF. Drain the dried mushrooms, reserving the liquid, and chop finely. Trim the morels and chop them.

2 Heat 1 tablespoon of the olive oil in a skillet and cook the shallots and garlic for 2–3 minutes until soft, stirring occasionally. Add the butter to the pan. When it begins to foam, add the mushrooms and cook for 3–4 minutes more, stirring occasionally.

3 Scrape the mixture into the bowl of rice and stir in the marjoram and parsley. Season to taste.

4 Cut the pastry into four and roll out each piece into a 7-inch circle. Trim the top and bottom edges.

5 Heat the remaining olive oil in the pan and cook the beef for about 30 seconds on each side until browned. Spread a little mustard over each tenderloin, then place on one side of a piece of pastry. Spoon a quarter of the mushroom and rice mixture on top of each tenderloin.

6 Fold the pastry over to make a pasty, sealing the join with a little of the egg wash. Repeat to make four pasties, then place them on an oiled baking sheet. Slit the top of each pasty, decorate with the pastry trimmings, and glaze with more egg wash. Bake in the oven for about 15 minutes, until the pastry is golden.

CHICKEN PILAF

THE FRENCH MARMITE POT IS IDEAL FOR THIS RECIPE. THE TALL SIDES SLANT INWARDS, REDUCING EVAPORATION AND ENSURING THAT THE RICE COOKS SLOWLY WITHOUT BECOMING DRY.

SERVES THREE TO FOUR

INGREDIENTS
    15–20 dried chanterelle mushrooms
    1–2 tablespoons olive oil
    1 tablespoon butter
    4 thin rindless smoked lean bacon
        strips, chopped
    3 skinless, boneless chicken breasts,
        cut into thin slices
    4 scallions, sliced
    generous 1 cup basmati rice,
        soaked
    scant 2 cups hot chicken stock
    salt and freshly ground black pepper

1 Preheat the oven to 350°F. Soak the mushrooms for 10 minutes in warm water. Drain, reserving the liquid. Slice the mushrooms, discarding the stems.

2 Heat the olive oil and butter in a skillet. Cook the bacon for 2–3 minutes. Add the chicken and stir-fry until the pieces are golden brown all over. Transfer the chicken and bacon mixture to a bowl using a slotted spoon.

3 Briefly cook the mushrooms and scallions in the fat remaining in the pan, then add them to the chicken pieces. Drain the rice and add it to the pan, with a little olive oil if necessary. Stir-fry for 2–3 minutes. Spoon the rice into an earthenware marmite pot or casserole.

4 Pour the hot chicken stock and reserved mushroom liquid over the rice in the marmite pot or casserole. Stir in the reserved chicken and mushroom mixture and season.

5 Cover with a double piece of foil and secure with a lid. Cook in the oven for 30–35 minutes until the rice is tender.

RED RICE AND ROASTED BELL PEPPER SALAD

BELL PEPPERS, SUN-DRIED TOMATOES AND GARLIC GIVE A DISTINCTLY MEDITERRANEAN FLAVOR TO THIS SALAD DISH. IT MAKES AN EXCELLENT SIDE DISH TO SPICY SAUSAGES OR FISH.

SERVES FOUR

INGREDIENTS
generous 1 cup Camargue red rice
vegetable or chicken stock or water
    (see method)
3 tablespoons olive oil
3 red bell peppers, seeded and sliced
    into strips
4–5 sun-dried tomatoes
4–5 whole garlic cloves, unpeeled
1 onion, chopped
2 tablespoons chopped fresh parsley,
    plus extra to garnish
1 tablespoon chopped cilantro
2 teaspoons balsamic vinegar
salt and freshly ground black pepper

1 Cook the rice in stock or water, following instructions on the packet. Heat the oil in a skillet and add the bell peppers. Cook over medium heat for 4 minutes, shaking occasionally.

2 Lower heat, add the sun-dried tomatoes, whole garlic cloves and onion, cover the pan and cook for 8–10 minutes more, stirring occasionally. Remove the lid and cook for 3 minutes more.

3 Off the heat, stir in the parsley, cilantro and vinegar, and season. Spread the rice out on a serving dish and spoon the bell pepper mixture on top. Peel the whole garlic cloves, cut the flesh into slices and sprinkle these over the salad. Serve at room temperature, garnished with more fresh parsley.

CREAMY FISH PILAU

THIS DISH IS INSPIRED BY A FUSION OF CUISINES – THE METHOD COMES FROM INDIA AND USES THAT COUNTRY'S FAVORITE RICE, BASMATI, BUT THE DELICIOUS WINE AND CREAM SAUCE IS VERY MUCH FRENCH IN FLAVOR.

SERVES FOUR TO SIX

INGREDIENTS
1 pound fresh mussels, scrubbed
1½ cups white wine
fresh parsley sprig
about 1½ pounds salmon
8 ounces scallops
about 1 tablespoon olive oil
3 tablespoons butter
2 shallots, finely chopped
3 cups white mushrooms, halved
    if large
1½ cups basmati rice, soaked
1¼ cups fish stock
⅔ cup heavy cream
1 tablespoon chopped fresh parsley
8 ounces large cooked shrimp,
    shelled and deveined
salt and freshly ground black pepper
fresh Italian parsley sprigs,
    to garnish

1 Preheat the oven to 325ºF. Place the mussels in a pan with 6 tablespoons of the wine and parsley, cover and cook for 4–5 minutes until they have opened. Drain, reserving the cooking liquid. Remove the mussels from their shells, discarding any that have not opened.

2 Cut the fish into bite-size pieces. Detach the corals from the scallops and cut the white scallop flesh into thick pieces.

3 Heat half the olive oil and butter and cook the shallots and mushrooms for 3–4 minutes. Transfer to a large bowl. Heat the remaining oil in the skillet and fry the rice for 2–3 minutes, stirring until it is coated in oil. Spoon the rice into a deep casserole.

4 Pour the stock, remaining wine and reserved mussel liquid into the skillet, and bring to a boil. Off the heat, stir in the cream and parsley; season lightly. Pour over the rice and then add the salmon and the scallop flesh, together with the mushroom mixture. Stir carefully to mix.

5 Cover the casserole tightly. Bake for 30–35 minutes, then add the corals, replace the cover and cook for 4 minutes more. Add the mussels and shrimp, cover and cook for 3–4 minutes until the seafood is heated through and the rice is tender. Serve garnished with the parsley sprigs.

ZUCCHINI ROULADE

THIS MAKES A REALLY IMPRESSIVE BUFFET SUPPER OR DINNER-PARTY DISH, OR CAN BE WRAPPED AND SERVED CHILLED AS THE PIÈCE DE RÉSISTANCE AT A PICNIC.

5 Bake for 10–15 minutes until the roulade is firm and lightly golden on top. Carefully turn it out onto a sheet of waxed or baking parchment sprinkled with 2 tablespoons shredded Parmesan. Peel away the lining paper. Roll the roulade up, using the paper as a guide, and let cool.

6 To make the filling, mix the goat cheese, ricotta cheese, rice and herbs in a bowl. Season with salt and pepper. Heat the olive oil and butter in a small pan and cook the mushrooms until soft.

7 Unwrap the roulade, spread with the rice filling and lay the mushrooms along the center. Roll up again. The roulade can be served warm or chilled. To heat, place on a baking sheet, cover with foil and heat for 15–20 minutes in a moderately hot oven. To eat cold, wrap in plastic wrap and chill in the fridge. Serve with a herb and green leaf salad.

SERVES SIX

INGREDIENTS
 3 tablespoons butter
 ½ cup all-purpose flour
 1¼ cups milk
 4 eggs, separated
 3 zucchini, shredded
 ⅓ cup freshly shredded Parmesan
  cheese
 salt and freshly ground black pepper
 herb and green leaf salad, to serve
For the filling
 ⅔ cup soft goat cheese
 4 tablespoons ricotta cheese
 2 cups cooked rice, such as
  Thai fragrant rice or Japanese
  short grain
 1 tablespoon chopped mixed fresh
  herbs
 1 tablespoon olive oil
 1 tablespoon butter
 generous 1 cup white mushrooms,
  very finely chopped

1 Preheat the oven to 400°F. Line a 13 x 9-inch jelly roll pan with baking parchment.

2 Melt the butter in a pan, stir in the flour and cook for 1–2 minutes, stirring all the time. Gradually add the milk, stirring until the mixture forms a smooth sauce. Remove from the heat and cool for a few minutes.

3 Stir the egg yolks into the sauce, one at a time, and then add the shredded zucchini and the Parmesan, and check the seasoning.

4 Beat the egg whites until stiff, fold them into the zucchini mixture and scrape into the prepared pan. Spread evenly, smoothing the surface with a metal spatula.

PROVENÇAL RICE

ONE OF THE GLORIOUS THINGS ABOUT FOOD FROM THE SOUTH OF FRANCE IS ITS COLOR, AND THIS DISH IS NO EXCEPTION. TO SERVE AS A MAIN COURSE, ALLOW 1/4 CUP RICE PER PERSON.

SERVES FOUR

INGREDIENTS

   2 onions
   6 tablespoons olive oil
   scant 1 cup brown long grain
      rice
   2 teaspoons mustard seeds
   2 cups vegetable stock
   1 large or 2 small red bell peppers,
      seeded and cut into chunks
   1 small eggplant, cut into cubes
   2–3 zucchini, sliced
   about 12 cherry tomatoes
   5–6 fresh basil leaves, torn into
      pieces
   2 garlic cloves, finely chopped
   4 tablespoons white wine
   4 tablespoons passata or tomato
      juice
   2 hard-cooked eggs, cut into wedges
   8 stuffed green olives, sliced
   1 tablespoon capers
   3 drained sun-dried tomatoes in oil,
      sliced (optional)
   butter
   sea salt and freshly ground black
      pepper

1 Preheat the oven to 400°F. Finely chop one onion. Heat 2 tablespoons of the oil in a pan and cook the chopped onion over a gentle heat for 5–6 minutes until softened.

2 Add the rice and mustard seeds. Cook, stirring, for 2 minutes, then add the stock and a little salt. Bring to a boil, then lower heat, cover and simmer for 35 minutes until the rice is tender.

3 Meanwhile, cut the remaining onion into wedges. Put these in a roasting pan with the bell peppers, eggplant, zucchini and cherry tomatoes. Scatter over the torn basil leaves and chopped garlic. Pour over the remaining olive oil and sprinkle with sea salt and black pepper. Roast for 15–20 minutes until the vegetables begin to char, stirring halfway through cooking. Reduce the oven temperature to 350°F.

4 Spoon the rice into an earthenware casserole. Put the roasted vegetables on top, together with any vegetable juices from the roasting pan, then pour over the wine and passata.

5 Arrange the egg wedges on top of the vegetables, with the sliced olives, capers and sun-dried tomatoes, if using. Dot with butter, cover and cook for 15–20 minutes until heated through.

VEGETABLE TARTE TATIN

THIS UPSIDE-DOWN TART COMBINES MEDITERRANEAN VEGETABLES WITH A MEDLEY OF RICE, GARLIC, ONIONS AND OLIVES.

SERVES FOUR AS AN APPETIZER

INGREDIENTS
 2 tablespoons sunflower oil
 about 1½ tablespoons olive oil
 1 eggplant, sliced lengthwise
 1 large red bell pepper, seeded and
  cut into long strips
 5 tomatoes
 2 red shallots, finely chopped
 1–2 garlic cloves, crushed
 ⅔ cup white wine
 2 teaspoons chopped fresh basil
 2 cups cooked white or brown long
  grain rice
 ⅔ cup pitted black olives, chopped
 12 ounces puff pastry, thawed if
  frozen
 freshly ground black pepper

VARIATION
Zucchini and mushrooms could be used as well, or instead of, the eggplant and bell peppers, or use strips of lightly browned chicken breast and serve for two as a light lunch.

1 Preheat the oven to 375°F. Heat the sunflower oil with 1 tablespoon of the olive oil in a skillet and cook the eggplant slices for 4–5 minutes on each side until golden brown. Lift out and drain on paper towels.

2 Add the bell pepper strips to the oil remaining in the pan, turning them to coat. Cover the pan with a lid and sweat the bell peppers over a moderately high heat for 5–6 minutes, stirring occasionally, until the bell pepper strips are soft and flecked with brown.

3 Slice two of the tomatoes and set them aside. Plunge the remaining tomatoes briefly into boiling water, then peel them, cut them into quarters and remove the core and seeds. Chop them coarsely.

4 Heat the remaining oil in the skillet and cook the shallots and garlic for 3–4 minutes until softened. Add the chopped tomatoes and cook for a few minutes until softened. Stir in the wine and basil, with black pepper to taste. Bring to a boil, then remove from heat and stir in the cooked rice and black olives.

5 Arrange the tomato slices, eggplant slices and peppers in a single layer over the bottom of a heavy, 12-inch, shallow ovenproof dish. Spread the rice mixture on top.

6 Roll out the pastry to a circle slightly larger than the diameter of the dish and place on top of the rice, tucking the overlap down inside the dish.

7 Bake for 25–30 minutes, until the pastry is golden and risen. Cool slightly, then invert the tart onto a large, warmed serving plate. Serve in slices, with a leafy green salad or simply dressed corn salad.

COOK'S TIP
This vegetable tart would make a lovely lunch or supper dish for two people. Serve it hot with buttered new potatoes and a green vegetable, such as snow peas or French Beans.

SOUFFLEED RICE DESSERT

USING LOW-FAT MILK TO MAKE THIS DESSERT IS A HEALTHY OPTION, BUT YOU COULD USE WHOLE MILK IF YOU PREFER A CREAMIER TASTE.

SERVES FOUR

INGREDIENTS
⅓ cup short grain dessert rice
3 tablespoons honey
3 cups low-fat milk
1 vanilla pod or ½ teaspoon vanilla
   extract
butter, for greasing
2 egg whites
1 teaspoon freshly shredded
   nutmeg
wafer biscuits, to serve (optional)

1 Place the rice, honey and milk in a heavy or non-stick pan, and bring the milk to just below boiling point, watching it closely to prevent it from boiling over. Add the vanilla pod, if using.

2 Reduce the heat to lowest setting and cover the pan. Let cook for about 1–1¼ hours, stirring occasionally to prevent sticking, until most of the liquid has been absorbed.

3 Remove the vanilla pod or, if using vanilla extract, add this to the rice mixture now. Preheat the oven to 425°F. Grease a 4 cup baking dish with butter.

4 Place the egg whites in a large grease-free bowl and beat them until they hold soft peaks. Using either a large metal spoon or a spatula, carefully fold the egg whites evenly into the rice and milk mixture. Turn into the baking dish.

5 Sprinkle with nutmeg and bake in the oven for about 15–20 minutes, until the rice dessert has puffed and the surface is golden brown. Serve the dessert hot, with wafer biscuits, if desired.

COOK'S TIP
This dessert is delicious topped with a stewed, dried fruit salad.

PEAR, ALMOND <u>AND</u> GROUND RICE DESSERT

GROUND RICE GIVES A DISTINCTIVE, SLIGHTLY GRAINY TEXTURE TO DESSERTS THAT GOES PARTICULARLY WELL WITH FALL FRUIT. PEARS AND ALMONDS ARE A DIVINE COMBINATION.

2 Combine the butter and sugar until light and fluffy, then beat in the eggs and almond extract. Fold in the flour and ground rice.

3 Carefully spoon the almond-flavored egg and ground rice mixture over the quartered pears and level the surface with a metal spatula.

SERVES SIX

INGREDIENTS
    4 ripe pears
    2 tablespoons brown sugar
    ½ cup unsalted butter
    generous ½ cup superfine sugar
    2 eggs
    a few drops of almond extract
    ⅔ cup self-rising flour
    ⅓ cup ground rice
    ¼ cup slivered almonds
    custard or crème fraîche, to serve
        (optional)

1 Preheat the oven to 350°F. Grease a shallow 10-inch tart dish. Peel and quarter the pears and arrange them in the tart dish. Sprinkle with the brown sugar.

4 Sprinkle the top with the slivered almonds, then bake the dessert for 30–35 minutes until the topping is golden. Serve with custard or crème fraîche.

CAJUN, CREOLE AND LATIN AMERICA

Rice is grown in all parts of Louisiana, in the south of the United States, and across the border in Central and South America and Mexico. The rice dishes from these regions use of a wealth of ingredients, and many are world classics — jambalayas and gumbos from Cajun country, tortillas from Mexico and a rice casserole from Brazil.

LOUISIANA RICE

EGGPLANT AND PORK COMBINE WITH HERBS AND SPICES TO MAKE A HIGHLY FLAVORSOME DISH.

SERVES FOUR

INGREDIENTS

4 tablespoons vegetable oil
1 onion, chopped
1 small eggplant, diced
8 ounces ground pork
1 green bell pepper, seeded and
  chopped
2 celery stalks, chopped
1 garlic clove, crushed
1 teaspoon cayenne pepper
1 teaspoon paprika
1 teaspoon freshly ground black
  pepper
½ teaspoon salt
1 teaspoon dried thyme
½ teaspoon dried oregano
2 cups chicken stock
8 ounces chicken livers, chopped
¾ cup white long grain rice
1 bay leaf
3 tablespoons chopped fresh parsley

1 Heat the oil in a skillet. When it is piping hot, add the onion and eggplant and stir-fry for about 5 minutes.

2 Add the pork and cook for 6–8 minutes until browned, using a wooden spoon to break up any lumps.

3 Stir in the green bell pepper, celery and garlic, with all the spices and herbs. Cover and cook over high heat for 5–6 minutes, stirring frequently from the bottom of the pan to scrape up and distribute the crispy brown bits.

4 Pour in the chicken stock and stir to remove any sediment from the bottom of the pan. Cover and cook for 6 minutes over moderate heat. Stir in the chicken livers and cook for 2 minutes more.

5 Stir in the rice and add the bay leaf. Lower heat, cover and simmer for 6–7 minutes. Turn off the heat and let stand, still covered, for 10–15 minutes more until the rice is tender. Remove the bay leaf and stir in the chopped parsley. Serve the rice hot.

DIRTY RICE

CONTRARY TO POPULAR BELIEF, THIS DISH DOESN'T GET ITS NAME FROM ITS APPEARANCE, BUT FROM ITS ASSOCIATION WITH NEW ORLEANS, THE HOME OF JAZZ, WHICH HAS OFTEN BEEN REFERRED TO AS "DIRTY MUSIC."

<u>SERVES FOUR</u>

INGREDIENTS
4 tablespoons vegetable oil
¼ cup all-purpose flour
4 tablespoons butter
1 large onion, chopped
2 garlic cloves, crushed
7 ounces ground pork
8 ounces chicken livers, trimmed and
  finely chopped
dash of Tabasco sauce
1 green bell pepper, seeded and sliced
2 celery stalks, sliced
1¼ cups chicken stock
generous 1 cup cooked white long
  grain rice
4 scallions, chopped
3 tablespoons chopped fresh parsley
salt and freshly ground black pepper
celery leaves, to garnish

1 Heat half the oil in a heavy-based pan. Stir in the flour and cook over low heat, stirring constantly, until the roux is smooth and the color is a rich chestnut-brown. Immediately remove the pan from the heat and place it on a cold surface such as the draining board of a sink.

2 Heat the remaining oil with the butter in a skillet and stir-fry the onion for 5 minutes.

3 Add the garlic and pork. Cook for about 5 minutes, breaking up the pork and stirring until it is evenly browned, then stir in the chicken livers and cook for 2–3 minutes until they have changed color all over. Season with salt, pepper and Tabasco sauce. Stir in the green bell pepper and celery.

4 Stir the roux into the stir-fried mixture, then gradually add in the stock. When the mixture begins to bubble, cover and cook for 30 minutes, stirring occasionally. Stir in the rice, scallions and parsley. Toss over the heat until the rice has heated through. Serve garnished with celery leaves.

LOUISIANA SEAFOOD GUMBO

GUMBO IS A SOUP, BUT IS SERVED OVER RICE AS A MAIN COURSE. IN LOUISIANA, OYSTERS ARE CHEAP AND PROLIFIC, AND WOULD BE USED HERE INSTEAD OF MUSSELS.

SERVES SIX

INGREDIENTS

1 pound fresh mussels
1 pound shrimp, in the shell
1 cooked crab, about 2¼ pounds
small bunch of parsley, leaves
  chopped and stalks reserved
⅔ cup vegetable oil
1 cup all-purpose flour
1 green bell pepper, seeded and
  chopped
1 large onion, chopped
2 celery stalks, sliced
3 garlic cloves, finely chopped
3 ounces smoked spiced sausage,
  skinned and sliced
1½ cups white long grain rice
6 scallions, shredded
cayenne pepper, to taste
Tabasco sauce, to taste
salt

3 Peel the shrimp and set them aside, reserving a few for the garnish. Put the shells and heads into the pan.

4 Remove all the meat from the crab, separating the brown and white meat. Add all the pieces of shell to the pan with 2 teaspoons salt.

6 Heat the oil in a heavy-based pan and stir in the flour. Stir constantly over medium heat with a wooden spoon or beater until the roux reaches a golden-brown color. Immediately add the bell pepper, onion, celery and garlic. Continue cooking for about 3 minutes until the onion is soft. Stir in the sausage. Reheat the stock.

7 Stir the brown crab meat into the roux, then ladle in the hot stock a little at a time, stirring constantly until it has all been smoothly incorporated. Bring to a low boil, partially cover the pan, then simmer the gumbo for 30 minutes.

8 Meanwhile, cook the rice in plenty of lightly salted boiling water until the grains are tender.

9 Add the shrimp, mussels, white crab meat and scallions to the gumbo. Return to a boil and season with salt, if necessary, cayenne and a dash or two of Tabasco sauce. Simmer for a further minute, then add the chopped parsley leaves. Serve immediately, ladling the soup over the hot rice in soup plates.

1 Wash the mussels in several changes of cold water, pulling away the black "beards." Discard any mussels that are broken and do not close when you tap them firmly.

2 Bring 1 cup water to a boil in a deep pan. Add the mussels, cover the pan tightly and cook over high heat, shaking frequently, for 3 minutes. As the mussels open, lift them out with tongs into a strainer set over a bowl. Discard any that fail to open. Shell the mussels, discarding the shells. Return the liquid from the bowl to the pan and make the quantity up to 8 cups with water.

5 Bring the shellfish stock to a boil, skimming it regularly. When there is no more froth on the surface, add the parsley stalks and simmer for 15 minutes. Cool the stock, then strain it into a measuring cup and make up to 8 cups with water.

COOK'S TIP

It is vital to stir constantly to darken the roux without burning. Should black specks occur at any stage of cooking, discard the roux and start again. Have the onion, green bell pepper and celery ready to add to the roux the minute it reaches the correct golden-brown stage, as this arrests its darkening.

CHICKEN AND SHRIMP JAMBALAYA

THE MIXTURE OF CHICKEN, SEAFOOD AND RICE SUGGESTS A CLOSE RELATIONSHIP TO THE SPANISH PAELLA, BUT THE NAME IS MORE LIKELY TO HAVE DERIVED FROM JAMBON (THE FRENCH FOR HAM), À LA YA (CREOLE FOR RICE). JAMBALAYAS ARE A COLORFUL MIXTURE OF HIGHLY FLAVORED INGREDIENTS, AND ARE ALWAYS MADE IN LARGE QUANTITIES FOR FEASTS AND CELEBRATION MEALS.

SERVES TEN

INGREDIENTS
2 chickens, each about 3–3½ pounds
1 pound piece raw smoked cured ham
4 tablespoons shortening or bacon fat
½ cup all-purpose flour
3 medium onions, finely sliced
2 green bell peppers, seeded and sliced
1½ pounds tomatoes, peeled and
  chopped
2–3 garlic cloves, crushed
2 teaspoons chopped fresh thyme or
  1 teaspoon dried thyme
24 jumbo shrimp, shelled and
  deveined
3 cups white long grain rice
5 cups water
2–3 dashes Tabasco sauce
3 tablespoons chopped fresh Italian
  parsley, plus tiny fresh parsley
  sprigs, to garnish
salt and freshly ground black pepper

4 Add the diced cured ham, onions, green bell peppers, tomatoes, garlic and thyme. Cook, stirring regularly, for 10 minutes, then add the shrimp and mix lightly.

5 Stir the rice into the pan and pour in the water. Season with salt, pepper and Tabasco sauce. Bring to a boil, then cook gently until the rice is tender and all the liquid has been absorbed. Add a little extra boiling water if the rice looks like drying out before it is cooked.

6 Mix the parsley into the finished dish, garnish with tiny sprigs of Italian parsley and serve immediately.

1 Cut each chicken into 10 pieces and season with salt and pepper.Dice the cured ham, discarding the rind and fat.

2 Melt the shortening or bacon fat in a large, heavy-based skillet. Add the chicken pieces in batches, brown them all over, then lift them out with a slotted spoon and set them aside.

3 Reduce the heat. Sprinkle the flour into the fat in the pan and stir until the roux turns golden brown. Return the chicken pieces to the pan.

BRAZILIAN PORK AND RICE CASSEROLE

WE TEND TO ASSOCIATE BRAZIL WITH BEEF, BUT THERE ARE ALSO SOME EXCELLENT PORK RECIPES, INCLUDING THIS HEARTY DISH OF MARINATED PORK, VEGETABLES AND RICE.

SERVES FOUR TO SIX

INGREDIENTS
   1¼ pounds lean pork, such as
      tenderloin, cut into strips
   4 tablespoons corn oil
   1 onion, chopped
   1 garlic clove, crushed
   1 green bell pepper, cut into
      pieces
   about 1¼ cups chicken stock
   generous 1 cup white long grain
      rice
   ⅔ cup heavy cream
   ½ cup freshly shredded Parmesan
      cheese
   salt and freshly ground black pepper
For the marinade
   ½ cup dry white wine
   2 tablespoons lemon juice
   1 onion, chopped
   4 juniper berries, lightly crushed
   3 cloves
   1 fresh red chili, seeded and finely
      sliced

1 Mix all the marinade ingredients, add the pork and set aside to marinate for 3–4 hours, turning occasionally. Transfer the pork to a plate and pat dry. Strain the marinade and set aside.

2 Heat the oil in a heavy-based pan and cook the pork for a few minutes until evenly brown. Transfer to a plate using a slotted spoon.

3 Add the chopped onion and the garlic to the pan and cook for 3–4 minutes. Stir in the bell pepper, cook for 3–4 minutes more, then return the pork to the pan. Pour in the reserved marinade and the stock. Bring to a boil and season with salt and fresh black pepper, then lower heat, cover and simmer gently for 10 minutes until the meat is nearly tender.

4 Preheat the oven to 325°F. Cook the rice in plenty of lightly salted boiling water for 8 minutes or until three-quarters cooked. Drain well. Spread half the rice over the bottom of a buttered, oval baking dish. Using a slotted spoon, make a neat layer of meat and vegetables on top, then spread over the remaining rice.

5 Stir the cream and 2 tablespoons of the Parmesan into the liquid in which the pork was cooked. Tip into a measuring cup. Pour the cream mixture over the rice and sprinkle with the remaining Parmesan cheese. Cover with foil and bake for 20 minutes, then remove the foil and cook for 5 minutes more, until the top is lightly brown.

CHICKEN FAJITAS

FAJITAS ARE WARMED SOFT TORTILLAS, FILLED AND FOLDED LIKE AN ENVELOPE. THEY ARE TRADITIONAL MEXICAN FAST FOOD, DELICIOUS AND EASY TO PREPARE, AND A FAVORITE FOR SUPPER.

SERVES FOUR

INGREDIENTS
  generous ½ cup white long grain rice
  3 tablespoons wild rice
  1 tablespoon olive oil
  1 tablespoon sunflower oil
  1 onion, cut into thin wedges
  4 skinless, boneless chicken breasts, cut into thin strips
  1 red bell pepper, seeded and finely sliced
  1 teaspoon ground cumin
  generous pinch of cayenne pepper
  ½ teaspoon ground turmeric
  ¾ cup passata
  ½–¾ cup chicken stock
  12 small or 8 large wheat tortillas, warmed
  sour cream, to serve
For the salsa
  1 shallot, coarsely chopped
  1 small garlic clove
  ½–1 fresh green chili, seeded and coarsely chopped
  small bunch of fresh parsley
  5 tomatoes, peeled, seeded and chopped
  2 teaspoons olive oil
  1 tablespoon lemon juice
  2 tablespoons tomato juice
  salt and freshly ground black pepper
For the guacamole
  1 large ripe avocado
  2 scallions, chopped
  1–2 tablespoons fresh lime or lemon juice
  generous pinch of cayenne pepper
  1 tablespoon chopped cilantro

COOK'S TIP
To warm the tortillas, either wrap them in foil and place them in a warm oven for 5 minutes, or wrap 4 or 5 at a time in plastic wrap and microwave for 20 seconds on 100% Full Power.

1 Cook the long grain and wild rice separately, following the instructions on the packets. Drain and set aside.

2 Make the salsa. Finely chop the shallot, garlic, chili and parsley in a blender or food processor. Spoon into a bowl. Stir in the chopped tomatoes, olive oil, lemon juice and tomato juice. Season to taste with salt and pepper. Cover with plastic wrap and chill.

3 Make the guacamole. Scoop the avocado flesh into a bowl. Mash it lightly with the scallions, citrus juice, cayenne, cilantro and seasoning, so that small pieces still remain. Cover the surface closely with plastic wrap and chill.

4 Heat the olive and sunflower oils in a skillet and cook the onion wedges for 4–5 minutes until softened. Add the chicken strips and red bell pepper slices and cook until evenly browned.

5 Stir in the cumin, cayenne and turmeric. Cook, stirring, for about 1 minute, then stir in the passata and chicken stock. Bring to a boil, then lower the heat and simmer gently for 5–6 minutes until the chicken is cooked through. Season to taste.

6 Stir both types of rice into the chicken and cook for 1–2 minutes until the rice is warmed through. Spoon a little of the chicken and rice mixture on to each warmed tortilla. Top with salsa, guacamole and sour cream and roll up. Alternatively, let everyone assemble their own fajita at the table.

VARIATION
Fajitas are very popular family fare, so don't be surprised if there are demands for this dish time and time again. To ring the changes, use brown long grain rice and red Camargue rice instead of the white rice and wild rice, and try pork fillet or beef steak in place of chicken.

MEXICAN SPICY BEEF TORTILLA

THIS DISH IS NOT UNLIKE A LASAGNE, EXCEPT THAT THE SPICY MEAT IS MIXED WITH RICE AND IS LAYERED BETWEEN MEXICAN TORTILLAS, WITH A HOT SALSA SAUCE FOR AN EXTRA KICK.

SERVES FOUR

INGREDIENTS
    1 onion, chopped
    2 garlic cloves, crushed
    1 fresh red chili, seeded and
        sliced
    12 ounces rump steak, cut into
        small cubes
    1 tablespoon oil
    2 cups cooked long grain rice
    beef stock, to moisten
    3 large wheat tortillas
For the salsa picante
    2 x 14 ounce cans chopped
        tomatoes
    2 garlic cloves, halved
    1 onion, quartered
    1–2 fresh red chilies, seeded and
        coarsely chopped
    1 teaspoon ground cumin
    ½–1 teaspoon cayenne pepper
    1 teaspoon fresh oregano or
        ½ teaspoon dried oregano
    tomato juice or water, if required
For the cheese sauce
    4 tablespoons butter
    ½ cup all-purpose flour
    2½ cups milk
    1 cup shredded Cheddar cheese
    salt and freshly ground black pepper

1 Preheat the oven to 350°F. Make the salsa picante. Place the tomatoes, garlic, onion and chilies in a blender or food processor and process until smooth. Pour into a small pan, add the spices and oregano and season with salt. Gradually bring to a boil, stirring. Boil for 1–2 minutes, then lower heat, cover and simmer for 15 minutes. The sauce should be thick, but of a pouring consistency. If it is too thick, dilute it with tomato juice or water.

2 Make the cheese sauce. Melt the butter in a pan and stir in the flour. Cook for 1 minute. Add the milk gradually, stirring, until the sauce boils and thickens. Stir all but 2 tablespoons of the cheese and season with salt and pepper. Cover closely and set aside.

3 Mix the onion, garlic and chili in a bowl. Add the steak cubes and mix well. Heat the oil in a skillet and stir-fry the meat mixture for 10 minutes until the meat cubes have browned and the onion is soft. Stir in the cooked rice and enough beef stock to moisten. Season to taste with salt and freshly ground black pepper.

4 Pour about a quarter of the cheese sauce into the bottom of a round ovenproof dish. Add a tortilla and then spread over half the salsa followed by half the meat mixture.

5 Repeat these layers, then add half the remaining cheese sauce and the final tortilla. Pour over the remaining cheese sauce and sprinkle the reserved cheese on top. Bake in the oven for 15–20 minutes until golden on top.

COOK'S TIP
You can use any type of beef for this dish. If chuck steak is used, it should be very finely chopped or even ground, and the bake should be cooked for an extra 10–15 minutes.

TOMATO RICE

PROOF POSITIVE THAT YOU DON'T NEED ELABORATE INGREDIENTS OR COMPLICATED COOKING
METHODS TO MAKE A DELICIOUS DISH.

SERVES FOUR

INGREDIENTS
2 tablespoons sunflower oil
½ teaspoon onion seeds
1 onion, sliced
2 tomatoes, chopped
1 orange or yellow bell pepper,
  seeded and sliced
1 teaspoon crushed fresh ginger root
1 garlic clove, crushed
1 teaspoon chili powder
1 potato, diced
1½ teaspoons salt
2 cups basmati rice, soaked
3 cups water
2–3 tablespoons chopped cilantro

1 Heat the oil and cook the onion seeds for about 30 seconds. Add the sliced onion and cook for about 5 minutes.

2 Stir in the tomatoes, bell pepper, ginger, garlic, chili powder, potato and salt. Stir-fry over medium heat for about 5 minutes more.

3 Drain the rice and add to the pan, then stir for about 1 minute until the grains are well coated.

4 Pour in the water and bring the rice to a boil, then lower the heat, cover the pan and cook the rice for 12–15 minutes. Remove from heat, without lifting the lid, and let stand for about 5 minutes. Stir in the chopped cilantro and serve.

PERUVIAN DUCK WITH RICE

THIS IS A VERY RICH DISH, BRIGHTLY COLORED WITH SPANISH TOMATOES AND FRESH HERBS.

SERVES FOUR TO SIX

INGREDIENTS
4 boned duck breasts
1 Spanish onion, chopped
2 garlic cloves, crushed
2 teaspoons shredded fresh ginger
  root
4 tomatoes (peeled, if desired),
  chopped
8 ounces Kabocha or onion squash,
  cut into ½-inch cubes
1½ cups long grain rice
3 cups chicken stock
1 tablespoon finely chopped
  cilantro
1 tablespoon finely chopped fresh
  mint
salt and freshly ground black
  pepper

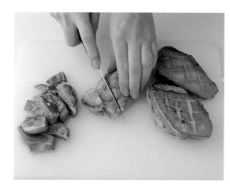

2 Pour all but 1 tablespoon of the fat into a cup, then fry the breasts, meat side down, in the fat remaining in the pan for 3–4 minutes until brown all over. Transfer to a board, slice thickly and set aside in a shallow dish. Deglaze the pan with a little water and pour this liquid over the duck.

4 Add the squash, stir-fry for a few minutes, then cover and allow to steam for about 4 minutes.

1 Heat a heavy skillet or flameproof casserole. Using a sharp knife, score the fatty side of the duck breasts in a criss-cross pattern, rub the fat with a little salt, then dry fry the duck, skin side down, for 6–8 minutes to render some of the fat.

3 Cook the onion and garlic in the same pan for 4–5 minutes until the onion is fairly soft, adding a little extra duck fat if necessary. Stir in the ginger, cook for 1–2 minutes more, then add the tomatoes and cook, stirring, for another 2 minutes.

5 Stir in the rice and cook, stirring, until the rice is coated in the tomato and onion mixture. Pour in the stock, return the slices of duck to the pan and season with salt and pepper.

6 Bring to a boil, then lower heat, cover and simmer gently for 30–35 minutes until the rice is tender. Stir in the cilantro and mint and serve.

COOK'S TIP
While rice was originally imported to Latin America, squash was very much an indigenous vegetable. Pumpkin could also be used for this recipe. Kabocha squash has a thick skin and lots of seeds, which need to be removed before the flesh is cubed.

PERUVIAN SALAD

THIS REALLY IS A SPECTACULAR-LOOKING SALAD. IT COULD BE SERVED AS A SIDE DISH OR WOULD MAKE A DELICIOUS LIGHT LUNCH. IN PERU, WHITE RICE WOULD BE USED, BUT BROWN RICE ADDS AN INTERESTING TEXTURE AND FLAVOR.

SERVES FOUR

INGREDIENTS
- 2 cups cooked long grain brown or white rice
- 1 tablespoon chopped fresh parsley
- 1 red bell pepper
- 1 small onion, sliced
- olive oil, for sprinkling
- 4 ounces green beans, halved
- ½ cup baby corn
- 4 quail eggs, hard-cooked
- 1–2 ounces Spanish ham, cut into thin slices (optional)
- 1 small avocado
- lemon juice, for sprinkling
- 3 ounces mixed salad
- 1 tablespoon capers
- about 10 stuffed olives, halved

For the dressing
- 1 garlic clove, crushed
- 4 tablespoons olive oil
- 3 tablespoons sunflower oil
- 2 tablespoons lemon juice
- 3 tablespoons plain yogurt
- ½ teaspoon mustard
- ½ teaspoon sugar
- salt and freshly ground black pepper

1 Make the dressing by placing all the ingredients in a bowl and beating with a fork until smooth. Alternatively, shake the ingredients together in a glass jar.

2 Put the cooked rice into a large, glass salad bowl and spoon in half the dressing. Add the chopped parsley, stir well and set aside.

3 Cut the bell pepper in half, remove the seeds and pith, then place the halves, cut side down, in a roasting pan. Add the onion rings. Sprinkle the onion with olive oil, place the pan under a hot broiler and cook for 5–6 minutes until the bell pepper blackens and blisters and the onion turns golden. You may need to stir the onion once or twice so that it grills evenly.

4 Stir the onion in with the rice. Put the bell pepper in a plastic bag and knot the bag. When the steam has loosened the skin on the bell pepper halves and they are cool enough to handle, peel them and cut the flesh into thin strips.

COOK'S TIP
This dish looks particularly attractive if served in a deep glass salad bowl. Guests can then see the various layers, starting with the white rice, then the green salad leaves, topped by the bright colors of bell peppers, corn, eggs and olives.

5 Cook the green beans in boiling water for 2 minutes, then add the corn and cook for 1–2 minutes more, until tender. Drain both vegetables, refresh them under cold water, then drain again. Place in a large bowl and add the red bell pepper strips, quail eggs and ham, if using.

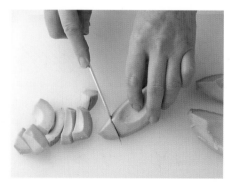

6 Peel the avocado, remove the pit, and cut the flesh into slices or chunks. Sprinkle with the lemon juice. Put the mixed salad in a bowl, add the avocado and mix lightly. Arrange the salad on top of the rice.

7 Stir about 3 tablespoons of the remaining dressing into the green bean and bell pepper mixture. Pile this on top of the salad.

8 Scatter the capers and stuffed olives on top and serve the salad with the remaining dressing.

CALAS

These sweet rice fritters are a Creole speciality, sold by "Calas" women on the streets of the French Quarter of New Orleans to residents and office workers, for whom they make a popular and tasty breakfast.

MAKES OVER 40

INGREDIENTS

    generous ½ cup short grain dessert
      rice
    3¾ cups mixed milk and water
    2 tablespoons sugar
    ½ cup plain all-purpose flour
    1½ teaspoons baking powder
    1 teaspoon shredded lemon rind
    ½ teaspoon ground cinnamon
    ¼ teaspoon ground ginger
    generous pinch of shredded nutmeg
    2 eggs
    oil, for deep frying
    salt
    confectioners' sugar, for dusting
    cherry or strawberry jam and heavy
      cream, to serve

1 Put the rice in a large pan and pour in the milk and water mixture. Add a pinch of salt and bring to a gentle boil. Stir, then cover the pan and simmer over very gentle heat for 15–20 minutes until the rice is tender.

2 Switch off the heat under the pan, then add the sugar. Stir well, cover and leave until completely cool, by which time the rice should have absorbed all the liquid and become very soft.

3 Put the rice in a food processor or blender and add the flour, baking powder, lemon rind, spices and eggs. Process for about 20–30 seconds so that the mixture is like a thick batter.

4 Heat the oil in a wok or deep fryer to 325°F. Scoop up a generous teaspoon of the rice batter and, using a second spoon, push this off carefully into the hot oil. Add four or five more and fry for 3–4 minutes, turning them occasionally, until the calas are a deep golden brown. Drain the calas on paper towels and keep warm while cooking successive batches.

5 Dust the calas generously with confectioners' sugar and serve warm with fruit jam and heavy cream.

FRUITY RICE DESSERT CUSTARD

THERE ARE MANY DELICIOUS VARIATIONS ON RICE DESSERTS IN LATIN AMERICA, THANKS TO SPANISH, PORTUGUESE AND FRENCH SETTLERS WHO ADAPTED FAVORITE RECIPES FROM THEIR NATIVE COUNTRIES AND ADDED LOCAL INGREDIENTS, LIKE RUM, THAT THEY HAD ACQUIRED A LIKING FOR.

SERVES FOUR TO SIX

INGREDIENTS
    4 tablespoons rum or brandy
    ½ cup golden raisins
    scant ½ cup short grain dessert
      rice
    2½ cups whole milk
    1 strip pared lemon rind
    ½ cinnamon stick
    scant ½ cup superfine sugar
    ⅔ cup light cream
    2 eggs, plus 1 egg yolk
    almond biscuits, to serve (optional)

1 Warm the rum or brandy in a small pan, then pour it over the golden raisins. Soak for 3–4 hours or overnight.

2 Cook the rice in boiling water for 10 minutes until slightly softened. Drain well and return to the pan.

3 Stir 1¼ cups of milk into the rice in the pan. Add the strip of lemon rind and the cinnamon stick, bring to a boil, then lower heat and simmer for about 5 minutes. Remove the pan from the heat and stir in half of the sugar. Cover tightly with a damp dish towel held firmly in place with the pan lid. Let the rice cool for 1–2 hours.

4 Preheat the oven to 350°F. Butter a medium-size baking dish and scatter the golden raisins (with any remaining rum or brandy) over the bottom. Stir the rice, which should by now be thick and creamy, most of the liquid having been absorbed, and discard the cinnamon stick and lemon rind. Spoon the rice over the golden raisins in the baking dish.

5 Heat the remaining milk with the cream until just boiling. Meanwhile, mix the eggs and egg yolk in a measuring cup. Beat in the remaining sugar, then the hot milk. Pour the mixture over the rice.

6 Stand the dish in a roasting pan, pour in hot water to come halfway up the sides of the dish and bake for 1–1¼ hours until the top is firm. Serve hot, with almond biscuits, if desired.

COOK'S TIP
This makes a light, creamy rice dessert. If you would prefer your dessert to be denser, cook it for longer.

AFRICA
AND THE
CARIBBEAN

Rice has been an important crop in Africa for centuries, and some of the oldest rice dishes, although not necessarily the best known, come from here. Traditional recipes and, probably, the rice seeds, were brought from Africa to the Caribbean, and a new cuisine evolved — a rich and unforgettable blend of tradition and exotic produce.

JOLOFF CHICKEN AND RICE

IN WEST AFRICA, WHERE IT ORIGINATED, THIS DISH IS USUALLY MADE IN LARGE QUANTITIES, USING JOINTED WHOLE CHICKENS. THIS VERSION IS SOMEWHAT MORE SOPHISTICATED, BUT STILL HAS THE TRADITIONAL FLAVOR.

SERVES FOUR

INGREDIENTS

2 garlic cloves, crushed
1 teaspoon dried thyme
4 skinless, boneless chicken breasts
2 tablespoons vegetable oil
14 ounce can chopped tomatoes
1 tablespoon tomato paste
1 onion, chopped
scant 2 cups chicken stock
2 tablespoons dried shrimps or
  crayfish, ground
1 fresh green chili, seeded and finely
  chopped
1¾ cups white long grain rice
2½ cups water
fresh thyme sprigs, to garnish

1 Mix the garlic and thyme in a bowl. Rub the mixture into the chicken breasts. Heat the oil in a skillet.

2 Add the chicken breasts to the pan to brown in the oil, then remove to a plate. Add the chopped tomatoes, tomato paste and onion to the pan. Cook over a moderately high heat for about 15 minutes until the tomatoes are well reduced, stirring occasionally at first and then more frequently as the tomatoes thicken.

3 Lower heat a little, return the chicken pieces to the pan and stir well to coat with the sauce. Cook for 10 minutes, stirring, then add the stock, the dried shrimps or crayfish and the chili. Bring to a boil, then simmer for 5 minutes or until the chicken is cooked, stirring occasionally.

4 Meanwhile, put the rice in a separate pan. Pour in 2½ cups of water, and top up with the sauce from the chicken. Bring to a boil, then lower the heat and cover the pan. Cook over low heat for 12–15 minutes until the liquid has been absorbed and the rice is tender.

5 Pack the rice in four individual molds and set aside. Lift out the chicken breasts from the sauce and put them on a board. If the sauce is runny, cook it over a high heat to reduce it a little. Unmold a rice timbale on each of four serving plates. Spoon the sauce around, then quickly slice the chicken breasts and fan them on the sauce. Garnish with fresh thyme sprigs and serve immediately.

TANZANIAN VEGETABLE RICE

SERVE THIS TASTY DISH WITH BAKED CHICKEN OR FISH. ADD THE VEGETABLES NEAR THE END OF COOKING SO THAT THEY REMAIN CRISP.

SERVES FOUR

INGREDIENTS

1¾ cups basmati rice
3 tablespoons vegetable oil
1 onion, chopped
2 garlic cloves, crushed
3 cups vegetable stock or
   water
⅔ cup fresh or drained canned corn
   kernels
½ red or green bell pepper, seeded
   and chopped
1 large carrot, shredded
fresh chervil sprigs, to garnish

1 Rinse the rice in a strainer under cold water, then leave to drain thoroughly for about 15 minutes.

2 Heat the oil in a large pan and cook the onion for a few minutes over a medium heat until it starts to soften.

3 Add the rice and cook for about 10 minutes, stirring constantly to prevent the rice sticking to the pan. Then stir in the crushed garlic.

4 Pour in the stock or water and stir well. Bring to a boil, then lower the heat, cover and simmer for 10 minutes.

5 Scatter the corn kernels over the rice, then spread the chopped bell pepper on top. Sprinkle over the shredded carrot. Cover the pan tightly. Steam over low heat until the rice is tender, then mix together with a fork, pile onto a platter and garnish with chervil. Serve immediately.

MOROCCAN PAELLA

PAELLA IS PERENNIALLY POPULAR. THIS VERSION HAS CROSSED THE SEA FROM SPAIN TO MOROCCO, AND ACQUIRED SOME SPICY TOUCHES. UNLIKE SPANISH PAELLA, IT IS MADE WITH LONG GRAIN RICE.

SERVES SIX

INGREDIENTS

2 large skinless, boneless chicken breasts
about 5 ounces prepared squid, cut into rings
10 ounces cod fillets, skinned and cut into bite-size chunks
8–10 jumbo shrimp, shelled and deveined
8 scallops, trimmed and halved
12 ounces fresh mussels
1⅓ cups white long grain rice
2 tablespoons sunflower oil
1 bunch scallions, cut into strips
2 small zucchini, cut into strips
1 red bell pepper, cored, seeded and cut into strips
1⅔ cups chicken stock
1 cup passata
salt and freshly ground black pepper
cilantro sprigs and lemon wedges, to garnish

For the marinade

2 fresh red chilies, seeded and roughly chopped
generous handful of cilantro
2–3 teaspoons ground cumin
1 tablespoon paprika
2 garlic cloves
3 tablespoons olive oil
4 tablespoons sunflower oil
juice of 1 lemon

1 Make the marinade. Place all the ingredients in a food processor with 1 teaspoon salt and process until thoroughly blended. Cut the chicken into bite-size pieces. Place in a bowl.

2 Place the fish and shellfish (apart from the mussels) in a separate glass bowl. Divide the marinade between the fish and chicken and stir well. Cover with plastic wrap and leave to marinate for at least 2 hours.

3 Scrub the mussels, discarding any that do not close when tapped sharply, and keep in a bowl in the fridge until ready to use. Place the rice in a bowl, cover with boiling water and set aside for about 30 minutes. Drain the chicken and fish, and reserve both lots of the marinade separately. Heat the oil in a wok, balti pan or paella pan and cook the chicken pieces for a few minutes until lightly browned.

4 Add the scallions to the pan, cook for 1 minute and then add the zucchini and red bell pepper and cook for 3–4 minutes more until slightly softened. Transfer the chicken and then the vegetables to separate plates.

5 Scrape all the marinade into the pan and cook for 1 minute. Drain the rice, add to the pan and cook for 1 minute. Add the chicken stock, passata and reserved chicken, season with salt and pepper and stir well. Bring the mixture to a boil, then cover the pan with a large lid or foil and simmer very gently for 10–15 minutes until the rice is almost tender.

6 Add the reserved vegetables to the pan and place all the fish and mussels on top. Cover again with a lid or foil and cook over a moderate heat for 10–12 minutes until the fish is cooked and the mussels have opened. Discard any mussels that remain closed. Serve garnished with cilantro and lemon wedges.

SAVORY GROUND RICE

SAVORY GROUND RICE IS OFTEN SERVED AS A SIDE DISH TO SOUPS AND STEWS IN WEST AFRICA.

SERVES FOUR

INGREDIENTS
- 1¼ cups water
- 1¼ cups milk
- ½ teaspoon salt
- 1 tablespoon chopped fresh parsley
- 2 tablespoons butter or margarine
- 1⅔ cups ground rice

COOK'S TIP
Ground rice is a creamy white color, with a slightly grainy texture. Although often used in sweet dishes, it is a tasty grain to serve with savory dishes too. The addition of milk gives a creamier flavor, but a double quantity of water can be used instead, if preferred.

1 Place the water in a pan. Pour in the milk, bring to a boil and add the salt and parsley.

2 Add the butter or margarine and the ground rice, stirring with a wooden spoon to prevent the rice from becoming lumpy.

3 Cover the pan and cook over low heat for about 15 minutes, beating the mixture every 2 minutes to prevent the formation of lumps.

4 To test if the rice is cooked, rub a pinch of the mixture between your fingers: if it feels smooth and fairly dry, it is ready. Serve hot.

MOROCCAN SPICY MEATBALLS WITH RED RICE

CAMARGUE RED RICE IS NATIVE TO FRANCE, BUT IS RAPIDLY GROWING IN POPULARITY THROUGHOUT THE MEDITERRANEAN. IN THIS MOROCCAN DISH, THE NUTTY FLAVOR OF THE RICE IS A PERFECT MATCH FOR THE SPICY MEATBALLS.

SERVES FOUR TO SIX

INGREDIENTS

    generous 1 cup Camargue red rice
    1½ pounds lamb leg steaks
    2 onions
    3–4 fresh parsley sprigs
    3 cilantro sprigs, plus 2 tablespoons
      chopped cilantro
    1–2 fresh mint sprigs
    ½ teaspoon ground cumin
    ½ teaspoon ground cinnamon
    ½ teaspoon ground ginger
    1 teaspoon paprika
    2 tablespoons sunflower oil
    1 garlic clove, crushed
    1¼ cups tomato juice
    scant 2 cups chicken or vegetable
      stock
    salt and freshly ground black pepper
    Moroccan flat bread and yogurt
      dressing, to serve (optional)

1 Cook the rice in plenty of lightly salted water or stock for 30 minutes or according to the instructions on the packet. Drain.

2 Meanwhile, prepare the meatballs. Chop the lamb roughly, then place it in a food processor and process until finely chopped. Scrape the meat into a large bowl.

3 Cut 1 onion into quarters and add it to the processor with the parsley, cilantro and mint sprigs; process until finely chopped. Return the lamb to the processor, add the spices and seasoning and process again until smooth. Scrape the mixture into a bowl and chill for about 1 hour.

4 Shape the mixture into 30 small balls. Heat half the oil in a skillet, add the meatballs, in batches if necessary, and brown them evenly. Transfer to a plate. Chop the remaining onion finely.

5 Drain off the excess fat, leaving around 2 tablespoons in the pan, and cook the chopped onion with the garlic for a few minutes until softened. Stir in the rice. Cook, stirring for 1–2 minutes, then stir in the tomato juice, stock and chopped cilantro. Season to taste with salt and pepper.

6 Arrange the meatballs over the rice, cover with a lid or foil and simmer very gently for 15 minutes. Serve solo, or with Moroccan flat bread and a yogurt dressing, if desired.

COOK'S TIP
A yogurt dressing is delicious with these meatballs. Simply stir 2 teaspoons finely chopped fresh mint into 6 tablespoons plain yogurt.

AFRICAN LAMB AND VEGETABLE PILAU

SPICY LAMB IS SERVED IN THIS DISH WITH BASMATI RICE AND A COLORFUL SELECTION OF DIFFERENT VEGETABLES AND CASHEWS. LAMB AND RICE ARE A POPULAR COMBINATION IN AFRICAN COOKING.

SERVES FOUR

INGREDIENTS

1 pound boned shoulder of lamb, cubed
½ teaspoon dried thyme
½ teaspoon paprika
1 teaspoon garam masala
1 garlic clove, crushed
1½ tablespoons vegetable oil
3¾ cups lamb stock
savoy cabbage or crisp lettuce leaves, to serve

For the rice

2 tablespoons butter
1 onion, chopped
1 medium potato, diced
1 carrot, sliced
½ red bell pepper, seeded and chopped
1 fresh green chili, seeded and chopped
1 cup sliced green cabbage
4 tablespoons plain yogurt
½ teaspoon ground cumin
5 green cardamom pods
2 garlic cloves, crushed
generous 1 cup basmati rice, soaked
about ½ cup cashews
salt and freshly ground black pepper

1 Put the lamb cubes in a large bowl and add the thyme, paprika, garam masala and garlic, with plenty of salt and pepper. Stir, cover, and leave in a cool place for 2–3 hours.

2 Heat the oil in a pan and cook the lamb, in batches if necessary, over medium heat for 5–6 minutes, until browned. Stir in the stock, cover the pan and cook for 35–40 minutes. Using a slotted spoon, transfer the lamb to a bowl. Pour the liquid into a measuring cup, topping it up with water, if necessary, to make 2½ cups.

COOK'S TIP

If the stock looks a bit fatty after cooking the lamb cubes, blot the surface with paper towels to remove the excess grease before pouring the stock into the measuring cup.

3 Melt the butter in a separate pan and cook the onion, potato and carrot for 5 minutes. Add the red bell pepper and chili and cook for 3 minutes more, then stir in the cabbage, yogurt, spices, garlic and the reserved lamb stock. Stir well, cover, then simmer gently for 5–10 minutes, until the cabbage has wilted.

4 Drain the rice and stir into the stew with the lamb. Cover and simmer over low heat for 20 minutes or until the rice is cooked. Sprinkle in the cashews and season to taste with salt and pepper. Serve hot, cupped in cabbage or lettuce leaves.

NORTH AFRICAN FISH WITH PUMPKIN RICE

THIS IS A DISH OF CONTRASTS — THE SLIGHTLY SWEET FLAVOR OF PUMPKIN, THE MILDLY SPICY FISH, AND THE CILANTRO AND GINGER MIXTURE THAT IS STIRRED IN AT THE END — ALL BOUND TOGETHER WITH WELL-FLAVORED RICE.

SERVES FOUR

INGREDIENTS

    1 pound sea bass or other firm fish fillets
    2 tablespoons plain flour
    1 teaspoon ground coriander
    ¼–½ teaspoon ground turmeric
    1 wedge of pumpkin, about 1¼ pounds
    2–3 tablespoons olive oil
    6 scallions, sliced diagonally
    1 garlic clove, finely chopped
    1½ cups basmati rice, soaked
    2½ cups fish stock
    salt and freshly ground black pepper
    lime or lemon wedges and cilantro sprigs, to serve
For the cilantro and ginger flavoring mixture
    3 tablespoons finely chopped cilantro
    2 teaspoons finely chopped fresh ginger root
    ½–1 fresh chili, seeded and very finely chopped
    3 tablespoons lime or lemon juice

1 Remove and discard any skin or stray bones from the fish, and cut into ¾-inch chunks. Mix the flour, ground coriander, turmeric and a little salt and pepper in a plastic bag, add the fish and shake for a few seconds so that the fish is evenly coated in the spice mixture. Set aside. Make the cilantro and ginger flavoring mixture by combining the ingredients in a bowl.

2 Cut away the skin and scoop out the seeds from the pumpkin. Cut the flesh into ¾-inch chunks.

3 Heat 1 tablespoon oil in a flameproof casserole and stir-fry the scallions and garlic for a few minutes until slightly softened. Add the pumpkin and cook over fairly low heat, stirring frequently, for 4–5 minutes or until the flesh begins to soften.

4 Drain the rice, add it to the mixture and toss over brisk heat for 2–3 minutes. Stir in the stock, with a little salt. Bring to simmering point, then lower heat, cover and cook for 12–15 minutes until both the rice and the pumpkin are tender.

5 About 4 minutes before the rice is ready, heat the remaining oil in a skillet and cook the spiced fish over moderately high heat for 3 minutes, until the outside is lightly browned and crisp and the flesh is cooked through but still moist.

6 Stir the cilantro and ginger flavoring mixture into the rice and transfer to a warmed serving dish. Lay the fish pieces on top. Serve immediately, garnished with cilantro, and offer lemon or lime wedges for squeezing over the fish.

COOK'S TIP
This dish can also be cooked – and served – in a wok, if desired.

CHICKEN AND VEGETABLE TAGINE

MOROCCAN TAGINES ARE USUALLY SERVED WITH COUSCOUS, BUT RICE MAKES AN EQUALLY DELICIOUS ACCOMPANIMENT. HERE, COUSCOUS IS STIRRED INTO THE RICE TO CREATE AN UNUSUAL AND TASTY DISH, ALTHOUGH YOU COULD USE RICE BY ITSELF.

SERVES FOUR

INGREDIENTS
  2 tablespoons groundnut oil
  4 skinless, boneless chicken breasts,
    cut into large pieces
  1 large onion, chopped
  2 garlic cloves, crushed
  1 small parsnip, cut into 1-inch
    pieces
  1 small turnip, cut into ¾-inch
    pieces
  3 carrots, cut into 1½-inch pieces
  4 tomatoes, chopped
  1 cinnamon stick
  4 cloves
  1 teaspoon ground ginger
  1 bay leaf
  ¼–½ teaspoon cayenne pepper
  1½ cups chicken stock
  14 ounce can chick-peas, drained
    and skinned
  1 red bell pepper, seeded and sliced
  5 ounces green beans, halved
  1 piece of preserved lemon peel,
    thinly sliced
  20–30 pitted brown or green
    olives
  salt
For the rice and couscous
  3 cups chicken stock
  generous 1 cup long grain rice
  ⅔ cup couscous
  3 tablespoons chopped cilantro

1 Heat half of the oil in a large, flameproof casserole and cook the chicken pieces for a few minutes until evenly browned. Transfer to a plate. Heat the remaining oil and cook the onion, garlic, parsnip, and carrots together over a medium heat for 4–5 minutes until the vegetables are lightly flecked with brown, stirring frequently. Lower the heat, cover and sweat the vegetables for 5 minutes more, stirring occasionally.

2 Add the tomatoes, cook for a few minutes, then add the cinnamon stick, cloves, ginger, bay leaf and cayenne. Cook for 1–2 minutes.

3 Pour in the chicken stock, add the chick-peas and browned chicken pieces, and season with salt. Cover and simmer for 25 minutes.

4 Meanwhile, cook the rice and couscous mixture. Bring the chicken stock to a boil. Add the rice and simmer for about 5 minutes until almost tender. Remove the pan from the heat, stir in the couscous, cover tightly and leave for about 5 minutes.

5 When the vegetables in the tagine are almost tender, stir in the bell pepper slices and green beans and simmer for 10 minutes. Add the preserved lemon and olives, stir well and cook for 5 minutes more, or until the vegetables are perfectly tender.

6 Stir the chopped cilantro into the rice and couscous mixture and pile it onto a plate. Serve the chicken tagine in the traditional dish, if you have one, or in a casserole.

RICE AND PEAS

THIS IS A POPULAR DISH ON THE ISLANDS OF THE EASTERN CARIBBEAN. THE BEANS MUST BE SOAKED OVERNIGHT, SO ALLOW PLENTY OF TIME FOR THIS RECIPE.

SERVES FOUR TO SIX

INGREDIENTS

¾ cup red kidney beans
2 fresh thyme sprigs
2-ounce piece of creamed coconut
2 bay leaves
1 onion, finely chopped
2 garlic cloves, crushed
½ teaspoon ground allspice
⅔ cup chopped red bell pepper
2½ cups water
2⅓ cups white long grain rice
salt and freshly ground black pepper

1 Place the red kidney beans in a large bowl. Cover with water and leave to soak overnight.

2 Drain the beans, place in a large pan and pour in enough water to cover them by 1 inch. Bring to a boil. Boil over high heat for 10 minutes, then lower the heat and simmer for 1½ hours or until the beans are tender.

3 Add the thyme, creamed coconut, bay leaves, onion, garlic, allspice and red bell pepper. Season well and stir in the measured water.

4 Bring to a boil and add the rice. Stir well, lower the heat and cover the pan. Simmer for 25–30 minutes, until all the liquid has been absorbed. Serve as a side dish to fish, meat or vegetarian dishes.

COOK'S TIP
To save time, use a 14 ounce can of red kidney beans. Add them along with the rice.

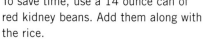

CARIBBEAN PEANUT CHICKEN

PEANUT BUTTER IS USED A LOT IN MANY CARIBBEAN DISHES. IT ADDS A RICHNESS, AS WELL AS A DELICIOUS DEPTH OF FLAVOR ALL OF ITS OWN.

SERVES FOUR

INGREDIENTS

    4 skinless, boneless chicken breasts,
      cut into thin strips
    generous 1 cup white long grain
      rice
    2 tablespoons groundnut oil
    1 tablespoon butter, plus extra
      for greasing
    1 onion, finely chopped
    2 tomatoes, peeled, seeded and
      chopped
    1 fresh green chili, seeded and
      sliced
    4 tablespoons smooth peanut butter
    scant 2 cups chicken stock
    lemon juice, to taste
    salt and freshly ground black pepper
    lime wedges and sprigs of fresh flat
      leaf parsley, to garnish
For the marinade
    1 tablespoon sunflower oil
    1–2 garlic cloves, crushed
    1 teaspoon chopped fresh thyme
    1½ tablespoons medium curry
      powder
    juice of half a lemon

1 Mix all the marinade ingredients in a large bowl and stir in the chicken. Cover loosely with plastic wrap and set aside in a cool place for 2–3 hours.

2 Meanwhile, cook the rice in plenty of lightly salted boiling water until tender. Drain well and turn into a generously buttered casserole.

3 Preheat the oven to 350°F. Heat 1 tablespoon of the oil and butter in a flameproof casserole and cook the chicken pieces for 4–5 minutes until evenly brown. Add more oil if necessary.

4 Transfer the chicken to a plate. Add the onion to the casserole and cook for 5–6 minutes until lightly browned, adding more oil if necessary. Stir in the chopped tomatoes and chili. Cook over gentle heat for 3–4 minutes, stirring occasionally. Remove from the heat.

5 Mix the peanut butter with the chicken stock. Stir into the tomato and onion mixture, then add the chicken. Stir in the lemon juice, season to taste, then spoon the mixture over the rice in the casserole.

6 Cover the casserole. Cook in the oven for 15–20 minutes or until piping hot. Use a large spoon to toss the rice with the chicken mixture. Serve immediately, garnished with the lime wedges and parsley sprigs.

COOK'S TIP

If the casserole is not large enough to allow you to toss the rice with the chicken mixture before serving, invert a large, deep plate over the casserole, turn both over and toss the mixture on the plate.

SPICY PEANUT BALLS

TASTY RICE BALLS, ROLLED IN CHOPPED PEANUTS AND DEEP-FRIED, MAKE A DELICIOUS SNACK.
SERVE THEM AS THEY ARE, OR WITH A CHILI SAUCE FOR DIPPING.

MAKES SIXTEEN

INGREDIENTS
 1 garlic clove, crushed
 ½-inch piece of fresh ginger root,
   peeled and finely chopped
 ¼ teaspoon ground turmeric
 1 teaspoon sugar
 ½ teaspoon salt
 1 teaspoon chili sauce
 2 teaspoons fish sauce or soy sauce
 2 tablespoons chopped cilantro
 juice of ½ lime
 2 cups cooked white long grain
   rice
 4 ounces peanuts, chopped
 vegetable oil, for deep frying
 lime wedges and chili dipping sauce,
   to serve

1 Process the garlic, ginger and turmeric in a food processor until the mixture forms a paste. Add the sugar, salt, chili sauce and fish sauce or soy sauce, with the chopped cilantro and lime juice. Process briefly to mix.

2 Add three-quarters of the cooked rice to the paste in the food processor, and process until smooth and sticky. Scrape into a mixing bowl and stir in the remainder of the rice. Wet your hands and shape the mixture into thumb-size balls.

3 Roll the balls in chopped peanuts, making sure they are evenly coated.

4 Heat the oil in a deep fryer or wok. Deep fry the peanut balls until crisp. Drain on paper towels and then pile onto a platter. Serve hot with lime wedges and a chili dipping sauce.

CARIBBEAN CHICKEN WITH PIGEON PEA RICE

GOLDEN, SPICY CARAMELIZED CHICKEN TOPS A RICHLY FLAVORED VEGETABLE RICE IN THIS HEARTY AND DELICIOUS SUPPER DISH. PIGEON PEAS ARE A COMMON INGREDIENT IN CARIBBEAN COOKING.

SERVES FOUR

INGREDIENTS

1 teaspoon allspice
½ teaspoon ground cinnamon
1 teaspoon dried thyme
pinch of ground cloves
¼ teaspoon freshly shredded
  nutmeg
4 skinless, boneless chicken
  breasts
3 tablespoons groundnut or
  sunflower oil
1 tablespoon butter
1 onion, chopped
2 garlic cloves, crushed
1 carrot, diced
1 celery stick, chopped
3 scallions, chopped
1 fresh red chili, seeded and
  thinly sliced
14 ounce can pigeon peas
generous 1 cup long grain rice
½ cup coconut milk
2½ cups chicken stock
2 tablespoons brown sugar
salt and cayenne pepper

1 Mix together the allspice, cinnamon, thyme, cloves and nutmeg. Rub the mixture all over the pieces of chicken. Set aside for 30 minutes.

2 Heat 1 tablespoon of the oil with the butter in a pan. Cook the onion and garlic over medium heat until soft and beginning to brown. Add the carrot, celery, scallions and chili. Saute for a few minutes, then stir in the pigeon peas, rice, coconut milk and chicken stock. Season with salt and cayenne pepper. Bring to simmering point, cover and cook over low heat for about 25 minutes.

COOK'S TIP
Pigeon peas are sometimes called gungo beans, especially when sold in ethnic markets. If they are not available, use borlotti beans instead.

3 About 10 minutes before the rice mixture is cooked, heat the remaining oil in a heavy skillet, add the sugar and cook, without stirring, until it begins to caramelize.

4 Carefully add the chicken to the pan. Cook for 8–10 minutes until the chicken has a browned, glazed appearance and is cooked through. Transfer the chicken to a board and slice it thickly. Serve the pigeon pea rice in individual bowls, with the chicken on top.

JAMAICAN FISH CURRY

ALTHOUGH THE RICE IS SIMPLY BOILED FOR THIS RECIPE, IT IS AN INTEGRAL PART OF THIS DISH AND IS AN EXCELLENT EXAMPLE OF HOW THE PLAINEST RICE TAKES ON THE FLAVOR OF THE SAUCE WITH WHICH IT IS SERVED. CURRIES HAVE A DEFINITE PART TO PLAY IN AFRICAN COOKING.

SERVES FOUR

INGREDIENTS
    2 halibut steaks or other firm white
      fish, total weight about
      1¼–1½ pounds
    2 tablespoons groundnut oil
    2 cardamom pods
    1 cinnamon stick
    6 allspice berries
    4 cloves
    1 large onion, chopped
    3 garlic cloves, crushed
    2–3 teaspoons grated fresh ginger
      root
    2 teaspoons ground cumin
    1 teaspoon ground coriander
    ½ teaspoon cayenne pepper or
      to taste
    4 tomatoes, peeled, seeded and
      chopped
    1 sweet potato, about 8 ounces,
      cut into ¾-inch cubes
    2 cups fish stock or water
    4 ounce piece of creamed
      coconut
    1 bay leaf
    generous 1 cup white long grain
      rice
    salt
    chopped cilantro, to garnish

COOK'S TIP
Sweet potato discolours very quickly.
If you are preparing the ingredients
in advance, put the cubed potato into
a large bowl and cover with cold water.
Add 2–3 tablespoons lemon juice, and
set aside until ready to use.
    This recipe uses some of the most
common spices to appear in dishes from
Africa and the Caribbean, where the
influence of India is clearly visible.
The taste is for pungent flavours rather
than fiery heat. Allspice is widely
used throughout the Caribbean, while
cardamom and cayenne pepper are
essential ingredients in curries.

1 Rub the fish steaks well with salt and
set aside.

2 Heat the oil in a flameproof
casserole and stir-fry the cardamom
pods, cinnamon stick, allspice berries
and cloves for about 3 minutes to
release the aroma.

3 Add the onion, garlic and ginger.
Continue cooking for 4–5 minutes over
a gentle heat until the onion is fairly
soft, stirring frequently, then add the
cumin, coriander and cayenne pepper
and cook briefly, stirring all the time.

4 Stir in the tomatoes, sweet potato,
fish stock or water, creamed coconut
and bay leaf. Season well with salt.
Bring to a boil, then lower heat, cover
and simmer for 15–18 minutes until the
sweet potato is tender.

5 Cook the rice according to your
preferred method. Meanwhile, add the
fish steaks to the pan of sauce and
spoon the sauce over to cover them
completely. Put a lid on the pan and
simmer for about 10 minutes until the
fish is just tender and flakes easily.

6 Spoon the rice into a warmed serving
dish, spoon over the curry sauce and
arrange the halibut steaks on top.
Garnish with chopped cilantro, if you
like, and serve immediately.

ORANGE RICE DESSERT

IN MOROCCO, AS IN SPAIN, GREECE AND ITALY, THICK, CREAMY RICE DESSERTS ARE VERY POPULAR, ESPECIALLY WHEN SWEETENED WITH HONEY AND FLAVORED WITH ORANGE.

SERVES FOUR

INGREDIENTS

   generous ¼ cup short grain dessert
     rice
   2½ cups milk
   finely shredded rind of ½ small orange
   2–3 tablespoons honey
   ⅔ cup heavy cream
   1 tablespoon chopped pistachios,
     toasted
   shredded orange rind, to garnish

3 Remove the lid and continue cooking and stirring for 15–20 minutes, until the rice is creamy.

4 Pour in the cream, stirring constantly, then simmer for 5–8 minutes more. Spoon the rice dessert into warmed individual bowls. Sprinkle with the toasted pistachios and serve.

1 Mix the rice with the milk and orange rind in a pan. Pour in the honey and stir well.

2 Bring to a boil, then lower heat, cover and simmer very gently for about 1¼ hours, stirring frequently.

VARIATION
Instead of adding heavy cream, stir in strained, plain yogurt. Serve immediately (without reheating), topped with toasted pine nuts and fresh orange segments.

CARIBBEAN SPICED RICE DESSERT

CARIBBEAN RECIPES CAN BE EXTREMELY SWEET, AND YOU MAY FIND YOU CAN REDUCE THE SUGAR QUANTITY IN THIS DESSERT BECAUSE OF THE NATURAL SWEETNESS OF THE FRUIT.

SERVES FOUR TO SIX

INGREDIENTS
   2 tablespoons butter
   1 cinnamon stick
   ½ cup brown sugar
   ⅔ cup ground rice
   5 cups milk
   ½ teaspoon allspice
   ⅓ cup golden raisins
   3 ounces chopped mandarin oranges
   3 ounces chopped pineapple

1 Melt the butter in a non-stick pan and then add the cinnamon stick and sugar. Heat over medium heat until the sugar begins to caramelize: remove from the heat as soon as this happens.

2 Carefully stir in the rice and three-quarters of the milk. Bring to a boil, stirring all the time, without letting the milk burn. Reduce the heat and simmer for 10 minutes until the rice is cooked, stirring constantly.

3 Add the remaining milk, the allspice and the golden raisins. Let simmer for 5 minutes, stirring occasionally.

4 When the rice is thick and creamy, allow to cool slightly, then stir in the mandarin and pineapple pieces. As an alternative, the fruit can be served separately, with warm or cold rice.

BRITAIN

Rice is a relative newcomer to
Britain. For a surprisingly long
time, the only way to use rice was
to cream it with milk and sugar
in a rice dessert, but the last
twenty years have seen rice earn its
rightful place at the dinner table.
Of today's rice dishes, some
have been adapted from Oriental
cuisines; others are entirely original.

PUMPKIN, RICE AND CHICKEN SOUP

THIS IS A WARM, COMFORTING SOUP WHICH, DESPITE THE SPICE AND BASMATI RICE, IS QUINTESSENTIALLY ENGLISH. FOR AN EVEN MORE SUBSTANTIAL MEAL, ADD A LITTLE MORE RICE AND MAKE SURE YOU USE ALL THE CHICKEN FROM THE STOCK.

SERVES FOUR

INGREDIENTS
  1 wedge of pumpkin, about 1 pound
  1 tablespoon sunflower oil
  2 tablespoons butter
  6 green cardamom pods
  2 leeks, chopped
  generous ½ cup basmati rice,
    soaked
  1½ cups milk
  salt and freshly ground black pepper
  generous strips of pared orange rind,
    to garnish
For the chicken stock
  2 chicken quarters
  1 onion, quartered
  2 carrots, chopped
  1 celery stalk, chopped
  6–8 peppercorns
  3¾ cups water

1 First make the chicken stock. Place the chicken quarters, onion, carrots, celery and peppercorns in a large pan. Pour in the water and slowly bring to a boil. Skim the surface if necessary, then lower heat, cover and simmer gently for 1 hour.

2 Strain the chicken stock into a clean, large bowl, discarding the vegetables. Skin and bone one or both chicken pieces and cut the flesh into strips. (If not using both chicken pieces for the soup, reserve the other piece for another recipe.)

3 Skin the pumpkin and remove all the seeds and pith, so that you have about 12 ounces of flesh. Cut the flesh into 1-inch cubes.

4 Heat the oil and butter in a pan and cook the cardamom pods for 2–3 minutes until slightly swollen. Add the leeks and pumpkin. Cook, stirring, for 3–4 minutes over medium heat, then lower heat, cover and sweat for 5 minutes more or until the pumpkin is soft, stirring once or twice.

5 Measure out 2½ cups of the stock and add to the pumpkin mixture. Bring to a boil, then lower the heat, cover and simmer gently for 10–15 minutes, until the pumpkin is soft.

6 Pour the remaining stock into a measuring cup and make up with water to 1¼ cups. Drain the rice and put it into a pan. Pour in the stock, bring to a boil, then simmer for about 10 minutes until the rice is tender. Add seasoning to taste.

7 Remove the cardamom pods, then process the soup in a blender or food processor until smooth. Pour back into a clean pan and stir in the milk, chicken and rice (with any stock that has not been absorbed). Heat until simmering. Garnish with the strips of pared orange rind and freshly ground black pepper, and serve with fresh whole-wheat bread.

RICE CAKES <u>WITH</u> SMOKED SALMON

THESE ELEGANT RICE CAKES ARE MADE USING A RISOTTO BASE. YOU COULD SKIP THIS STAGE AND USE LEFTOVER SEAFOOD OR MUSHROOM RISOTTO. ALTERNATIVELY, USE LEFTOVER LONG GRAIN RICE AND ADD EXTRA FLAVOR WITH SCALLIONS.

SERVES FOUR

INGREDIENTS
2 tablespoons olive oil
1 medium onion, chopped
generous 1 cup risotto rice
about 6 tablespoons white wine
about 3 cups fish or chicken
    stock
2 tablespoons dried porcini
    mushrooms, soaked for 10 minutes
    in warm water to cover
1 tablespoon chopped fresh parsley
1 tablespoon chopped fresh chives
1 teaspoon chopped fresh dill weed
1 egg, lightly beaten
about 3 tablespoons ground rice,
    plus extra for dusting
vegetable oil, for frying
4 tablespoons sour cream
6 ounces smoked salmon
salt and freshly ground black pepper
mixed salad leaves, tossed in
    French dressing, to serve

1 Heat the olive oil in a pan and cook the onion for 3–4 minutes until soft. Add the rice and cook, stirring, until the grains are thoroughly coated in oil. Pour in the wine and stock, a little at a time, stirring constantly over gentle heat until each quantity of liquid has been absorbed before adding more.

2 Drain the mushrooms and chop them into small pieces. When the rice is tender, and all the liquid has been absorbed, stir in the mushrooms, parsley, chives, dill weed and seasoning. Remove from heat and set aside for a few minutes to cool.

3 Add the beaten egg, then stir in enough ground rice to bind the mixture – it should be soft but manageable. Dust your hands with ground rice and shape the mixture into four patties, about 5-inches in diameter and about a ¾-inch thick.

4 Heat the oil in a shallow skillet and cook the rice cakes, in batches if necessary, for 5 minutes until browned on both sides. Drain on paper towels and cool slightly. Place each rice cake on a plate and top with 1 tablespoon sour cream. Twist two or three thin slices of smoked salmon on top, and serve with a dressed salad garnish.

COOK'S TIP
For a sophisticated occasion, garnish the rice cakes with roasted baby asparagus spears, lemon slices and dill weed.

SALMON IN PUFF PASTRY

THIS IS AN ELEGANT PARTY DISH, MADE WITH RICE, EGGS AND SALMON AND ENCLOSED IN PUFF PASTRY.

<u>SERVES SIX</u>

INGREDIENTS

1 pound puff pastry, thawed if
  frozen
1 egg, beaten
3 hard-cooked eggs
6 tablespoons light cream
1¾ cups cooked long grain rice
2 tablespoons finely chopped fresh
  parsley
2 teaspoons chopped fresh
  tarragon
1½ pounds fresh salmon fillets
3 tablespoons butter
juice of ½ lemon
salt and freshly ground black pepper

2 In a bowl, mash the hard-cooked eggs with the cream, then stir in the cooked rice. Add the parsley and tarragon and season well. Spoon this mixture onto the prepared pastry.

5 Roll out the remaining pastry and cut out a semi-circle piece to cover the head portion and a tail shape to cover the tail. Brush both pieces of pastry with a little beaten egg and place on top of the fish, pressing down firmly to secure. Score a criss-cross pattern on the tail.

1 Preheat the oven to 375ºF. Roll out two-thirds of the pastry into a large oval, measuring about 14-inches in length. Cut into a curved fish shape and place on a lightly greased baking sheet. Use the trimmings to make narrow strips. Brush one side of each strip with a little beaten egg and secure in place around the rim of the pastry to make a raised edge. Prick the base all over with a fork, then bake for 8–10 minutes until the sides are puffed and the pastry is lightly golden. Let cool.

COOK'S TIP

If the pastry seems to be browning too quickly, cover it with foil during cooking and remove from the oven for the last 5 minutes. It is important that the "fish" cooks for the recommended amount of time, so that the salmon is sufficiently cooked through.

3 Cut the salmon into ¾-inch chunks. Melt the butter until it starts to sizzle, then add the salmon. Turn the pieces over in the butter so that they begin to color but do not cook through.

4 Remove from the heat and arrange the salmon pieces on top of the rice, piled in the center. Stir the lemon juice into the butter in the pan, then spoon the mixture over the salmon pieces.

6 Cut the remaining pastry into small circles and, starting from the tail end, arrange the circles in overlapping lines to represent scales. Add an extra one for an eye. Brush the whole fish shape with the remaining beaten egg.

7 Bake for 10 minutes, then reduce the temperature to 325ºF and cook for a further 15–20 minutes until the pastry is evenly golden. Slide the fish onto a serving plate and serve.

VARIATION

For a simplified version of the recipe, roll out the pastry into a rectangle, then make the pastry edges to contain the filling. Part bake the "fish", top it with plain, rolled out pastry and return it to the oven to complete the cooking time.

KEDGEREE

A POPULAR VICTORIAN BREAKFAST DISH, KEDGEREE HAS ITS ORIGINS IN KITCHIRI, AN INDIAN RICE AND LENTIL DISH. KEDGEREE CAN BE FLAVORED WITH CURRY POWDER, BUT THIS RECIPE IS MILD.

SERVES FOUR

INGREDIENTS

1¼ pounds smoked haddock
generous ½ cup basmati rice
2 tablespoons lemon juice
⅔ cup light cream or sour cream
pinch of freshly shredded nutmeg
pinch of cayenne pepper
2 hard-cooked eggs, peeled and cut
  into wedges
4 tablespoons butter, diced
2 tablespoons chopped fresh
  parsley
salt and freshly ground black pepper

COOK'S TIP
Taste the kedgeree before you add salt, as the smoked haddock may already be quite salty.

1 Put the haddock in a skillet, pour in just enough water to cover and heat to simmering point. Poach the fish for about 10 minutes, until the flesh flakes easily when tested with the tip of a sharp knife. Lift the fish out of the cooking liquid, then remove any skin and bones and flake the flesh. Reserve the cooking liquid.

2 Pour the cooking liquid into a measuring cup and make up the volume with water to 1 cup.

3 Pour the measured liquid into a pan and bring it to a boil. Add the rice, stir, then lower the heat, cover and simmer for about 10 minutes, until the rice is tender and the liquid has been absorbed. Meanwhile, preheat the oven to 350°F and butter a baking dish.

4 When the rice is cooked, remove it from the heat and stir in the lemon juice, cream, flaked fish, nutmeg and cayenne. Add the egg wedges to the rice mixture and stir in gently.

5 Tip the rice mixture into the prepared baking dish. Level the surface and dot with butter. Cover the dish loosely with foil and bake for about 25 minutes.

6 Stir the chopped parsley into the baked kedgeree and add seasoning to taste. Serve immediately.

CHICKEN AND MANGO SALAD WITH ORANGE RICE

CONTEMPORARY BRITISH COOKING DRAWS ITS INSPIRATION FROM ALL OVER THE WORLD.

SERVES FOUR

INGREDIENTS
    1 tablespoon sunflower oil
    1 onion, chopped
    1 garlic clove, crushed
    2 tablespoons red curry paste
    2 teaspoons apricot jelly
    2 tablespoons chicken stock
    about 1 pound cooked chicken, cut
      into small pieces
    ⅔ cup plain yogurt
    4–5 tablespoons mayonnaise
    1 large mango, cut into ½-inch dice
    fresh Italian parsley sprigs, to
      garnish
    poppadums, to serve
For the orange rice
    scant 1 cup white long grain rice
    8 ounces carrots, shredded (about
      1⅓ cups)
    1 large orange, cut into segments
    ⅓ cup roasted slivered almonds
For the dressing
    3 tablespoons olive oil
    4 tablespoons sunflower oil
    3 tablespoons lemon juice
    1 garlic clove, crushed
    1 tablespoon chopped mixed fresh
      herbs (tarragon, parsley, chives)
    salt and freshly ground black
      pepper

1 Heat the sunflower oil in a skillet and cook the onion and garlic for 3–4 minutes until soft.

2 Stir in the curry paste, cook for about 1 minute, then lower heat and stir in the apricot jelly and stock. Mix well, add the chopped chicken and stir until the chicken is thoroughly coated in the paste. Spoon the mixture into a large bowl and let cool.

3 Meanwhile, boil the rice in plenty of lightly salted water until just tender. Drain, rinse under cold water and drain again. When cool, stir into the shredded carrots and add the orange segments and slivered almonds.

4 Make the dressing by whisking all the ingredients together in a bowl.

5 When the chicken mixture is cool, stir in the yogurt and mayonnaise, then add the mango, stirring it in carefully so as not to break the flesh. Chill for about 30 minutes.

6 When ready to serve, pour the dressing into the rice salad and mix well. Spoon onto a platter and mound the cold curried chicken on top. Garnish with Italian parsley and serve with poppadums.

COOK'S TIP
A simple way of dicing a mango is to take two thick slices from either side of the large flat pit without peeling the fruit. Make criss-cross cuts in the flesh on each slice and then turn inside out. The cubes of flesh will stand proud of the skin and can be easily cut off.

LOIN OF PORK WITH CASHEW AND ORANGE STUFFING

THE ORANGES AND CASHEWS ADD CONTRASTING FLAVORS AND TEXTURES TO THIS STUFFING, AND COMBINE WELL WITH THE BROWN RICE. DON'T WORRY IF THE STUFFING DOESN'T BIND — THE BEST THING ABOUT BROWN RICE IS THAT IT RETAINS ITS OWN TEXTURE.

SERVES SIX

INGREDIENTS
- 3–3½ pounds boned loin of pork
- 1 tablespoon all-purpose flour
- 1¼ cups dry white wine
- salt and freshly ground black pepper
- fresh rosemary sprig and orange slices, to garnish

For the stuffing
- 2 tablespoons butter
- 1 small onion, finely chopped
- scant ½ cup brown basmati rice, soaked and drained
- scant 1½ cups chicken stock
- ½ cup cashews
- 1 orange
- ⅓ cup golden raisins

1 First cook the rice for the stuffing. Melt the butter in a skillet and fry the chopped onion for 2–3 minutes until softened but not browned. Add the rice and cook for 1 minute, then pour in the chicken stock and bring to a boil. Stir, then lower heat, cover and simmer for 35 minutes until the rice is tender and the liquid has been absorbed. Preheat the oven to 425°F.

2 While the rice is cooking, open out the loin of pork and cut two lengthwise slits through the meat, making sure not to cut all the way through. Turn the meat over. Remove any excess fat, but leave a good layer; this will keep the meat moist during cooking.

3 Spread out the cashews for the stuffing in a roasting pan and roast for 2–4 minutes until golden. Allow to cool, then coarsely chop in a food processor or blender. Leave the oven on.

4 Shred 1 teaspoon of the orange rind into a bowl, then peel the orange. Working over a bowl to catch the juice, cut the orange into segments. Chop them coarsely.

5 Add the chopped orange segments to the cooked rice with the orange rind, roast cashews and golden raisins. Season well, then stir in 1–2 tablespoons of the reserved orange juice. Don't worry if the rice doesn't bind – it should have a fairly loose consistency.

6 Spread a generous layer of stuffing along the center of the pork. If you have any stuffing left over, put it in a heatproof bowl and set aside.

7 Roll up the loin and tie securely with kitchen string. Rub a little salt and pepper into the surface of the meat and place it in a roasting pan. Roast for 15 minutes then lower the oven temperature to 350°F. Roast for 2–2¼ hours more or until the meat juices run clear and without any sign of pinkness. Heat any extra stuffing in the covered bowl alongside the meat for the final 15 minutes.

8 Transfer the meat to a warmed serving plate and keep warm. Stir the flour into the meat juices remaining in the roasting pan, cook for 1 minute, then stir in the white wine. Bring to a boil, stirring until thickened, then strain into a gravy boat.

9 Remove the string from the meat before carving. Stud the pork with the rosemary and garnish with the orange slices. Serve with the gravy and any extra stuffing.

COOK'S TIP
Pork is usually roasted until well done, though cooking times depend on your oven and the size of the joint. As a rule, allow 35–40 minutes at 350°F per 1 pound of stuffed pork, plus an extra 15–20 minutes. If you like crackling, make sure the skin is completely dry. Just before cooking, score it in a diamond pattern and rub generously with salt.

STRAWBERRY SHORTCAKE

GROUND RICE ADDS A LIGHT, FINE TEXTURE TO SHORTCAKE.

SERVES EIGHT

INGREDIENTS
 3 cups strawberries
 1¼ cups heavy cream
 2 tablespoons superfine sugar
 1 tablespoon confectioners' sugar
  (optional)
For the shortcake
 1 cup all-purpose flour
 ⅓ cup ground rice
 6 tablespoons superfine sugar
 ½ cup unsalted butter
 1 egg yolk
 about 1 tablespoon milk

1 Preheat the oven to 350ºF. Make the shortcake. Sift the flour and ground rice into a bowl. Stir in the sugar, then rub in the butter. Stir in the egg yolk and milk, and mix to a cookie dough.

2 Knead the dough lightly, break in half and roll each piece into a 8-inch circle. Place on a greased baking sheet or in two fluted flan tins. Mark one of the rounds in to eight wedges.

3 Bake the shortcakes for 15–20 minutes until golden. Allow to cool a little on the baking sheet or in the tins. Cut the marked shortcakes into wedges, then transfer the whole circles and wedges to a wire rack and let cool.

4 Reserve the best-looking strawberry for the central decoration, and hull and slice the remainder. Set aside about eight of the strawberry slices to use as decoration. Whip the cream until it is thick, and stir in the superfine sugar.

5 Spoon about one-third of the cream into a pastry bag. Spread the remaining cream mixture over the whole shortcake base, and top with the sliced strawberries.

6 Top with the shortcake wedges, standing them at an angle and squeeze cream between them. Decorate with the reserved strawberry slices. Slice the whole strawberry almost, but not quite through and fan the slices. Place it in the center of the shortcake, dust with confectioners' sugar, if you like, and serve.

COOK'S TIP
Ground rice makes a good substitute for wheat flour, and is especially popular with people who cannot tolerate gluten.

TRADITIONAL ENGLISH RICE PUDDING

A PROPER ENGLISH RICE PUDDING IS SMOOTH AND CREAMY WITH JUST A HINT OF FRAGRANCE SUPPLIED BY A GENEROUS SPRINKLING OF FRESHLY SHREDDED NUTMEG. SERVE IT WITH A SPOONFUL OF THICK CHERRY JELLY, IF YOU LIKE.

SERVES FOUR

INGREDIENTS
 2½ cups whole milk or half-and-half
 1 vanilla pod
 generous ¼ cup short grain dessert
  rice
 3 tablespoons superfine sugar
 2 tablespoons butter
 freshly shredded nutmeg

1 Pour the milk into a pan and add the vanilla pod. Bring to simmering point, then remove from the heat, cover and leave to infuse for 1 hour. Preheat the oven to 300ºF.

2 Put the rice and sugar in an ovenproof baking dish. Strain the milk over the rice, discarding the vanilla pod. Stir to mix, then dot the surface with the butter.

3 Bake, uncovered, for 2 hours. After about 40 minutes, stir the surface skin into the pudding, and repeat this after a further 40 minutes. At this point, sprinkle the surface of the pudding generously with shredded nutmeg. Allow the pudding to finish cooking without stirring.

COOK'S TIP
If possible, always use a non-stick saucepan when heating milk, otherwise it is likely to stick to the bottom of the pan and burn.

NORTH AMERICA

North America is one of the world's
largest rice producing countries.
It is no surprise to find here
a large number of home-grown
rice recipes, as well as a diverse
collection of "imports" introduced
and adapted over generations by
the culturally rich migrant
communities, amongst them
Italians, Japanese and Chinese.

SEAFOOD CHOWDER

CHOWDER TAKES ITS NAME FROM THE FRENCH WORD FOR CAULDRON — CHAUDIÈRE — THE TYPE OF POT ONCE TRADITIONALLY USED FOR SOUPS AND STEWS. LIKE MOST CHOWDERS, THIS IS A SUBSTANTIAL DISH, WHICH COULD EASILY BE SERVED WITH CRUSTY BREAD FOR A LUNCH OR SUPPER.

SERVES FOUR TO SIX

INGREDIENTS
  generous 1 cup drained, canned
    corn kernels
  2½ cups milk
  1 tablespoon butter
  1 small leek, sliced
  1 small garlic clove, crushed
  2 rindless smoked lean bacon strips,
    finely chopped
  1 small green bell pepper, seeded
    and diced
  1 celery stalk, chopped
  generous ½ cup white long grain
    rice
  1 teaspoon all-purpose flour
  scant 2 cups hot chicken or
    vegetable stock
  4 large scallops, preferably with
    corals
  4 ounce white fish fillet, such as
    monkfish or flounder
  1 tablespoon finely chopped fresh
    parsley
  good pinch of cayenne pepper
  2–3 tablespoons light cream
    (optional)
  salt and freshly ground black pepper

1 Place half the corn kernels in a food processor or blender. Add a little of the milk and process until thick and creamy.

2 Melt the butter in a large pan and gently cook the leek, garlic and bacon for 4–5 minutes until the leek has softened but not browned. Add the green bell pepper and celery and sweat over very gentle heat for 3–4 minutes more, stirring frequently.

3 Stir in the rice and cook for a few minutes until the grains begin to swell. Sprinkle over the flour. Cook, stirring, for about 1 minute, then gradually stir in the remaining milk and the stock.

4 Bring the mixture to a boil over medium heat, then lower heat and stir in the creamed corn mixture, with the whole corn kernels. Season well.

5 Cover the pan and simmer the chowder very gently for 20 minutes or until the rice is tender, stirring occasionally, and adding a little more chicken stock or water if the mixture thickens too quickly or the rice begins to stick to the bottom of the pan.

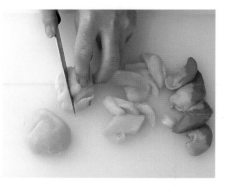

6 Pull the corals away from the scallops and slice the white flesh into ¼-inch pieces. Cut the fish fillet into bite-size chunks.

7 Stir the scallops and fish into the chowder, cook for 4 minutes, then stir in the corals, parsley and cayenne. Cook for a few minutes to heat through, then stir in the cream, if desired. Adjust the seasoning and serve.

THAI-STYLE SEAFOOD PASTIES

THAI-STYLE FOOD IS HUGELY POPULAR IN MANY PARTS OF AMERICA, ESPECIALLY ALONG THE WEST COAST, WHERE RICE IS ONE OF THE MOST IMPORTANT CROPS.

MAKES EIGHTEEN

INGREDIENTS
1¼ pounds puff pastry, thawed if frozen
1 egg, beaten with 2 tablespoons water
cilantro leaves and lime twists, to garnish
For the filling
10 ounces skinned firm white fish fillets, such as cod
all-purpose flour seasoned with salt and freshly ground black pepper
8–10 jumbo shrimp
1 tablespoon sunflower oil
about 6 tablespoons butter
6 scallions, finely sliced
1 garlic clove, crushed
2 cups cooked Thai fragrant rice
1½-inch piece of fresh ginger root, shredded
2 teaspoons finely chopped cilantro
1 teaspoon finely shredded lime rind

1 Preheat the oven to 375°F. Make the filling. Cut the fish into ¾-inch cubes and dust with the seasoned flour. Shell and devein the shrimp and cut each one into four pieces.

2 Heat half of the oil and 1 tablespoon of the butter in a skillet. Add the scallions and cook them over gentle heat for 2 minutes. Add the garlic and cook for about 5 minutes more, until the onions are very soft. Transfer to a large bowl.

3 Heat the remaining oil and a further 2 tablespoons of the butter in a clean pan. Cook the fish pieces briefly. As soon as they begin to turn opaque, use a slotted spoon to transfer them to the bowl with the scallions. Cook the shrimp in the fat remaining in the pan. When they begin to change color, lift them out and add them to the bowl.

4 Add the cooked rice to the bowl, with the ginger, cilantro and lime rind. Mix, taking care not to break up the fish.

5 Dust the counter with a little flour. Roll out the pastry and cut into 4-inch circles. Place spoonfuls of filling just off center on the pastry circles. Dot with a little butter. Dampen the edges of the pastry with a little of the egg wash, fold one side of the pastry over the filling and press the edges together firmly.

6 Place these on a lightly greased baking sheet. Decorate the pasties with the pastry trimmings, if you like. Brush them with egg wash and bake for 12–15 minutes or until golden.

7 Transfer to a plate and garnish with fresh cilantro leaves and lime twists.

COOK'S TIP
If you prefer, you could make 6 larger pasties to serve as a main course.

CALIFORNIAN CITRUS FRIED RICE

AS WITH ALL FRIED RICE DISHES, THE IMPORTANT THING HERE IS TO MAKE SURE THE RICE IS COLD.
ADD IT AFTER COOKING ALL THE OTHER INGREDIENTS, AND STIR TO HEAT IT THROUGH COMPLETELY.

SERVES FOUR TO SIX

INGREDIENTS

    4 eggs
    2 teaspoons Japanese rice vinegar
    2 tablespoons light soy sauce
    about 3 tablespoons groundnut oil
    ½ cup cashews
    2 garlic cloves, crushed
    6 scallions, diagonally sliced
    2 small carrots, cut into julienne
      strips
    8 ounces asparagus, each spear cut
      diagonally into 4 pieces
    2¼ cups white mushrooms,
      halved
    2 tablespoons rice wine
    2 tablespoons water
    4 cups cooked white long grain
      rice
    about 2 teaspoons sesame oil
    1 pink grapefruit or orange, to serve
    thin strips of orange rind, to garnish
For the hot dressing
    1 teaspoon shredded orange rind
    2 tablespoons Japanese rice wine
    3 tablespoons oyster sauce
    2 tablespoons freshly squeezed pink
      grapefruit or orange juice
    1 teaspoon medium or hot chili sauce

3 Heat the remaining oil and add the garlic and scallions. Cook over medium heat for 1–2 minutes until the onions begin to soften, then add the carrots and stir-fry for 4 minutes.

4 Add the asparagus and cook for 2–3 minutes, then stir in the mushrooms and stir-fry for a further 1 minute. Stir in the rice wine, the remaining soy sauce and the water. Simmer for a few minutes until the vegetables are just tender but still firm.

5 Mix the ingredients for the dressing, then add to the wok and bring to a boil. Add the rice, scrambled eggs and cashews. Toss over low heat for 3–4 minutes, until the rice is heated through. Just before serving, stir in the sesame oil and the grapefruit or orange segments. Garnish with strips of orange rind and serve at once.

1 Beat the eggs with the vinegar and 2 teaspoons of the soy sauce. Heat 1 tablespoon of the oil in a wok and cook the eggs until scrambled. Transfer to a plate and set aside.

2 Add the cashews to the wok and stir-fry for 1–2 minutes. Set aside.

WALDORF RICE SALAD

WALDORF SALAD TAKES ITS NAME FROM THE WALDORF HOTEL IN NEW YORK, WHERE IT WAS FIRST MADE. THE RICE MAKES THIS SALAD SLIGHTLY MORE SUBSTANTIAL THAN USUAL. IT CAN BE SERVED AS A SIDE DISH, OR AS A MAIN MEAL FOR TWO.

SERVES TWO TO FOUR

INGREDIENTS
generous ½ cup white long grain rice
1 red apple
1 green apple
4 tablespoons lemon juice
3 celery stalks
2–3 slices thick cooked ham
6 tablespoons good quality mayonnaise, preferably home-made
4 tablespoons sour cream
generous pinch of saffron, dissolved in 1 tablespoon hot water
2 teaspoons chopped fresh basil
1 tablespoon chopped fresh parsley
several cos or iceberg lettuce leaves
½ cup walnuts, coarsely chopped
salt and freshly ground black pepper

1 Cook the rice in plenty of boiling salted water until tender. Drain and set aside in a bowl to cool.

2 Cut the apples into quarters, remove the cores and finely slice one red and one green apple quarter. Place the slices in a bowl with half the lemon juice and reserve for the garnish. Peel the remaining apple quarters and cut into julienne strips. Place in a separate bowl and toss with another 1 tablespoon of the lemon juice.

3 Cut the celery into thin strips. Roll up each slice of ham, slice finely and add to the apple sticks, with the celery.

4 Mix together the mayonnaise, sour cream and saffron water, then stir in salt and pepper to taste.

5 Stir the mayonnaise mixture and herbs into the rice. Add the apple and celery, with the remaining lemon juice.

6 Arrange the lettuce leaves around the outside of a salad bowl and pile the rice and apple mixture into the center. Scatter with the chopped walnuts and garnish with fans of apple slices.

SMOKED SALMON AND RICE SALAD PARCELS

FETA, CUCUMBER AND TOMATOES GIVE A GREEK FLAVOR TO THE SALAD IN THESE PARCELS, A COMBINATION WHICH GOES WELL WITH THE RICE, ESPECIALLY IF A LITTLE WILD RICE IS ADDED.

SERVES FOUR

INGREDIENTS
scant 1 cup mixed wild rice and basmati rice
8 slices smoked salmon, total weight about 12 ounces
4-inch piece of cucumber, finely diced
about 8 ounces feta cheese, cubed
8 cherry tomatoes, quartered
2 tablespoons mayonnaise
2 teaspoons fresh lime juice
1 tablespoon chopped fresh chervil
salt and freshly ground black pepper
lime slices and fresh chervil, to garnish

1 Cook the rice according to the instructions on the packet. Drain, turn into a bowl and let cool.

2 Line four ramekins with plastic wrap, then line each ramekin with two slices of smoked salmon. Reserve any extra pieces of smoked salmon for the tops of the parcels.

3 Add the cucumber, feta and tomatoes to the rice, and stir in the mayonnaise, lime juice and chervil. Mix together well. Season with salt and pepper to taste.

4 Spoon the rice mixture into the salmon-lined ramekins. (Any leftover mixture can be used to make a rice salad.) Place any extra pieces of smoked salmon on top, then fold over the overlapping pieces of salmon so that the rice mixture is completely encased.

5 Chill the parcels in the fridge for 30–60 minutes, then invert each parcel onto a plate, using the plastic wrap to ease them out of the ramekins. Carefully peel off the plastic wrap, then garnish each parcel with slices of lime and a sprig of fresh chervil and serve.

STUFFED PANCAKES WITH TURKEY AND CRANBERRIES

THIS IS A WONDERFUL WAY OF USING LEFTOVER ROAST TURKEY. CRANBERRIES ADD THEIR OWN BITTER-SWEET FLAVOR, WHILE THE WILD RICE CONTRIBUTES A NUTTY FLAVOR AND TEXTURE.

MAKES SIX TO EIGHT

INGREDIENTS
  generous ¼ cup wild rice
  stock or water
  1 tablespoon butter
  ½ teaspoon sunflower oil
  1 small onion, finely chopped
  ½ cup small brown mushrooms,
    quartered
  ¾ cup cranberries, fresh or
    frozen
  1½ tablespoons sugar
  4–5 tablespoons water
  about 10 ounces cooked turkey
    breast, cut into ¾-inch cubes
  ⅔ cup sour cream
  2 tablespoons freshly shredded
    Parmesan
  salt and freshly ground black pepper
For the pancakes
  1½ cups plain flour
  1 egg
  1½ cups milk, preferably low-fat
  oil, for frying

1 Cook the wild rice in simmering stock or water for 40–50 minutes or according to the instructions on the packet. Drain. Preheat the oven to 375°F.

2 Meanwhile, make the pancakes. Sift the flour and a pinch of salt into a bowl. Beat in the egg and milk to make a smooth batter. Heat a little oil in a skillet, pour in about 2 tablespoons of the batter and tilt to cover the bottom of the pan. Cook until the underside is a pale brown color, then flip the pancake over and cook the other side briefly. Carefully slide it out of the pan and cook 5–7 more pancakes in the same way.

3 Heat the butter and sunflower oil in a separate skillet and cook the chopped onion for 3–4 minutes until soft. Add the mushrooms and cook for 2–3 minutes, until they are a pale golden color.

4 Put the cranberries in a small pan and add the sugar and measured water. Bring to simmering point and then cover and simmer over very low heat until the cranberries burst. This will take about 10 minutes if the cranberries are fresh, and about 2–3 minutes if frozen.

5 Transfer the cooked cranberries to a bowl, using a slotted spoon, and pour in 3 tablespoons of the cooking liquid. Add the rice, turkey, onion and mushroom mixture and 4 tablespoons of the sour cream. Season with a little salt and pepper and stir to mix, taking care not to break up the cranberries.

6 Fold the pancakes in four and spoon the stuffing into one of the pockets. Arrange in a lightly greased baking dish. Mix the remaining sour cream with the shredded Parmesan and spoon over the top of the pancakes. Bake for 10 minutes to heat through, then serve.

FISH PIE WITH SWEET POTATO TOPPING

*THIS TASTY DISH IS FULL OF CONTRASTING FLAVORS — THE SWEET, SLIGHTLY SPICY SWEET POTATO
MAKING AN INTERESTING PARTNER FOR THE MILD-FLAVORED FISH. WITH ITS BRIGHT TOPPING,
IT LOOKS ATTRACTIVE, TOO, AND IS DELICIOUS SERVED WITH SNOW OR SUGAR SNAP PEAS.*

SERVES FOUR

INGREDIENTS
    scant 1 cup basmati or Texmati rice,
        soaked
    scant 2 cups well-flavored stock
    1½ cups podded fava beans
    1½ pounds firm white fish fillets,
        skinned
    scant 2 cups milk
For the sauce
    3 tablespoons butter
    2–3 tablespoons all-purpose
        flour
    1 tablespoon chopped fresh
        parsley
    salt and freshly ground black pepper
For the topping
    1 pound sweet potatoes, peeled and
        cut in large chunks
    1 pound floury white potatoes,
        peeled and cut in large chunks
    milk and butter, for mashing
    2 teaspoons freshly chopped parsley
    1 teaspoon freshly chopped dill
        weed
    1 tablespoon single cream
        (optional)

1 Preheat the oven to 375°F. Drain the
rice and put it in a saucepan. Pour in
the stock, with a little salt and pepper,
if needed, and bring to a boil. Cover the
pan, lower heat and simmer for about
10 minutes or until all the liquid has
been absorbed.

2 Cook the fava beans in a little lightly
salted water until tender. Drain
thoroughly. When cool enough to
handle, pop the bright green beans
out of their skins.

3 To make the topping, cook the sweet
and white potatoes separately in boiling
salted water until tender. Drain them
both, mash them with a little milk and
butter and spoon them into separate
bowls. Beat parsley and dill into the
sweet potatoes, with the cream, if using.

4 Place the fish in a large skillet and
pour in enough of the milk (about
1½ cups) to just cover. Dot with
1 tablespoon of the butter and season
with salt and pepper. Heat gently and
simmer for 5–6 minutes until the fish
is just tender. Lift out the fish and
break it into large pieces. Pour the
cooking liquid into a measuring cup
and make up to **scant** 2 cups with the
remaining milk.

5 Make a white sauce. Melt the butter
in a pan, stir in the flour and cook for
1 minute. Gradually add the cooking
liquid and milk mixture, stirring, until
a fairly thin white sauce is formed. Stir
in the parsley, taste and season with a
little more salt and pepper, if necessary.

6 Spread out the cooked rice on the
bottom of a large oval gratin dish. Add
the fava beans and fish and pour over
the white sauce. Spoon the mashed
potatoes over the top, to make an
attractive pattern. Dot with a little extra
butter and bake for 15 minutes until
lightly browned.

COOK'S TIP
There are several types of sweet potato.
The lighter skinned variety, surprisingly,
has the redder flesh. If liked, you could
top this pie entirely with sweet potatoes,
or you could mash the two types
together. Cook them separately, however,
as the sweet potato tends to cook slightly
more quickly.

WILD RICE PILAF

WILD RICE ISN'T A RICE AT ALL, BUT IS ACTUALLY A TYPE OF WILD GRASS. CALL IT WHAT YOU WILL, IT HAS A WONDERFUL NUTTY FLAVOR AND COMBINES WELL WITH LONG GRAIN RICE IN THIS FRUITY MIXTURE. SERVE AS A SIDE DISH.

SERVES SIX

INGREDIENTS
    1 cup wild rice
    3 tablespoons butter
    ½ onion, finely chopped
    1 cup long grain rice
    2 cups chicken stock
    ¾ cup sliced or slivered almonds
    ⅔ cup golden raisins
    2 tablespoons chopped fresh
        parsley
    salt and freshly ground black pepper

1 Bring a large pan of water to a boil. Add the wild rice and 1 teaspoon salt. Lower heat, cover and simmer gently for 45–60 minutes, until the rice is tender. Drain well.

2 Meanwhile, melt 1 tablespoon of the butter in another pan. Add the onion and cook over medium heat for about 5 minutes until it is just softened. Stir in the long grain rice and cook for 1 minute more.

3 Stir in the stock and bring to a boil. Cover and simmer gently for 30–40 minutes, until the rice is tender and the liquid has been absorbed.

COOK'S TIP
Like all rice dishes, this one must be made with well-flavored stock. If you haven't time to make your own, use a carton or can of good quality stock.

4 Melt the remaining butter in a small pan. Add the almonds and cook until they are just golden. Set aside.

5 Put the rice mixture in a bowl and add the almonds, golden raisins and half the parsley. Stir to mix. Taste and adjust the seasoning if necessary. Transfer to a warmed serving dish, sprinkle with the remaining parsley and serve.

WILD RICE WITH BROILED VEGETABLES

THE MIXTURE OF WILD RICE AND LONG GRAIN RICE IN THIS DISH WORKS VERY WELL, AND MAKES AN EXTREMELY TASTY VEGETARIAN MEAL.

SERVES FOUR

INGREDIENTS
   generous 1 cup mixed wild and long
      grain rice
   1 large eggplant, thickly sliced
   1 red, 1 yellow and 1 green bell
      pepper, seeded and cut into quarters
   2 red onions, sliced
   generous 3 cups brown or shiitake
      mushrooms
   2 small zucchini, cut in half
      lengthwise
   olive oil, for brushing
   2 tablespoons chopped fresh thyme,
      plus extra to garnish
For the dressing
   6 tablespoons extra virgin olive oil
   2 tablespoons balsamic vinegar
   2 garlic cloves, crushed
   salt and freshly ground black pepper

1 Put all the rice in a pan of cold salted water. Bring to a boil, then lower heat, cover and cook gently for 30–40 minutes (or according to the instructions on the packet) until tender.

2 Make the dressing. Whisk the olive oil, vinegar, garlic and seasoning together in a bowl or shake in a screw-top jar until thoroughly blended. Set aside while you broil the vegetables.

3 Arrange all the vegetables on a broiler rack. Brush with olive oil and cook for about 5 minutes.

4 Turn the vegetables over, brush them with more olive oil and cook for 5–8 minutes more, or until tender and charred in places.

5 Drain the rice, turn into a bowl and toss in half the dressing. Spoon onto individual plates and arrange the vegetables on top. Pour over the remaining dressing, sprinkle over the chopped thyme and serve.

SOUTH-WESTERN RICE DESSERT

COCONUT IS THE SECRET INGREDIENT IN THIS UNUSUAL RICE DESSERT. DO NOT OVERCOOK THE RICE OR IT WILL BECOME STODGY. FRESH FRUITS, SUCH AS STRAWBERRIES, MAKE THE IDEAL PARTNER.

SERVES FOUR

INGREDIENTS

¼ cup raisins
about 2 cups water
1 cup short grain dessert rice
1 cinnamon stick
2 tablespoons sugar
2 cups milk
1 cup canned sweetened coconut
    cream
½ teaspoon vanilla extract
1 tablespoon butter
⅓ cup shredded coconut
ground cinnamon, for sprinkling

1 Put the raisins in a small bowl and pour over enough water to cover. Let the raisins soak.

2 Pour the measured water into a heavy or non-stick pan and bring it to a boil. Add the rice, cinnamon stick and sugar and stir. Return to a boil, then lower heat, cover, and simmer gently for 15–20 minutes until the liquid has been absorbed.

3 Remove the cinnamon stick from the rice. Drain the raisins and add them to the rice with the milk, coconut cream and vanilla essence. Stir to mix. Replace the lid and cook the mixture for about 20 minutes more, until it is just thick. Do not overcook the rice. Preheat the broiler.

4 Transfer the mixture to a serving dish that can safely be used under the broiler. Dot with the butter and sprinkle coconut evenly over the surface. Cook about 5 inches from the heat until the top is just browned. Sprinkle with cinnamon. Serve the dessert warm or cold.

CARAMEL RICE DESSERT

THIS RICE DESSERT IS DELICIOUS SERVED WITH CRUNCHY FRESH FRUIT.

SERVES FOUR

INGREDIENTS
    1 tablespoon butter
    ¼ cup short grain dessert rice
    5 tablespoons demerara sugar
    14 ounce can evaporated milk
      made up to 2½ cups with water
    2 fresh baby pineapples
    2 figs
    1 crisp eating apple
    2 teaspoons lemon juice
    salt

1 Preheat the oven to 300°F. Grease an ovenproof souffle dish lightly with a little of the butter. Put the rice in a strainer and wash it thoroughly under cold water. Drain well and put into the souffle dish.

2 Add 2 tablespoons of the sugar to the dish, with a pinch of salt. Pour on the diluted evaporated milk and stir gently.

3 Dot the surface of the rice with butter. Bake for 2 hours, then let cool for 30 minutes.

4 Meanwhile, quarter the pineapple and the figs. Cut the apple into segments and toss in the lemon juice. Preheat the broiler.

5 Sprinkle the remaining sugar evenly over the rice. Place under the hot broiler for 5 minutes or until the sugar has caramelized. Let the rice stand for 5 minutes to allow the caramel to harden, then serve with the fresh fruit.

INDEX

ACKNOWLEDGMENTS

The photographs in this book are by Dave King and David Jordan except those which appear on the following pages:

page 8 Life File/Emma Lee; *page 9 top* e.t. archive/Free Library Philadelphia; *bottom* e.t. archive/Domenica del Corriere; *page 10 top* e.t. archive/Freer Gallery of Art; *bottom* e.t. archive/ Freer Gallery of Art; *page 11* Life File/Emma Lee; *page 12* Life File/Emma Lee; *page 13 top and bottom* Life File/ Emma Lee.